Saints

DATE DUE			

Saints

APOSTLE OF CHARITY

APOSTLE
OF CHARITY

THE LIFE OF ST. VINCENT DE PAUL

by

Theodore Maynard

THE DIAL PRESS   NEW YORK

MCMXXXIX

Nihil Obstat

Arthur J. Scanlan, S.T.D.
Censor Librorum

Imprimatur

✠Stephen J. Donahue, D.D.
Adm., New York
March 23, 1939

TO PHILIP, CHRISTINE, CLARE **AND** KEVIN

CONTENTS

APOSTLE OF CHARITY

ℂ Introduction

In the writing of a life of Vincent de Paul one all but insuperable difficulty must be acknowledged at the outset: it is that of telling his story in chronological progression. If up to the time he was entering middle age the difficulty does not arise, this is because, until then, though there is plenty of incident, he was concerned only with the performance of duties that would not have brought him lasting fame: his life-work had not yet begun. But after middle age he initiated, and continued to the day of his death, a number of very varied enterprises, driving his projects in tandem. The fact that no man ever lived who was less a man of one work makes strict sequence virtually impossible to any biographer and necessitates a topical rather than a chronological plan.

For this reason his first biographer, Louis Abelly, the Bishop of Rodez, found it advisable to devote one volume to the biographical details, another to Vincent's multifarious activities, and yet a third to his distinctive virtues. And indeed that, with some important modifications, is the pattern adopted by Vincent's latest biographer, Père Coste. Though I, because of working on a smaller scale, am able to attempt to relate this astonishing life in the story-method, I am aware that I am forced to make compromises which, in the nature of things, can hardly hope to be altogether successful. Further compromises would have resulted in too many sacrifices of things that need to be told, and I wish not merely to paint a portrait but to give a fairly adequate account of what the Saint did. As it is, I fear that I have not been able to pay proper attention to every aspect of Vincent de Paul's activities.

There is, however, one point of unity: all these many enterprises appear to have been started in much the same way—because circumstances obliged him to undertake them, or because they were suggested to him by other people. In nearly every case we find him taking what must have seemed to his associates an unconscionable time in making a beginning; but, once a decision was made, it was never abandoned, though he managed to exercise his gift for organization while keeping himself as far as possible in the background. Nobody could be less like the modern efficiency expert than this saint. And yet no efficiency expert has ever come near rivalling his success.

But at this point—since I do not propose to give a bibliography (a very full one being in Coste's Life), or even footnotes, except when these are unavoidable—it might be as well to mention my chief authorities and to indicate their importance.

The first biography, as has been said, is the one published by Abelly only four years after Vincent's death. For the times in which he wrote, the author is remarkable for his scientific method. He makes, for instance, no attempt to adduce miracles; on the contrary he ends his work by telling a pleasant story of an aged cardinal who at the process for Canonization was so bored by such matters that he composed himself to sleep. He woke up, however, and showed a most lively interest when it was related how the holy man had endured with perfect patience and charity the injuries he had received from others. "Now there's a great miracle!" was his comment.

Abelly had at his disposal the vast mass of letters and documents which was then still extant. And though he did not examine all of it personally the Fathers of the Congregation of the Mission did, so that he got everything of importance. On the other hand, some of these letters were discreetly "doctored," or even suppressed.[1] Moreover the Bishop was a little too ready

---

[1] This, however, seems to have occurred before Abelly received the documents for the biography. For he protests on oath that he changed nothing,

to admit hearsay evidence, though it should be added that he generally did so with a phrase of reservation. There can be no doubt, however, that he depicted his friend's character exactly as it was. Subsequent investigation has changed nothing in this respect. Indeed, one still gets the "feel" of St. Vincent de Paul better in Abelly than elsewhere.

Pierre Collet, writing in 1748, does not improve on Abelly, from whom he derives most of his material, even while correcting certain details. And Louis-Emile Bougaud, the Bishop of Laval, performs (1889) the same operation on Collet. If he added nothing of great significance, he arranged his material and wrote more attractively than any of his predecessors. His study is still the most readable of the longer lives of the saint, and, though in two volumes, may be described as a popular work.

Ulysse Maynard, who published a four-volume biography in 1861 and issued a revised edition in 1874, somewhat ungraciously attacked Bougaud. The Abbé had even ventured to announce, in his second edition, that his labours had rendered all future biographies of Vincent de Paul superfluous, since there was now nothing left to discover. Unfortunately, despite his brilliance, there remained a great deal to correct and even to add. So far from having examined his material critically, he was one of the worst offenders in the matter of embellishing the accretion of legends.

Nevertheless, his criticism of his predecessors, while rather too drastic, was acute. Abelly, he roundly affirmed, had neither

and Alméras, the Superior General of the Congregation of the Mission, certified in 1668 that "The words of M. Vincent reported therein are in agreement with the said memoranda." The phrase Alméras employed may of course mean either that Abelly used his documents with absolute exactitude, or merely that the agreement was substantial. It is perhaps not altogether unreasonable to surmise that a deliberate ambiguity was introduced by way of safeguarding the Superior General's conscience.

order, nor method, nor style, but had really produced three distinct works, each of which told Vincent's life over again.

Further, taking his cue from Claude-Joseph Lacour, he said that Abelly had merely acted as god-father, that his was no more than *un livre de famille*, and that the Vincentian Fathers, particularly Fournier, should be credited with the authorship. The contention can no longer be sustained, but it must be admitted that there is a good deal in his point that the work is one of edification rather than of historical scholarship.

Collet is similarly dismissed as "Cold and dry, after the fashion of too many theologians," and the charge is brought that his effort to follow a chronological order only too often results in an extreme disorder. But despite all that, these works—including the one by my not over modest namesake—must be taken into account by all who wish to learn what manner of man Vincent was. Much may be gathered also from some seventeenth century memoirs, especially that of Vincent's not very edifying pupil, the Cardinal de Retz.

Only recently (1920-25) a French Vincentian, Père Pierre Coste, has published in fourteen volumes all the existing source material under the title of *Saint Vincent de Paul. Correspondance, Entretiens, Documents;* and he has followed this editorial task with a monumental biography which has been translated into English by Father Joseph Leonard, C. M., as *The Life and Labours of St. Vincent de Paul.* Nothing in hagiography has ever been written with a more scrupulous adherence to the principles of historical criticism. The only objection that can be brought against it is that it makes somewhat difficult reading, and should mainly be regarded as a quarry from which subsequent biographers must excavate their facts rather than as a symmetrical work of art. With far more justice than the Abbé Maynard Père Coste might say, "It is all there." My indebtedness to it is enormous, as must be that of everyone who in future may desire to give an accurate account of its subject.

Of Vincent's letters, thirty thousand, we are told, were in existence at the time of his death. When Collet wrote less than a quarter of that number remained. Now we have only about twenty-five hundred. Many were probably destroyed during the sack of Saint-Lazare in the French Revolution. But the disappearance of others may be due to the Fathers of the Congregation having gradually got rid of those which seemed to them of slight importance or which merely repeated what had been said elsewhere. What we have left, however, is amply adequate to give us so complete an idea of the Saint's mind and work that it is likely that our loss is not so great as it might appear to be. At all events, about few saints have we such full information.

Until Coste's edition of the documents appeared, the Conferences Vincent gave to the Sisters of Charity were jealously guarded from the world. Even Bougaud, though as a bishop he seems to have been allowed to see them, threw dust in the eyes of the over-curious by giving foot-note references that were apparently designed for that specific purpose. This attempt to keep the Conferences as a household treasure was a pity, for nothing reveals Vincent de Paul in a clearer or more attractive light. Only now is a translation intended for general circulation about to appear in English, though unfortunately too late to be of service to me. This work is being performed by Father Leonard, to whom we are already deeply in debt for the English version of Coste's Life and for a large volume of selected Letters.

Only now, therefore, are all the biographical materials available. Yet Père Coste's exhaustive study based on that material has resulted in the cry "destructive criticism!" being raised by those who are scandalized by the scientific scrutiny of anything which, though doubtful, is sacrosanct. Père Verdier, however, the late Superior General of the Congregation of the Mission, in commending Coste's labours, remarks, "There is nothing so beautiful as truth," though he, too, throws a sop to the more tender-minded by adding that the legends "will continue to be told, written and published for the consolation of pious souls."

I confess to a feeling of relief at being able to take shelter in the fact that Coste has gone before me and has received the highest approbation from his own Congregation. But our Saint loses nothing by having a few preposterous stories removed from his tradition. Such piety as I may possess needs no nourishment from legend. Nor is St. Vincent lessened an inch in stature merely because it has to be confessed that some charming things related of him repose on no solid historical basis, and are even inherently impossible. Rather, as the Abbé Bremond remarks, "The legend and the quasi-official portrait [he was writing before Coste], each lending the other support, have sadly simplified, vulgarised and impoverished the figure of St. Vincent de Paul."

When one approaches this very great man, at first sight he does not appear to be endowed with much more than the *bon sens français*. If we put aside his sanctity, the comment of Saint-Beuve on Louis XIV would almost apply—that he had little more than common-sense, only common-sense to an extraordinary degree. So far from wishing to be original, he constantly disclaimed being the originator of anything he undertook. He abhorred every sort of singularity; he shunned publicity. And however much we set this down to his humility, it is true that he can hardly be described as a man of ideas, except of the single idea of devotion to God through service toward men. He was indeed a fine psychologist, and never tired of describing the direction of souls as the art of arts. But though we should misread him if we miss the complexity of what many think a simple character, he had (or at any rate, displayed) slight aptitude for speculation, and he incessantly enforced upon his Missionaries and the Daughters of Charity that their vocation was not for contemplation (though this was by no means ruled out) but for practical work. Yet he insisted with equal vehemence that activity could be effective only if based upon prayer; but when there was any conflict of claims, he said, God should be left for God—in other words, the immediate claims of charity came, so far as his institutions were concerned, before the exercises of piety. As he put it, "Beneficent and perfect action is the true characteristic of the love of God." It was for this reason that the members of what we may, at this point, call for convenience his two "Orders" were obliged to rise at four every morning so as to dispose of their prayers before their long day's work began. At the same time he kept reminding them that all the duties of the day were to be discharged in the spirit of prayer. His reported Conferences prove him to be one of the great masters of the spiritual life.

He showed in himself the union of qualities which are generally opposed, or are at least rarely found conjoined in the same man: intense fervour and cautious prudence—to both of which he added a child-like simplicity. If we recall St. Augustine's remark that simplicity without prudence is likely to be taken for folly, and prudence without simplicity to degenerate into cunning, we shall see how there was in Vincent together, and in level balance, a union of absolute openheartedness and hard-headed shrewdness.

His peasant origin makes us wonder that his first appointment was as almoner to Queen Marguerite (during her later years, long after her marriage to Henry IV had been annulled), and that subsequently, until he was in his middle forties, he acted as tutor in one of the noblest houses of France. This would be quite inexplicable had he lacked fine intellectual parts.

Though we find him in one of his last letters apologising to his former patron for his rustic manners, we may safely conclude that, whether or not kind hearts are more than coronets, his benignity was so genuine and profound as to have bestowed upon him a charm much greater than is to be conferred by a merely courtly polish.

His destined career as an organizer of charity did not begin until he was ageing. Then it went forward, steadily broadening, up to his death, and his work has continued to our own day. Not only did he get some of the greatest ladies in the land to contribute lavishly to his charities but—what is still more astonishing—he actually set them to work. The royal house itself was at his command. Anne of Austria became president of one of his confraternities. Louis XIII died in his arms.

In an age full of tortuous intrigue he managed to keep clear of all entanglements. Richelieu backed his undertakings; under Mazarin he held an official position. Only because he remained resolutely disengaged from politics and never asked the least favour for himself was this achieved. Somehow he kept in harness together the niece of the Marillacs (Richelieu's victims after the "Day of Dupes"), and Richelieu's own niece. The former, now canonized as St. Louise de Marillac, was his right hand in his works of charity; the latter, who became the Duchesse d'Aiguillon, was, of many women distinguished for their munificence, the one most constant in her generosity.

Yet this eminently practical mind—his sole excursion into the field of theological controversy was his brush with the early group of Jansenists—functioned always without set design. Even if we take literally his assertions that he moved only when circumstances obliged him to do so and that all his projects were prompted by other people—perhaps this cannily simple man contrived to lead people to offer the suggestions he wanted them to make!—it is quite certain that it was his habit to defer decision until it could no longer be delayed. His contemporary, Oliver Cromwell, made the point: "No one rises so high as he who knows not whither he is going." Vincent would have thoroughly concurred. Of all men he was the least precipitate. "Good establishments," he used to say, "are not called into being suddenly, but little by little"; and that "In this world, things that are naturally destined to endure for a long time are the slowest in reaching maturity." The deficiency of imagination noted by Abelly was therefore probably more apparent than real: Vincent went forward slowly so as to have the chance of examining every side of a question.[2]

There can be no doubt that a mind capable of directing simultaneously so many different undertakings must have been extremely flexible. Even while dealing with immediate matters, his eyes always saw into the future. What St. Francis de Sales had tried to do—that is, establish a religious community of women devoted to work among the poor—Vincent succeeded in doing. He managed it by a stroke of genius—by not allowing the Daughters of Charity to be, strictly speaking, a religious order at all: they were to be no more than a band of good strong country girls ready for any kind of hard work they were asked to perform. No innovator of ideas, Vincent was a wonderful innovator of methods and practices. And the secret of it all was that he left everything in the hands of Providence. "Time and I," Mazarin was accustomed to boast, "can accomplish all things." Vincent would have changed the terms to "God and time"; he never brought himself in except as the instrument to be used by God. He stands virtually alone among

[2] And in saying this I may perhaps show the disinterestedness of my admiration by adding that the Vincentian characteristics are totally at variance with my own rashly impetuous ones. Nobody would have found it harder than myself to have endured Vincent's slow and cautious progress. Indeed, many of those who served under him found him exasperating, even when they were afterwards forced to admit that his was the sounder method.

men of action in his lack of imperiousness. Instead of asserting himself, he subdued and disparaged his personal talents.

His triumphs therefore were neither dazzling nor ostentatious, but were the result of dogged hard work and complete dependence on divine guidance. In the same way, he did not reach sanctity at a bound, but by degrees so slow that they can hardly be perceived. There is no crisis of conversion upon which one can place one's finger confidently (except that we may reasonably surmise that there was such a crisis shortly after 1610); instead his spiritual development seems to be synchronous with the gradual development of his work, which grew out of beginnings so small as to be scarcely noticeable. Therefore perhaps the main lesson to be drawn from his life is that of how much may be accomplished by gifts less than supreme—gifts which in any other man might even strike one as rather moderate—provided these are put unreservedly at the disposal of God. But the doing of that was, of course, his greatest gift, one that lifted all his other gifts to a special plane in which they became, in their own order, supreme.

My thanks are due the Rev. John W. Dunn, C.M., Librarian of St. John's University, Brooklyn, and to the Vincentian Fathers and the Sisters of Charity at Emmitsburg, Maryland, for the loan of books, and to Miss Jessie Marson for the making of the index. Father Joseph Leonard, C.M., of London, read my MS. and made many valuable suggestions, for which I am grateful. As I did not in every instance follow his advice in some minor matters, he of course has no responsibility for my incidental opinions. Most of all I am indebted to Professor Henry A. Lappin of D'Youville College, Buffalo, N. Y., for the generosity equal to the skill with which, at a time prolonged illness delayed this book, he put it in order for me, and to my wife who helped in the typing.

ℭ 1. Drop-Scene

VINCENT DE PAUL in his early manhood saw that compromise under which a Protestant prince professed conversion to Catholicism to save his crown, and later—this time from closer quarters—watched the intricate policy by which Cardinal Richelieu allied France to the rebellious Protestant subjects of the Emperor Ferdinand so as to relieve the pressure Spain was applying on three sides of the "Square Field." How far he understood the significance of these events must be doubtful, for we can hardly credit him with the insight to perceive an outcome which Richelieu himself did not in all particulars intend. Political questions were beyond Vincent's special province, and to have shown himself a partizan would have been to hamper his own work. At most we can say that he probably viewed with misgiving much of what was going on.

It would nevertheless seem advisable to provide here a kind of historical drop-scene against which he and what he did may be viewed. For his times conditioned his undertakings in a sense more true than usually happens in such cases; indeed, some of his most important charitable activities were the direct result of social conditions which, in turn, were occasioned by political events. He was above all others the distinctive saint—at all events, the distinctive French saint—of the seventeenth century. God raised him up because just such a man was needed; but we may add that the age also called him forth.

The Concordat of 1516 made between Francis I and the Pope was used by the French Crown as a fruitful opportunity for endowing royal mistresses or bastards or favourites with the revenues of the Church. Thus Henry IV's illegitimate sons were made bishops, and Sully—though a Huguenot—held no less than four abbeys *in commendam*. Even when this system gave, as it sometimes did, a means of livelihood to a man of genius, or, by some lucky chance, put a worthy prelate in office, it no less firmly held the Church in a shameful servitude. Almost all that can be said in its favour is that it removed the incentive for direct plunder which promoted the Reformation in Germany and England. That it gave Catholicism a kind of breathing-space during the days when the nobles rather inclined toward the side of the reformers was an incidental advantage; the monarchy more often thought the main advantage lay in a means of buying one by one, the nobles who had taken up Calvinism as a weapon to be used against the Crown. The corruption engendered was as ignominious as it was dangerous.

Lutheranism, it must be remembered, was—at least in its French form—hardly more than a critical attitude toward the Church; its theological implications were vague. It was the appearance of Calvin's *Institution Chretiénne* that gave Protestantism in France a discipline and a body of doctrine. From that moment the issue was clear and the battle joined. In that battle it looked for a time as though victory would go to the Huguenots. Had this happened, they would have achieved their design: the capture of the monarchy and the destruction of Catholicism. For though they demanded toleration for themselves, they had not the slightest intention of showing it to others. Nothing less, therefore, than the fate of Catholicism throughout all Europe was at stake in this conflict.

All that saved France was the steadfastness of Paris to the Faith and the courageous leadership of the Catholic League. The stern measures of Henry II and Francis II had served only to fan the embers of heresy, and the conciliatory policy initiated by Catherine de' Medici led the Huguenots to believe, with some justice, that the Crown was too weak to arrest their progress. The Catholics were accordingly obliged to take their own cause in hand, and this brought about a long internal religious war which, though it left the country devastated, made Paris all the more resolute in refusal to accept a Protestant king.

There were massacres on both sides, but the most famous of these—that of Saint Bartholomew—was political rather than religious in origin, and was resolved upon in a moment of panic when Catherine de' Medici and her son, the young King Charles IX, were made to believe that the Huguenots assembled in Paris for the wedding of the King's sister and Henry of Navarre were planning a *coup d'état*. The Court—lax in its religion and even under some suspicion by Catholics, so far as the royal family was concerned—had intended to get rid of five people; but the populace seized the opportunity for a general massacre of the Reformers they so feared and hated. The result, on the one hand, was that the Protestants became convinced that carefully planned treachery had been practised upon them, and, on the other, that the Duc de Guise became, during the reign of the perfumed, frivolous and effeminate Henry III, the virtual king of France. The noble bearing of the young hero endeared him to the people; even the scar to which he owed the name of *le Balafré* seemed to make his features more majestic; and Henry III was exasperated by his awareness that he was more and more sinking into insignificance. Upon the murder of Guise and his brother the Cardinal, Henry made the famous exclamation, "Now I alone am the King!" Actually that murder rendered him even more inpotent. Almost his only support was that given by the Protestant heir, Henry of Navarre. His own assassination followed speedily enough.

Henry IV, an affable, loose-living, but able man, who was quite devoid of the furious fanaticism of his mother, Jeanne d'Albret (who had in the South carried out the work of devastation with peculiar thoroughness), had long recognised that,

if he was ever to wear the crown, he would have to become a
Catholic, and so had long intended to become one. But his ac-
cession, with his conversion, though it made him equally dis-
trusted by the Huguenots and the more fervent of the Catholics,
brought about the collapse of the League and the gradual ad-
hesion of the whole nation to his support. Rome hesitated for
some time in acknowledging this rather dubious son, but
in the end accepted a man who, however indifferent he might
be about religion, was at least known to have the intention of
keeping his word. No other course was open to Rome or to
France, since no other claimant had even a moderately good
case. Yet the religious war, though it kept the monarchy Catholic, ended in nothing more than a stalemate: the Edict of Nantes
was an admission that the battle had resulted in a draw. From
then on the policy of the Crown, even under the reign of a king
so sincerely pious as Louis XIII, was directed towards the rein-
forcement of the monarchy rather than the promotion of religion.

That policy did not immediately make itself manifest. Under
Henry IV there was from 1600 to 1610 a period of comparative
repose, one essential to a country exhausted by civil war; and
this period has given Henry the reputation for wise statesman-
ship that he still enjoys. He was, however, harbouring grandiose
dreams of glory when he fell beneath the dagger of Ravaillac
and the kingdom passed into the hands of the foolish and obstinate Marie de' Medici who, as Regent for her young son,
allowed the real power to pass into the hands of her ill-favoured,
wizened and stupid waiting-woman, Leonora Galigai, and her
husband Concini, who was soon created Marshal and Marquis
d'Ancre. Arrogant and rapacious, they had their way, until
Louis XIII in 1617, daring to do what nobody else would do,
had Concini assassinated. Like Henry III before him, he cried,
"Now I am really King!"

It was not, however, until 1624, when Richelieu came into

power, that the process of building up the monarchy can be truly said to have begun. Yet at first Louis accepted Richelieu with reluctance, for the young provincial bishop had commenced his political career under the patronage of Concini and the Queen Mother, and for this reason was suspect. But the King was by no means the weakling portrayed by many historians, and had the good sense to perceive the transcendent ability of his First Minister and to note that the plans projected by him usually succeeded. Accordingly, although Louis had no great liking for Richelieu—who indeed was loved probably only by Father Joseph, and who loved probably nobody but his niece—the Cardinal remained in power until his death at the end of 1642, only a few months before Louis himself died.

The long tenure of office is all the more astonishing in view of the recurrent intrigues of the vivacious, inept and chicken-hearted Gaston, in alliance with the Queen (whose Spanish birth understandably made her dislike Richelieu's foreign policy), and the Queen Mother. Indeed, Marie de' Medici, finding herself opposed (though with obsequious deference) by the man she had made and whose gratitude she expected, turned upon Richelieu with all the fury of a woman scorned.

A firm will, a brain of exceeding subtlety, an elaborate spy system, and the prompt and ruthless execution of enemies maintained the Cardinal's authority. Nevertheless, this authority was once so seriously threatened that it was generally assumed that the terrible Minister had actually fallen at last. But the Day of Dupes retrieved everything, and resulted in the execution of one Marillac and the imprisonment of the other and the flight of the meddlesome Marie de' Medici—just as the later plot of 1632, in which the King's brother was implicated, ended in Montmorency's ascending the scaffold. Richelieu, supported by Louis, spared the life of no conspirator who was not in the full sense royal, and he tolerated no interference with his policy.

With regard to that policy, it must in justice to him be said that he had hardly any alternative, or none from the point of view of strict statecraft. Its ultimate effects—of making possible the domination of the Germanies by a Protestant Prussia, and the permanent division of Europe into two cultures—were veiled from him. In its ultimate outcome we can now see that, even in its temporal aspect, his policy was a mistake. At that time that outcome could hardly have been so much as imagined. Richelieu was sincerely attached to Catholicism, even though his enemies derisively dubbed him "the Cardinal of the Huguenots," and it was his strategy that reduced La Rochelle after a famous siege and, in 1629, put an end to the new religious war. Yet the temper of his mind was secular; he put the interests of the Church below those of the State. Supremely clever as he was, he lacked spiritual vision. There are many times when the sons of light turn out to be, after all, wiser in their generation than the sons of this world.

In his dealings with foreign foes, however, it is not easy to see how he could have done otherwise than he did, though many of the details of his policy—especially his employment of Gustavus Adolphus against the Emperor Ferdinand—may be open to damaging criticism. But in all this we have the somewhat smug advantage of the perspective of history, which was lacking to Richelieu himself, as it also was to those of his contemporaries who, while doubtful about his methods, had nothing better to propose.

The fact only too evident was that France was hemmed in on three sides by a Spain then far more powerful than herself. The Spanish pressure had at all costs to be relieved, and it was the aim of Richelieu to weaken the King of Spain and the Emperor Ferdinand (both Hapsburgs) for France's benefit. Nothing, however, was further from his intention than to weaken Catholicism in the Empire; consequently, when buying the serv-

ices of Gustavus Adolphus, he stipulated that the Swedish mer-
cenaries should do no harm to the Church. Those stipulations,
as we know, were not very scrupulously observed, and for this
reason something never foreseen by Richelieu—a divided
Europe—was the result of the Thirty Years' War.

In the light of later knowledge we may deplore Richelieu's
policy, just as some of the more fervent Catholics of the time
viewed it with uneasiness. Only in doing so we should not forget
that nobody then knew precisely what the eventual outcome
would be. The concept of the *Insignia Peculiaria Christianissima
Francorum* was in the Gallic blood. No doubt Richelieu was
firmly convinced that by making France strong under a Catholic Crown he was fostering the interests of the Church of which
he was a prelate and a prince. He could not imagine that what
he regarded as the ephemeral heresy of England and Holland
and a few unimportant Baltic states was going to bring about,
because of his political support, permanent disunion in Christendom. What he did realize was that it was his duty to save
France; and he must be admitted to have saved her.

Occupied with this paramount concern, he had relatively little
time to spare for internal affairs. Moreover his knowledge of
finance was imperfect. This meant that, for the sake of the
glory of France, which he in common with nearly everybody of
his age identified with the glory of the French Crown, the French
people were neglected. And here degeneration is always likely
to be progressive. Sully, the surly old Huguenot who served
Henry IV, sitting at work all day in his bare room in the Arsenal
under the portraits of Luther and Calvin, drastically imposed
financial order upon what had been chaos, even while diligently
feathering his own nest. It was he who uttered the famous
aphorism that the two breasts of France are agriculture and
pasturage. He did his best to foster both. But Richelieu—when
free from preoccupation with his foreign policy—could attend

only to the humbling of recalcitrant nobles and to the collection
of taxes, although, being a Frenchman, he was not indifferent
to internal matters, as was the Sicilian Mazarin who succeeded
him, and whose indifference persisted even after the lesson of
the Fronde.

It was a consequence of Mazarin's neglect that France, which
had already suffered so severely from religious wars, now had
to suffer again for nearly twenty years the depredations of foreign and civil war. Province after province was laid waste by
a mercenary soldiery that was seldom paid and was therefore
obliged to live by plunder, and from plunder derived a taste for
destruction for its own sake. Though the horrors of the Thirty
Years' War in Germany were unquestionably greater than anything that France had to suffer, the miseries of France were
nevertheless well-nigh unendurable. To the ravages of the armies
was added a succession of plagues, and—during 1631, 1633, 1635,
1648 and 1652—famines that were largely due to war obliged
the peasantry to desert their fields.

It was during these years that Vincent de Paul did his heaviest
work. And fortunate indeed it was for his country that he was
raised up to do it. Just what was most urgently needed then was
his extraordinary union of peasant practicality with breadth of
vision.

Indeed in all his work the same qualities were called for and
were employed. For in France there was at that time a strange
contrast of intellectual forces. A wave of mysticism had swept
up from the Pyrenees, yet there was a great deal of religious lax-
ity and even of scepticism, so that Paris alone is said to have
numbered forty thousand "Libertines" among the half million
of her population during the early years of Louis XIII. Meanwhile in many of the provincial towns Protestantism flourished.
To cope with the situation neither fiery oratory nor subtle dialectic was required, but patient organization and the practical

fruits of charity. Only one who had intimate knowledge of the condition of the peasantry could bring them the help they required; only one who was himself a country priest could reform the clergy; only one of rare gifts of mind and heart could inspire and direct the charity of the rich.

Though the labours of Vincent's Missionaries and Daughters of Charity were mainly carried out in the provinces, it was from Paris that they were directed. Yet Paris itself needed help, as thousands of destitute people swarmed in from the ravaged country-side, living as beggars or bandits in the *Cours des Miracles*, and roving the darkened streets at night.

Paris, too, was the religious, intellectual and administrative centre. Because of the policy which was leading to the concentration of the nobles around the Court, the city contained a great many wealthy people. Their magnificence and frivolity stood out in shocking relief against the general misery, but there were among them devoted Christian souls upon whose wealth Vincent was able to draw to succour the poor. He penetrated to the generous instincts often discoverable behind a worldy exterior, and found tasks for these rich women to perform. The response to the appeal of the simple priest was one of the most astonishing things we come across in that astonishing time. Seventeenth century spirituality met its leader in a great saint. Steel and flint struck.

It was an appeal that could have been made only by one whose absolute disinterestedness was never in doubt, and who could be depended upon to turn whatever help might be given to the best account. But we must add that it could have been successfully made only by one in whom religion showed itself always in its gentlest form. For, even apart from the aberrations of Jansenism, the general tendency of Catholic fervour during the seventeenth century was only too often in the direction of a reaction toward medieval austerity, or the rigour of primitive times, as pictured by a very imperfect knowledge. Such piety being often too stern and exacting, Vincent sometimes found it no easy matter to restrain an aristocratic charity from being rather high-handed in its dealings with poverty, so that one feels that, admirable as were, for example, most of the members of the secret society of the Blessed Sacrament (to which he belonged, if in only an honorary capacity), a certain self-righteousness was also frequently engendered among them— a spirit that was to be satirised a little later by Molière in his *Tartuffe*. It was therefore necessary that Vincent should preach and practice a perfect humility and that he should make the great Court ladies, as well as the Daughters of Charity, understand that they were the servants of the poor, and that all they did for the most abject of God's creatures was to be done as though for Christ Himself.

ℂ 2. Birth and Boyhood

PERHAPS the most important fact that can be recorded of Vincent de Paul's upbringing—apart from his peasant origin—is the purely negative one that he was not born by the sea. Had he grown accustomed to boats in his boyhood, he would not in early manhood have been subject to sea-sickness. In that event, for reasons which will later be manifest, we should, humanly speaking, never have heard of him. It is a curious reflection.

Yet the district of the Landes where he was born bordered upon the sea. Fortunately the little village of Pouy was twenty miles or so inland, and the little shepherd boy never had any occasion to go to the coast, but rather to wander with his flocks away from the sandy marshes in search of fatter pasturage. Even today the Landes, after centuries of reclamation, is a rather desolate region; during the seventeenth century it must have been hard work to wring a living from that soil.

Yet the district was not without a charm to one who was prepared to make a friend of solitude. At certain seasons of the year rich colours glowed from the stagnant pools and the lupines under a blue or flaming sky, though at others everything lay burnt brown or were covered with a faint mist from the distant sea. Past Pouy the Adour slowly flows, and here and there the country was dotted with oaks. The de Pauls must have been industrious indeed to have made a living there. That Vincent came from such a place gave him tenacity and the disposition to take dogged hard work for granted. By such a life he was prepared for the things that were to come.

The "de" might suggest that the family was one of aristocratic blood that had come down in the world, and some of

Vincent's biographers have attempted to maintain as much. But against this there is the fact that the still-preserved parish registers show that everybody in Pouy had a particle before his name; it indicated no more than the name of the house or the farm he occupied. But so as to have nobody under misapprehension, the Saint usually employed the form "Depaul," and was known to everybody simply as "Monsieur Vincent." We are not sure of the Christian name of Vincent's father. Abelly gives it as "Jean"; Collet, as "Guillaume"; on the ordination papers of the young priest it was left blank. Most likely it was Jean; there is no question that Vincent's mother was Bertrande de Moras, and that he had three brothers and a couple of sisters. But none of the members of the family played a large rôle in his life. He left home while still a boy and returned only once, and then for a very brief visit.

Though there are few if any canonized saints about whom we have fuller or more exact documentation, we know little about his early life. In later years he did not talk much about it, except in the most general terms, and the information Abelly tried to gather at Pouy after Vincent's death did not come from a first-hand or very reliable source. We can be sure, however, that the de Pauls had a somewhat bare life, even if they also appear to have been among the more prosperous inhabitants of the village. The country had suffered the depredations of the religious war, and this particular district had been ravaged by one of the most furious of Calvinists, Jeanne d'Albret, the mother of the future Henry IV. The de Pauls' survival may be due merely to luck; more likely it was due to their seeming to be too poor to be worth plundering, or possibly to their ability to retrieve disaster.

La Bruyère, writing in a later generation, after peace had at last come to France, describes the peasantry in a famous passage: "One sees certain wild animals, male and female, scattered over the country, black, livid, and sunburnt all over, allied to the earth, which they search and rake up with invincible persistency. They have, as it were, an articulate voice, and when they raise themselves to their feet they show a human face. They are in fact men. At night they get them away to their dens, where they live on black bread, water and roots. They save other people the trouble of sowing, ploughing, and reaping in order to live, and therefore they deserve the bread they have helped to produce." The portrait, however vivid, is full of contempt; and the words of this usually kind man show already how the wrath of the Revolution was bound to occur. But it does not seem to correspond to what we know of the de Pauls. Their poverty was certainly not abject, nor their mode of life without a simple dignity.

Vincent himself tells us that the peasants in his part of the country lived on millet, though we need not draw the inference that they never had better fare. In a country of pasturage there must have been abundance of butcher's meat, and the sea was not so far away that fish could not be brought there. Cider and a coarse red wine were drunk, and the Gascon gaiety of temperament was not to be extinguished by a laborious existence.

It is safe to assume that almost as soon as they could walk all the children had small tasks allotted to them. We know that Vincent looked after the live-stock. If in his infancy he was sometimes frightened by what Padraic Colum has called

> "The peering of things
> Across the half-door"

—for the cattle-sheds opened directly upon the room in which the family lived—the various horned and woolly creatures must have soon become his friends. In later years, when Vincent had become a famous man, he used, now and then, to abash his aristocratic friends by telling them bluntly that he had been a swine-herd. Nevertheless that designation was not quite exhaustive, for he also permitted it to be known that he frequently had to travel as far afield as thirty miles to find good grass for his sheep. What we may conclude is that he spent his childhood among animals of various kinds—an excellent training for anyone.

We may imagine him trudging barefoot along the dusty roads dressed in knee-breeches and a cape, with a dog at his side, or bringing in a straggling sheep. With a slice or two of bread and cheese in his wallet he would spend the whole day out in the lonely fields. And as he was an intelligent boy, possessing indeed a spark of genius that had not yet come to flame, we may surmise that he thought of many deep things—though what those things were we have not the faintest idea, because whatever else he was, he was not a poet and so could not express the vague dreams of youth.

Abelly, digging up what memories he could find of him nearly eighty years later, assures us that he was already very compassionate and pious. And while it is not very safe to accept all the stories told about the boyhood of great men, it is likely enough that the incidents he relates correspond to the essential truth if not to the truth in all its details. They are at all events naïve and harmless.

Thus, the old oak still standing near the site of his birthplace (the house itself fell down before the end of the seventeenth century and the rebuilt one was afterwards moved a few feet) has a hollow in it in which Vincent is said to have set up a shrine to the Blessed Virgin. Thousands of children have done precisely the same thing, though unfortunately not all of them continued pious.

In the same way, there is the story of Vincent, when sent home to fetch a bag of flour from the mill, giving a few handfuls of it to a poor man. It is what one would expect. Though this saint, like others, had faults to overcome, grace builds upon nature; and the seed of what was to rise into a great fire of supernatural charity was no doubt embedded in the kindliness of disposition the child had from birth. More heroic is the account of how the impetuous little Gascon, after having carefully scraped together what seemed to him the enormous sum of thirty sous, handed it all in an impulse of pity to a beggar he met.

Such stories are very pleasant and also very natural. But, while they are hardly to be regarded as authentic history, only a cross-grained pedant would, on that account, wish to dismiss them as valueless. We have something here essentially different from those edifying (or, according to one's make-up, disedifying) yarns to be encountered in the Second Nocturn about precociously ascetic infants who refused their mother's breast on Fridays. I have therefore no wish to deprive Vincent de Paul of his shrine in the hollow oak or his thirty sous. Everything we know points to his having been a boy of good disposition. The only reserve I should like to make is against confusing the generous instincts of boyhood with something that is to be attained only after bitter struggles with the passions of maturity. Vincent was not yet a saint, and was not, for a long time, to become one.

On the other hand it should be said at once that we can find nothing in his life that is to be regarded as serious sin. He was always well behaved, and his worst early faults are those of a tinge of snobbery and of the ambition from which that snobbery sprang. But the tinge is very slight, and the ambition was a quite legitimate one even if it was not quite consonant with positive sanctity. He never deviated from the road that was to lead him to holiness, so that we cannot assign any definite date to the spiritual crisis after which he became something more than an ordinarily decent man. About that he always showed the greatest reticence.

But now we come to a legend. Harmless enough, but still a legend. To this must be added what I am afraid can be described only as a positive falsehood on the part of those responsible for his first biography.

The legend concerns Vincent's devotion to Our Lady of Buglose. That he was all his life distinguished for a tender devotion to the Blessed Virgin is of course perfectly true; but there was in his time no devotion to Our Lady of Buglose. The following would seem to be the germ of fact in the later fiction: in 1570 Montgomery (the same man who accidentally killed the King in the jousting-lists) led a party of marauding Calvinists into Béarn, and the local Catholics, fearful lest the statue of the Virgin should be destroyed, hid it in a marsh. There, according to subsequent embellishments, it was found in 1620. An ox was discovered cleaning the statue with its tongue! But precisely the same fable is to be found in at least fifty places in France.[1] Further, the image in question, though its body is of sixteenth century workmanship, is mended with a head that belongs to the seventeenth century. There was, in other words, no cult in Vincent's boyhood of Our Lady of Buglose. All that we can say is that he may have had some unconscious share in establishing the cult by the piety he showed when he prayed before this statue during his visit to Buglose in 1623; he could not so much as have seen it before that date.

The story, however, is charming, and in this case at least there is no occasion to "Chase myths like moths and fight them with a pin." If it does nothing more, it exemplifies the spirit

[1] We are also told that the oxen of the cart that was to take the image to Pouy advanced only so far as the oratory of Buglose, and then refused to move a step further!

of Catholicism and the horror of the French Catholics at seeing the wanton iconoclasm of Jeanne d'Albret's Huguenots. The other matter is far more serious, not only because it concerns a biographical detail of great importance, but because it shows that there must have been a deliberate intention to mislead. It concerns the date of Vincent's birth.

Abelly, who published his biography in 1664, four years after Vincent's death, gave the Saint's birth-date as April 24, 1576. He should have said 1581. Yet it was not until Père Coste wrote that the truth was at last established, though one wonders at the long delay, since Vincent over and over again in letters and the reports of his Conferences made no secret of his actual age. The subsequent biographers were either careless, or thought that Abelly ought to know, or shared his motive for concealment.

Père Coste, aware that Abelly had been supplied with his documents by the Fathers of the Mission, is kind enough to admit the possibility that he wrote in good faith. It *is* a bare possibility, but an unlikely one; for though it is more than likely that Abelly worked only with copies of documents which had already been touched up, he so often had been in Vincent's company that it is only reasonable to believe that he must have heard the truth from Vincent's own lips. Moreover we know that the good Bishop did suppress passages from the letters that might have given scandal—unless this, too, was done by the Vincentians before the letters came into Abelly's hands.

Whether Abelly is to be acquitted of deception or not, we cannot acquit Père Alméras, who was Vincent's successor as Superior. For the date 1576 was engraved by his orders upon the tomb-stone. As Vincent himself once said, the terms "Catholic" and "honest man" do not necessarily mean the same thing.

But there is this to be said in the defence of Alméras and Abelly. The biography was intended for edification, and we must not expect from a man of the seventeenth century the scientific historical standard prevailing in our own time. Also, if the 1581 birth-date had been divulged, the Jansenists would have whooped with glee, as this would have shown that the man they took delight in disparaging had, in spite of his having taken the lead in establishing seminaries and reforming the clergy, himself been ordained five years before the canonical age. Faced with this quandary, Abelly and the Fathers of the Mission evidently decided that it would never do to reveal the facts. They may well have argued that they were not only justified in the difficult circumstances but that, apart from other considerations, five years one way or the other were of little consequence.

There was another consideration we may assume to have weighed with them. They were already laying plans for the introduction of the cause of Vincent's beatification, and they were aware that the *Advocatus Diaboli* would be looking for something upon which he might pounce. And though at the end of the sixteenth century, and even later, the regulations of canon law upon this point were far from being scrupulously observed either by bishops or the priests ordained by them— Richelieu, for example, had not hesitated to resort to forgery in his own ordination papers—Rome in a stricter age might well take a somewhat serious view of the irregularity. Accordingly they thought it advisable to take no chances.

What is interesting to note is that Vincent, even if his ordination before he was twenty troubled his conscience in later life, was presumably not troubled at the time. Contrary to canon law as the procedure may have been, it was sanctioned in practice. He had completed his studies, and no doubt he felt that there was no reason to wait. His way in the world had to be made, and his family was looking to him to make it. No blame can fairly be attached to him. One might even maintain that he believed he was doing no more than his duty.

For he must have thought of his father, that little grey wiry man with a limp who had already worked himself into his grave. And he knew that his mother—though she had three other sons and a couple of daughters—was expecting him to do something by way of repaying the hard-earned money spent upon his education. He would have been hardly human if his heart had not gone out to them or if he had shown himself absurdly punctilious about a mere peccadillo. Not yet had the saint emerged from his chrysalis.

When that did happen, he often said that he thought so highly of the humble life of the peasantry as to wonder whether it would not have been better for him to have remained in the state of life in which he had been born. The reflection did him great credit; but we, looking back upon his extraordinary career, can see that it was just those conditions which gave him the special knowledge he needed for his life's work.

Yet, even with the advantage of this perspective, it remains an almost miraculous thing that one born to such lowliness should have risen to such heights. Genius alone will not quite account for it; to a man of his origin that could hardly have brought more than what was the goal of his early ambition— a comfortable benefice, in which he would have eaten his heart out in angry obscurity. But grace allied to genius, and trans- forming it, led him to an illustrious career of poverty which became the endowment of the poor of France and the whole world.

ℭ 3. Student Days

JEAN DE PAUL noticed that his son was not only a good but a clever boy, and being himself ambitious for him, he decided to have him educated for the priesthood. Already Vincent had probably picked up a certain amount of instruction from the priest of Pouy, when, at the age of twelve (though he himself says "about fourteen") he was sent to a school run by the Franciscans at the neighbouring town of Dax. In this he may well have been following the advice of a relative of his named Stephen de Paul who was in charge of a priory-hospice, and the Prior (who may also have had a hand in Vincent's early education) no doubt recognised the ability of his young kinsman and urged that the Church offered opportunities for advancement of a kind that no other profession gave to a peasant. Vincent's father was obviously impressed, both by the arguments and the prosperity of Stephen de Paul, and decided that the money to be expended on an education would prove to be a good investment. Probably he had to make sacrifices to raise the sixty livres a year of the school fees; that he was able to raise them at all shows that he must have been fairly well-to-do for his station in life.

The school, though under the general direction of the Friars, seems to have drawn most of its masters from wandering scholars down on their luck or under a cloud, or from among those unbeneficed secular priests of whom France was then full. But some of these may well have been able men, and it is clear that Vincent made rapid progress, for we soon find him taken into the house of a M. de Comet, a local magistrate, to coach his sons, while pursuing his own studies.

Abelly, having started with a false date for Vincent's birth,

estimates that the boy was at Dax for nine years. Père Coste
estimates two years, which is, no doubt, much nearer the mark.
For as Vincent later used to refer to himself as a "fourth form
scholar," it is clear that his residence at the school and in
the magistrate's household could not have been of long duration.

That Vincent "worked his way" through school, at any rate
during his second year, would indicate that he wished to save
his father expense, probably also that he already felt in his
blood and bones that it would have been inadvisable to put
himself under too heavy an obligation to his family. There is
also some indication that his success in his studies made him
at this time—he who was to be so notable for his extreme
humility—somewhat conceited and even a bit of a snob. He
must have got it into his head that he was going to rise in the
world, for we find him showing not merely that trace of a swollen
head which is almost universal among gifted youths but a shame
of his humble origin. It was not until he was a saint that he
expressed the opinion that it would have been better for him
had he remained a peasant. At this time, as he confessed in later
life with deep contrition, he was once told that his father had
called at the school,—and the future saint refused to see him,
because he knew that the limping old man would be sure to
look shabby.

Again, one must not make too much of the fact. If this was
the worst fault that Vincent ever committed—and many who
knew him thought that it was—his conscience must have been
extraordinarily clear. Those who have been educated at such
schools will know how cruel boys can be in their comments on
the relatives of their school-mates, and how anxious boys are
to do nothing to excite derision. The incident is worth recording only because we shall see how completely Vincent eventually
succeeded in overcoming this sort of frailty.

His general conduct at the school must have been exemplary,

because we find that he was allowed to take minor orders before he was sixteen, after which he proceeded to the University of Toulouse to follow his theological studies. To provide the initial expenses, his father sold a yoke of oxen. After that Vincent relied on himself, even though his family was still willing to contribute, so far as it could, to his support.

In those days, it must be remembered, there were, despite the regulations on the subject laid down by the Council of Trent, no theological seminaries in France, or few in any country, and therefore many priests had hardly more learning than was sufficient to enable them to say Mass. The establishment of seminaries had to wait for a full generation, and then was largely due to Vincent's own efforts. That he went to the University of Toulouse shows that he was using the best available means for equipping himself for the priesthood.

Yet it must be said that Toulouse, like all the French universities of the time, was not a very orderly place. Taverns and disreputable houses gathered around them, and the students indulged not merely in horse-play and fist fights but aped the aristocracy in the sport of duelling. This state of affairs was no doubt much more common among those belonging to the departments of law and medicine and arts than in that of theology; but probably even among clerical students conduct was not always so edifying as it should have been.

The men from each province had their presidents, or priors, who too frequently became leaders in the pitched battles. Thus we find orders from the Parlement on one occasion to arrest the priors, and other orders imposing heavy fines upon keepers of lodging houses who received armed students, and even the erection of a gallows for the punishment of refractory students. Whether any of them were actually hanged we do not know, but there is a record of two who received a capital sentence and were pardoned only on account of their youth. Even so, they were banished for five years and had to do public penance kneeling in their shirts with ropes around their necks. This seems hardly the proper environment for sacerdotal development.

Abelly states that after the death of Vincent's father, which occurred during the second year at Toulouse, Vincent made his way to Saragossa. Collet improves upon this by saying that Vincent did not remain there because he was disgusted by the wrangling that went on among the professors upon the subject of predestination. But there is no proof that he ever went to Saragossa at all, and Coste acidly comments on Collet: "It is an unlikely hypothesis fabricated to explain a still more unlikely fact." Of course all this is not impossible, but it is on the face of it improbable that an impoverished young man, who now knew he could get no support from his father, should have made a long and difficult journey to a foreign country.[1] If it did happen, I offer the conjecture that it was because somebody had assured Vincent that discipline was better at Saragossa. What is certain is that (if he ever went to Spain) he was soon back at Toulouse, and that he remained there until he obtained on October 12, 1604 the decree of bachelor of theology.

Certain facts must now be noted. On September 13, 1599 he received permission from the Bishop of Dax to be ordained to the priesthood. All this was quite contrary to the decrees of the Council of Trent, which set the canonical age for ordination at twenty-four. It must be remembered, however, that scant attention was paid to those decrees in France, where, in fact, they were not accepted until 1615, and that it was no unusual thing for a boy of eighteen and a half to be "priested." Even so—possibly because of some scruple of conscience—

[1] There is, however, a case—which has perhaps more to be said for it than Coste will allow—that Vincent's family was Spanish in origin. If so, this might account for his going to Saragossa.

Vincent put off, or was advised to put off, his ordination for a year. In this he may have considered that he was complying with the spirit, if not the letter, of the law; certainly he was much better qualified in every way for ordination than most of those who received it. No doubt it was this irregularity, which involved Papal censure and which was viewed in a much more serious light by the time the cause for Vincent's beatification was introduced at Rome, that occasioned the pious tarradiddle which set his age back by five years. The Fathers of the Congregation of the Mission may well have thought themselves justified for the reasons that I have already indicated, or for reasons which will never be known.

Further it should be noted that Vincent, instead of seeking a benefice immediately after ordination, went on with his theological studies for another four years. In all likelihood he shrewdly calculated that he could get a better benefice with a degree than without one; but I think he also deserves to be credited with a love of learning for its own sake. Obscure and modest though he was, we must suppose that he was not unconscious of his powers, and that greatness of soul, as well as ambition, prompted him to remain at the university.

Finally it should be remarked that, though Vincent never became a great scholar, this degree and the one he subsequently obtained in canon law at the Sorbonne, prove that at least he had more than respectable learning. And this learning is further proved not only by the diplomas found in his room after his death, but by his correspondence. The attacks made on him later by the Jansenists on the ground of his ignorance are therefore quite absurd, for that ignorance is disproved by the actions of the earliest Jansenists themselves, who did their utmost to attach him to their party. Equally absurd are the efforts made by some of his anti-Jansenist biographers to prove that he was a licentiate, and even a doctor of theology. What he had was a well-trained practical mind, not a speculative intelligence of a high order. If he was neither one of those dull, plodding fellows who make a good showing in examinations, nor one who sparkled with epigrams, he was naturally vivacious, and never did or said a stupid thing. His balance was certainly superior to that of his more brilliant friend Saint-Cyran, who had also inordinate conceit. It would have been waste of time in Vincent's case to go on to the doctorate.

A somewhat crude and cruel sentence is to be found in a letter written by Flaubert to George Sand. It is this: "The purely intellectual type of man has done more for the human race than all the Saint Vincent de Pauls in the world." I do not know whether this sprang from Flaubert's having come across some echo of the old Jansenist gibes, though probably it did. But if he was merely expressing his conviction that the life of contemplation is—abstractly considered—higher than the life of action, he was saying no more than the Catholic Church has always affirmed and than Vincent de Paul would have been the first to admit. Contemplation—that is, the purely intellectual or spiritual life—is not, however, better in every given case. St. Thomas Aquinas would accept no administrative office, lest it should interfere with his speculative vocation; and he was right. St. Vincent de Paul was equally right in seeking only that amount of education which would equip him to perform adequately the active functions to which he was called.

Before we leave the life led by Vincent at Toulouse, we should note that he supported himself during his later years at the university by conducting a small school, or coaching establishment for boys, at Buzet. As this was fifteen miles away from the city, he no doubt found it inconveniently situated and so after a time moved with his pupils to Toulouse. Again we have a testimony to his ability and energy. The school flourished; it numbered among its students, if we are to believe the Canon de Saint-Martin, two grand-nephews of no less a personage than the Master of the Order of St. John of Jerusalem. But I have my doubts as to whether Vincent liked being a pedagogue, or was a particularly good one. We know at any rate that the school supported him, and that it enabled him to pay off some of his debts. We also may assume that, soon after he had obtained his degree, he disbanded this establishment and began to look for a benefice.[2] He was still very far from having found his life's work.

[2] Or this may be inferred from what follows. Vincent could hardly have gone to Rome (presumably at the end of 1604, for we know that he did go early in life) had his school still been in existence. His disappearance the following year would have been even more sensational than it was had he been attached to any definite employment. His degree qualified him to expound the Master of the Sentences at the University, but there is not the slightest indication that he ever did so.

(4. By the Waters of Babylon

THE offer of a benefice was not long in forthcoming,—a very good one at Tilh, not far from Vincent's own home. It must have been a keen disappointment to him that another claimant appealed to Rome, and won his case.[1] There is no need to credit him at this stage of his career with the admirable disinterestedness he showed in later life. He thought Tilh a plum worth all the time and expense of a journey to Rome to pluck. As for the "disinclination for lawsuits" some of his biographers point out, that too was a later development, and probably took its origin quite as much from good-sense as from sanctity.

We hear another—and (considering Vincent's youth and humble origin) a more startling story—about the proffer of a great ecclesiastical benefice. According to this tale, the Duc d'Épernon summoned him to Bordeaux and held out hopes of a bishopric. Abelly, who says that this was in 1606, adds that the Duke had two relatives at the school, but again our authority is the questionable one of Canon de Saint-Martin. We know, however, from a letter by Vincent that he did go to Bordeaux "on a matter I do not even dare to mention." In the same letter he speaks of his urgent need of money to pay his debts. If the Duc d'Épernon really did offer a bishopric— against this is the fact mentioned by Père Coste that the

[1] Abelly says that Vincent withdrew his claim, and in this he is followed by Coste. I cannot believe that there was any withdrawal, for Vincent went to Rome himself, which does not look as though he was willing to give up without a fight. He may, however, have been advised there that he had no chance of success. The date of this is put by Abelly immediately after Vincent's ordination. Coste, who puts it after the obtaining of the degree, would seem to make a better case. Vincent could hardly have gone to Rome while he was conducting the school at Buzet, yet, as he himself tells us, he was in Rome during the reign of Clement VIII, which fixes the date of the visit during the winter of 1604-5.

Duke did not become Governor of Guienne until 1622—Vincent
would assuredly have snapped it up. More likely, as is so often
the case with great personages, there was a large vague promise
of the use of influence, and small performance. At any rate
nothing came of the affair, except another disappointment.

But now there arrived an unexpected little windfall. An old
lady in Toulouse died and left him some property. It consisted
of a debt owed her by a young man who had absconded to
Marseilles. Needing the money, Vincent set off in pursuit, selling, as he tells us, in order to defray the expenses of the
journey, a hired horse, with the intention of paying for it as
soon as he got what was due him. He found his debtor, had
him arrested, and then compounded for three hundred crowns.
"There is certainly very little resemblance," comments Coste,
"between this Vincent de Paul and the Saint we all know." The
net result of this transaction seems to have been a new debt
—to the owner of the horse. We are left with a suspicion that
this young priest was living beyond his means, in the hope
that his influential friends would secure for him a good appointment. Perhaps he really did believe that he was going to
get a bishopric. It should be added that the debts were all
eventually paid, and that Vincent had for the rest of his life
such a horror of them that he would never keep a man waiting
a day for his due, and even made a practice of sending the
money to a creditor's house so that he should not have the
trouble of calling for it. But his present crop of debts had to
wait a couple of years for settlement.

Instead of the looked-for advancement, which would have
buried Vincent in some sleepy snuggery in the South of France,
where we should never have heard of him, sudden disaster overwhelmed him, from which he emerged not yet indeed a saint
but still with a soul strengthened by suffering. He became a
slave.

With three hundred crowns in his pocket he was about to set back to Toulouse overland, where he meant to clear up the little matter of the horse, when an acquaintance suggested that, as the weather was so fine, it would be pleasanter to go by sea to Narbonne. Vincent no doubt knew that there was danger in this from the Barbary pirates, who were all the more numerous because the Fair of Beaucaire was attracting many ships to Marseilles. But he was young, and a Gascon, and the spice of danger was, perhaps, an added attraction. Neither young man was going to admit he was afraid, and they sailed out of the harbour in a bright blue July day.

The ship had not gone very far when it was attacked by three brigantines. Several of the sailors and passengers on board were killed; the rest were taken to Tunis and sold. One can picture their despair, for it was rare indeed that any so captured ever succeeded in getting back to their native land.

Vincent, who was himself wounded in the encounter, was, like the rest of his companions, stripped naked and given a pair of linen drawers and a cap, before being marched round the city in chains and then sold like an ox to the highest bidder. Our authority for all this is that of two letters written by himself to M. Comet, the authenticity of which has never been questioned. The only thing open to question is perhaps the literal accuracy of some of the details in what Bremond calls "the last chapter of the *Arabian Nights*."

In escaping being assigned to the galleys Vincent was extremely lucky. Possibly the fact that he was rather undersized and not very brawny saved him from that terrible fate or from being put to work in the marble quarries. Instead he fell to a fisherman.

Again his luck held. The fisherman discovered that this young man, who had been bred in an inland village, was unable to stand the choppy waves. As one who was perpetually

seasick could be of little use, Vincent was sold to an old alchemist, with whom he had about as pleasant a time as was
possible under the circumstances. Therefore, as has already
been pointed out, his whole career turned upon his never having been used to boats and so being peculiarly subject to *mal
de mer*. Had this not been the case he must inevitably have
remained a slave in Barbary for the rest of his life.

But with his new master he found congenial employment
—and in the end freedom. It is easy to surmise that the learned
Mohammedan thought that a bachelor of theology was just
the kind of assistant he was looking for. He evidently took a
fancy to his young Christian slave, for he initiated him into
some of his secrets, promising to impart all he knew and to
give him boundless wealth, if only Vincent would accept the
faith of the Prophet.

This, however, Vincent resolutely refused to do, though he
had a prodigious and what may even strike us as a rather simple-
minded respect for his master, and writes in his letter of "a
thousand beautiful geometrical matters," of which, however,
he mentions only two. These were a mirror of Archimedes,
not yet perfected, and a skull in which a spring had been so
placed as to make the jaws open and shut and speak. Ven-
triloquism was probably part of the trick.

Vincent solemnly assures us that the alchemist really did
possess the power of transmuting metals and that it was his
own duty as slave to look after the furnaces which turned
silver into gold. By a reverse process mercury was frozen into
silver. Whatever the devices of this venerable humbug may
have been, Vincent clearly enjoyed taking part in these strange
rites. The fact that he did so was skilfully used by the *Advocatus Diaboli* a hundred years later when the cause of
canonization was introduced at Rome. Then it had to be shown

that there was a "scientific" alchemy which had nothing to do with the black arts. But Abelly (or those who prepared his documents) found it advisable to omit the portions of Vincent's letters dealing with these curious affairs. One trace (apart from the letters) still lingers of Vincent's employment in Tunis. He brought back with him a prescription for the cure of the gravel, and what purports to be this may still be seen in a provincial French hospital.

The bondage was not severe and the young scholar and the old got on excellently together. But "God," Vincent records, "always gave me a firm conviction that I should escape by the unceasing prayers I offered up to Him and the Virgin Mary."

His prayers were answered, as often happens, in an altogether unexpected way. Fame is always a dangerous thing to possess, and that of the alchemist had reached the ears of the Sultan in Turkey, who sent an order to the old man that he wished to see him exhibit his marvels. There was nothing for it but to obey; Vincent therefore passed into the hands of the alchemist's nephew.

Again he was sold, this time to a renegade named William Gautier who had once been a Franciscan friar but who was now living a jovial life with three wives on an inland farm.[2] This man—probably because he had once been a Christian— did not keep his harem strictly enclosed but permitted the members of it to go out and converse at length with the slave as he worked in the fields under a burning sky.

Two of these women, one of whom was a Greek Schismatic, felt compassion for their husband's slave. Though it is hard to picture Vincent as ever having been handsome, since the portraits of him in old age show him with a bulbous nose

[2] Recent research, however, has made this doubtful. The matter has been discussed in some recent numbers of the *Annales de la Congrégation de la Mission*.

and abnormally big ears, he may not have been bad looking in his youth. At least in those days he had all his teeth, and probably a vivacious presence. Since, even when he was very old, his eyes had fire and a humorous twinkle, we may be sure that at this time his animated bearing was attractive. Already we have seen that he had the faculty of impressing people. The hearts of the good Mohammedan ladies were not hard and went out to a young man who had been so unfortunate.

Besides, there was a certain feminine curiosity to hear something about the strange land of the Franks. From that, Vincent went on to talk about religion. Wisely, however, the young bachelor of theology, instead of giving them formal expositions of doctrine, sang Christian songs. With a fine sense of the fitness of things, he chose the classic dirges of exile, no doubt explaining to the ladies afterwards the meaning, and the occasion of the composition of the plaints of captivity, *Quomodo cantabimus in terra aliena* and *Super flumina Babylonis*. "We wept when we remembered Zion," "There they that carried us away captive required of us a song." The wives of Gautier must have been insensitive indeed had they not been touched. He went on to the *Salve Regina*, again translating, "To thee do we cry, poor banished children of Eve." And though the conclusion *"O clemens, O pia, O dulcis Virgo Maria!"* did not form part of the prayer until St. Bernard added it, and appears to many[3] a weak ending from the literary point of view, there

[3] Here Dr. Lappin makes the following comment, which I gratefully append as footnote:

"But not to once-Anglican Edward Hutton (who was received into the Church on Trinity Sunday, 1928, at S. Maria degli Angeli, Assisi, by Frate Bernadas Ibaldi—*vide* the *Tablet*, June 16, 1928). In his third book, *Studies in the Lives of the Saints* (pp. 48-9), (1902), he writes the following exquisitely Pateresque passage: "[St. Bernard] was buried, as indeed was fit, before our Lady's altar at Clairvaux, the Church adapting his song of praise to the Blessed Virgin for her own, welding it into her song, giving it thereby a serene immortality. To that sweet and glorious hymn, 'Salve Regina,' St. Bernard has alone of all saints been allowed to add the

is no question that the music to which these words are set is almost unbearably beautiful. The women wept and were entranced with compassion.

In particular the wife who had been born a Mohammedan was moved. She told her husband of what had happened and said that he had done wrong to abandon his religion. William Gautier knew that already. He, like so many others, had apostatised merely because he had no hope of ever returning to his native land and because he could buy his freedom by accepting the turban. No doubt his conformity was no more than external and he was counting upon finding on his death-bed some priest-slave who would reconcile him to the Church. It was for him a choice between that and the galleys or the marble-quarries.

Now with Vincent to help him he began to plan his escape. We must suppose that the two men were careful not to say anything about this to the wives. For while no doubt Gautier could set them all free to marry other husbands by the simple procedure called for by Mohammedan law of pronouncing the

---

three magnificent vocatives at the end, 'O clemens, O pia, O dulcis Virgo Maria.'

"The three pearls that he laid so softly at the feet of Mary come to us across nearly a thousand years without loss of perfection or pathos. Place them beside the crown of the Rosary and you will find they are, not less perfect, only a little simpler and sweeter and more loving. Her feet, where he laid them, are already too white for any gold to burn beside; it is only the simplest and most perfect jewels she can bear after the human tears of the 'Salve Regina.' Upon her head have fallen all the life and sweetness and hope of mankind, but her eyes are satiated with tears and her head is weary of bending to catch our faint supplications. The gold and jewels of the Rosary have wearied her, and she who is our advocate almost avoids the weeping eyes of a world that never gives her peace. The cries of a world concerned with its own salvation, eternally busied with invoking her aid, her pity and prayers are but the music she has heard for a thousand years. But a new song arises, and she hears for the first time the three new names that man has given her: 'O clemens, O pia, O dulcis Virgo Maria,' and her eyelids are no longer weary with heaviness, nor her ears deaf with a repeated song, and it is almost with a new joy that she listens to the versicle 'Ora pro nobis, sancta Dei genetrix, ut digni efficiamur promissionibus Christi.' "

formula, "I divorce you," they may not have wanted to let
him go. It could hardly have been part of their calculations
that he would carry matters to such an extreme as to desert
them. Besides, would a secret entrusted to a woman—to *three*
women!—be safely kept? We may surmise that it was these
domestic complications that made Vincent and Gautier defer
their flight for ten months.

At last in June, 1607 the two Christians got into a small
boat and set out to sea, landing on the 28th of that month
at Aiguesmortes. The following day, the feast of St. Peter and
St. Paul, the Papal Vice-Legate, Peter Montorio, reconciled
William Gautier in the church of St. Peter at Avignon. So
thrilled was Montorio by the story the two fugitives had to
tell that he promised to take them with him to Rome, where
he intended to place the Friar in a penitential monastery of
his order and to find the young secular priest a benefice.

It would seem that Montorio had an additional motive in all
this: he knew that by presenting his protegé in Rome he would
create a sensation there. And as he was himself a life-long dab-
bler in alchemy, he perhaps wanted to produce a witness to
its marvels at the Papal court.

Even if Vincent was unable to explain how the old magician
had succeeded in transmuting metals, he could at least testify
to the fact. And Vincent's letters tell us how the Vice-Legate
did actually exhibit the Archimedes Mirror and the talking
skull to His Holiness and the cardinals, being, however, very
careful to keep to himself the method by which these conjuring
tricks were performed. Vincent, for his part, was to say nothing
to anybody else; Montorio wished to enjoy the credit alone.
By way of reward he was to be given a benefice. Then he intended to return to France, pay off his debts, and settle down.

All this took some time. Vincent lived with his Lordship for
over a year (continuing his theological studies in the meantime,

it should be noted), but waiting for the documents he needed
from the Bishop of Dax. The affair was entrusted to the discreet handling of the lawyer, M. Comet, to whose sons he had
once been tutor, and Vincent wrote to him asking him to obtain a letter of recommendation from the Bishop, who, he added,
was welcome to make any inquiries he chose, "as I have always
been regarded as a good-living man."

Once again we see a Vincent de Paul acting with a perfectly
proper human prudence but showing nothing of that humility
which made him, after he had arrived at sanctity, declare himself to all and sundry "The greatest of sinners." Providentially,
the documents when they arrived, were not in the correct form,
and had to be sent back twice before they were in order. I have
a suspicion—it can be no more than a suspicion—that the in-
advertence of the Bishop of Dax was by design. He can hardly
be blamed if he wanted to know a little bit more about Vincent's
disappearance before giving him an appointment in his diocese.
At all events, no appointment came from that quarter, though
of course this may have been on account of there being no
vacancy. It resulted in the young priest going to Paris instead
of to the Landes.

And now, having recorded these adventures, there is need
to offer some comment upon them. M. Pierre Grandchamp has
recently written two articles (in *La France en Tunisie au
XVIIᵉ Siècle*) whose thesis is contained in their title, *La Pré-
tendue Captivité de Saint Vincent de Paul à Tunis*. He does
not contest the authenticity of the letters to Comet, which is
beyond question, but he does suggest that the whole story is
a fabrication. I am inclined to believe that there was a certain
amount of mild romancing and that Vincent may have touched
up a few of the more romantic details. But Vincent clearly *was*
in Rome with the Vice-Legate when he wrote his letters to
Comet; and there *are* documents (or at least copies of docu-

ments) which attest to the reconciliation of William Gautier at Avignon on June 29, 1607. The very fact that one of these refers to Gautier as a "minister" who had once been a Friar Minor seems to me to demonstrate the existence of earlier records: a later copyist would naturally suppose that this was the case of a man who had apostatised to Calvinism.

The point is made by M. Grandchamp that Vincent never spoke of these matters to his confrères, and this has some weight in view of Vincent's habit of speaking disparagingly of himself, and of his having abundant opportunities, at the time he sent missionaries to work among the slaves of Barbary, of saying, "I, too, was once a slave there."

Against this there are other considerations: to have spoken about his captivity would have revealed the patience and the faith with which he had endured it; and to have spoken in this way would have been abhorrent to Vincent. But I think the capital point is that he was afraid he would have given serious scandal—as would assuredly have happened—had he let it out that he had once taken part in alchemical experiments. What would not the Jansenists have made of this had they ever heard of it! It is one thing to say in general terms, "I am a great sinner," and quite another to specify in public the nature of the sin.

I cannot help feeling that Vincent was oppressed with his knowledge that when writing to Comet he had done a bit of romancing; to a man of cautious and sober speech that would be likely to be a canker in the conscience. What we do know is that these letters came to light only shortly before Vincent's death, when copies of them were sent to him by the descendants of Comet. Immediately he wrote begging that the originals should be returned so that he might destroy them. That this did not happen was due to the action of Brother Ducournau, the Saint's secretary, who took it upon himself, after consulting some of the Fathers at Saint-Lazare, to slip in a letter of his own asking that the originals be sent instead to him for safekeeping. He added, "In case he should ask you again for his letters, you might write to him and say you had sent them on and were very sorry that he had not received them." It is to this piece of pious duplicity that we owe their preservation.

But it would seem, from two phrases in Brother Ducournau's letter, that the fathers at Saint-Lazare did after all have some inkling of Vincent's adventures in Tunis, for the secretary writes, "None of us had ever heard *with any degree of certainty* that he had been in Barbary and *still less* that he had converted his master." I have ventured to italicise the words which indicate that there was at least some rumour of the affair. Vincent's reticence about himself is also manifested in "[The Fathers] would very much like to know . . . when and why he came to Paris, in what year and in what place he was ordained priest. . . . He never speaks to us about himself except to humble himself."

The letters tell us nothing about Vincent's coming to Paris; for that we have to go to Abelly. According to him Vincent was sent at the end of 1608 on a diplomatic mission from Cardinal d'Ossat, the French agent at Rome, to Henry IV. With that scrap to go on, some of the biographers have given rein to their fancy. M. Henri Lavedan, for instance, describes the meeting between the Béarnais King and the Gascon priest, even down to the detail of their tossing off bumpers of ruby Jurançon together.

Again we know very little, if anything at all. Père Coste raises the objection, as did Bougaud before him, that Cardinal d'Ossat had died in 1604. But of course it is quite possible for Abelly to have made a slip on this minor matter and nevertheless to be correct on the main question. It is not at all improbable that a priest, to whose capacity for holding his tongue

Montorio could testify, should have been employed to carry a message to the King. Montorio may have thought that, since he had failed to obtain any benefice for Vincent in Dax, he might now be giving him the opportunity of advancing his own fortunes. By this time too he had got out of Vincent all that he was ever going to learn about those fascinating alchemical secrets, and the patronage of great men is apt to grow tired quickly. The most we can positively affirm is that Vincent was in Paris by the early days of 1609.

ℂ 5. In Search of a Benefice

VINCENT was now twenty-seven. From Montorio he may have obtained some money, and if he really did carry any diplomatic document to Henry IV, no doubt he got something out of that. But little could have been left out of the hundred and twenty crowns Gautier had gratefully handed over to him before entering his monastery. And in Toulouse debts were still owing, as in Pouy a widowed mother was wondering when her son was going to do something for the family. It was a matter of urgent necessity that Vincent find employment. In those days no priest was guaranteed a livelihood merely by virtue of his priesthood. A search for a benefice was therefore absolutely necessary.

So far from getting that at once in Paris, he nearly landed in jail. As he was fond of saying later, "One of the most certain marks that God has great designs on a person is when He sends desolation upon desolation, and sorrow upon sorrow." He spoke out of personal experience.

Being without an income and with his funds diminishing, he shared, for the sake of economy, a small apartment with a magistrate from Sore in the Landes. One morning Vincent, not being very well, kept his bed while his friend went out on business. Then the chemist's assistant, arriving with some medicine, while looking in the cupboard for a glass, saw a purse containing four hundred crowns left there by the magistrate. Perceiving his chance, the young rascal went off with the money, and the magistrate, upon his return that evening, accused Vincent of having stolen it. Why he did not go to the police about it is not clear, unless it was that he did not have sufficient evidence; but he made a scene, one day embarrassing Vincent very

much by going up to him while he was talking with the celebrated Père Bérulle and hissing, "Thief and hypocrite!" That
the reply was merely a "God knows the truth," has been taken
as an indication that Vincent had already attained great virtue.
That he did not fly into a rage with his accuser was no doubt
to his credit, but it seems to me to prove little more than that
Vincent had self-control. It was the wisest thing that he could
do under the circumstances; he knew that, after all, appearances were against him.

But he must have suffered from this false accusation, which
was all the harder to bear because he was looking for employment, for which the imputation of theft was anything but a
recommendation. However, it does not seem to have done Vincent much harm, because a year later he did obtain a most
surprising and unexpected position, though it was not until six
months later still that the real thief confessed his crime to the
magistrate, who at once wrote Vincent a most handsome letter
of apology for having suspected him.[1]

How Vincent obtained his appointment as Almoner to Marguerite, the former wife of Henry IV, we do not know; except
that it is generally understood that Charles du Fresne, one of
her secretaries, probably introduced the young priest to her.
However that may be, there is reason to suppose that Pierre
de Bérulle, the future Cardinal, had something to do with it,
for in his unobtrusive way, he was already an immensely influential person. Vincent had become acquainted with him soon
after his arrival in Paris, and for the next fifteen years or so
he did practically nothing without Bérulle's advice. Indeed, that

---

[1] Abelly wrote "six years," which his editor corrected to "six months."
One cannot always rely on Abelly's reckonings of time. Though Père
Coste says that the correction was an "obvious mistake," the shorter period
strikes me as being more likely. For had Vincent been under a cloud for
six years, it seems hardly likely that he would have obtained the position he
did about a year later—or the one after that.

is to put the situation too weakly: though he gradually came to stand on his own feet—without any lessening of the tie of friendship, however—at this stage of his career he practically put himself at Bérulle's disposal; and it was the making of him. It is to the insight that Bérulle had of the capabilities of his new friend and of the designs God had for him that we owe Vincent's career, as we owe so much else. For Bérulle, who had already directed Madame Acarie in the introduction of the Carmelites to France, and who was within two years to found the Oratory—which was to do a work in some respects similar to Vincent's own—was already encouraging Adrian Bourdoise and John Eudes in their plans for establishing seminaries, and his house was the centre of all that was best in the spiritual life in Paris.

At the moment he was too cautious to attempt to launch a man as yet untried on anything too ambitious; it was enough that Vincent should be provided with work that would give him a livelihood and in which he could be kept under his own eye. But wires were pulled, probably with the aid of the amiable Du Fresne, and Vincent found a position in Queen Marguerite's household.

Marguerite de Valois had been married in 1572 to Henry of Navarre. She had been forced into it very reluctantly as a pawn in the political game; but her unhappy marriage had been annulled by Rome on the double grounds of lack of consent and consanguinity in 1599, whereupon she had been replaced by the Rubenesque Marie de' Medici, who was neglected in her turn by the over-gallant King.

Henry must often have regretted the exchange. Where Marie was unhandsome and cantankerous, Marguerite had been vivacious, intelligent and beautiful. Though her comment, "Don't let anyone say that marriages are made in heaven; the gods are not so unjust," was somewhat acidulous, she was on the whole a good-natured and kind hearted person. But her own gallantries in youth had been almost as notorious as those of her husband.

By the time Vincent got to know her all that had changed. No longer did she have the

"Cheveux ondelez,
Nouez, retors, recrespez, annelez"

that Ronsard had praised in her. Nor could it be said now, as Brantôme once said, "If ever there was a perfect beauty, it is she . . . her carriage and majesty of bearing are such that she seems rather a goddess from heaven than an earthly princess." On the other hand, now that old age was approaching, she had left her former follies and was devoting herself to works of religion and charity. She was on good terms with her former husband and his new wife and they and the Dauphin frequently visited her in her magnificent palace.

Her benefactions were immense. She supported a hundred poor people and forty exiled English priests. Despite her scathing remark about marriage, she provided dowries for poor girls. On the feasts of the Church she distributed gold among the needy, and during Holy Week visited the hospitals. At Mass every day, and at Communion three times a week, she managed to impart a courtly air to her piety. Her penances were of a large and luxurious sort. But she was genuinely kind, if in a rather high-handed way, and universally liked.

Perhaps the most amusing thing to recall of her devotional exercises is that she had built a circular and domed chapel in which she established a community of Augustinian canons who had the obligation of singing day and night in pairs without ceasing hymns of her own composition. But one wonders how much of this verse was actually composed by herself. The fact that she had François Maynard, the disciple of Malherbe, as

one of her secretaries leads one to suspect that among the
duties of the hapless poet was that of improving her faltering
rhymes. Even so the Augustinians chanted without zest and
failed to do justice to her compositions, so that one day she
had an outburst of temper and summarily dismissed them. The
old soul was by way of being something of a character.

Vincent's duties were to look after the distribution of her
alms. For this he received no salary—that was not the way
of the times—but was provided with the *commendam* of the
Cistercian abbey of Saint-Léonard-de-Chaumes, from which he
derived a nominal revenue of twelve hundred livres but which
actually brought him in very little, since he found the abbey
was involved in several lawsuits.[2] But doubtless he felt elated
at the thought that he had at last begun to ascend the ladder
of fortune.

On the 17th of February that year, a few months before he
had received his appointment, he had written to his mother
telling her that he was still looking for "an opportunity of
advancement" and of obtaining "an honourable retirement so
that I may spend the rest of my days beside you." Though
Bougaud calls this letter one written in depression, it seems
to me remarkably cheerful under the circumstances, for Vincent
concludes with a suggestion that one of his nephews be sent to
college and, lest his own case should have disillusioned his
peasant family as to the value of education, he adds: "My mis-
fortunes and the little assistance I have so far been able to
render the family may possibly make him unwilling to do so;
but let him not forget that present ill-luck is indicative of future
prosperity."

[2] I reproduce Abelly's footnote: "The abbey of Saint-Léonard-de-Chaumes,
of the Cistercian order, was situated about a league from La Rochelle . . .
The brief conferred this abbey on Vincent de Paul, almoner to Queen
Marguerite . . . bachelor in theology, and is dated June 10, 1610, about
a month after the death of Henry IV. The Saint resigned it November 21,
1616."

That is a sensible and manly letter, but it is clear that Vincent was thinking mainly of "honourable retirement" and "opportunities for advancement." And when he entered the glittering household of Marguerite de Valois he must have supposed that his moment had come. Pierre Bérulle—to say nothing of God—thought otherwise.

What happened now was a mysterious spiritual crisis. It seems that among the clerics attached to the ex-Queen's house was a doctor of theology, who had won some renown by theological controversy, but who was at that time being overwhelmed with doubts as to the most fundamental Christian doctrines. Today I suppose we should say that he was suffering from a nervous breakdown. We hear of his being obsessed with the idea of throwing himself out of a window. As for praying, even if he began to say the *Paternoster* he was immediately assailed by terrifying spectres. Vincent, using his common-sense, told him that in this condition he should not attempt to pray at all but content himself with making an act of faith by pointing towards Rome or towards a church, if one were in sight. Perhaps with no other intention than that of cheering his friend up, Vincent offered to take the temptations upon himself. He was instantly overwhelmed in his turn.

If I may be allowed to venture a psychological explanation of this matter, it would be that the doubts Vincent now had to suffer offer the strongest possible proof of his faith. Though, supernaturally speaking, one may say that God allowed him to endure these temptations as a mode of proving his spiritual mettle, one may also say that this came about by the perfectly natural process of Vincent's feeling that, since he *had* made his offer, it was now incumbent upon him to be tempted. Precisely because he believed so vividly to the very roots of his being, it was inevitable that he should find his faith assaulted.

Abelly says that for three or four years he remained in this condition. The length of time is very open to question, for this period of acute mental torment did not begin until (at earliest) the middle of 1610 and must have been over by the end of the following year. But however long it may have lasted, Vincent had to endure an almost complete spiritual dereliction, during which the only way he could find relief was by making a physical act of faith, similar to that which he had suggested to the doctor of theology, by touching with his hand the articles of the Creed he had written out and wore over his heart.

Release came quite suddenly: it was when he made a promise to God to spend the rest of his life in the service of the poor. In other words, he got out of his chains as soon as he gave up the idea of making his way in the world. To every noble spirit an ambition less than noble is a bond. Having now renounced all for God, Vincent was at last free.

All this time Vincent had been living in constant touch with Bérulle, and for part of the time in the same house. If Bérulle said little as yet, he was carefully watching his protegé, probably understanding better than Vincent himself the nature of this spiritual crisis and waiting for the breaking-point. He must have noticed that the dangerous corner had been turned, that Vincent was not going to develop into another fashionable abbé. Instead he was aware of free time spent in work in the Charity Hospital nearby, and had heard of how when the Master of the Paris Mint made Vincent a personal gift of fifteen thousand livres, the whole amount was at once turned over to the Hospital. And when he was told of Vincent's determination to consecrate his life to the service of the poor, he devised a scheme for putting this into effect, one that would show whether it was only a passing fit of emotion or genuine determination.

It so happened that Bérulle was about this time planning to found the Oratory. And among the men who was going to join him was François Bourgoing, the Curé of Clichy, at that time a village of poor people, though one that took in a larger territory than the present Paris suburb. Well, let Vincent take Bourgoing's place. There would be hard work and plenty of it, and this would show of what stuff he was made.

The village Curé proved to be all that Bérulle had hoped. Appointed at the end of 1611, Vincent performed his pastoral duties with exemplary devotion, and expected nothing else than to remain among his rustic parishioners until his death. Unobtrusively he effected a reformation in Clichy, where his church still stands and where the font bears the date of his incumbency. But there was nothing sensational about it all. He got his people going regularly to confession and Communion; he founded sodalities; and he was happy.

This is why we know that Abelly must be mistaken about the "three or four years" of spiritual torment. For we hear of Vincent's saying one day to Cardinal de Retz (not the later and more famous cardinal but his uncle), "I think the Pope himself is not so happy as a parish priest in the midst of such kind hearted people. Not even you, My Lord, are as happy as I am."[3] To the end of his life he spoke of Clichy with emotion.

The one unusual feature of Vincent's work at Clichy was his taking into his house a number of young men and informally establishing a kind of *petite seminaire*. Of one of these young men we shall hear more later. He was then a student at the Sorbonne and was to become Vincent's first disciple. His name was Anthony Portail.

Vincent was not, however, destined to work long at Clichy, though he remained officially the Curé until 1625 or 1626, visiting his parish from time to time but leaving most of the actual work in the hands of substitutes. The keen eye of Bérulle

[3] Yet Coste dates Vincent's release as July, 1617, the time he went to Châtillon. Though surely it was by going to Clichy that Vincent indicated that he had dedicated his life to work among the poor.

had not lost sight of him, and what would seem to be a strange inspiration had come to the founder of the Oratory. Vincent was to take up work again in another great house.

To do so was quite contrary to the Curé's own inclinations. He must have felt that this was being unfaithful to his promise to God, and it could only have been his confidence in Bérulle that made him accept in the spirit of obedience what he was now asked to do. It proved to be the first step towards his distinctive lifework.

ℂ 6. Chaplain to a Great House

When Pierre Bérulle induced—we might say, practically ordered—Vincent de Paul to become chaplain to the Gondis he showed what amounted to genius. For though the opportunities provided by such a position only manifested themselves slowly and over a period of years, he had put Vincent in the way of fulfilling his vocation.

It should be added that all of Bérulle's dealings with his greater protegé show remarkable insight. It would probably have been easy enough for him to have persuaded Vincent in 1611 to join the newly-founded Oratory; had he done so, he would have obtained a valuable recruit, but have deflected a saint from his destiny. As we shall see, in the years that followed there were several occasions on which Vincent put the decision as to his career in Bérulle's hands, and Bérulle invariably made the right decision.

Yet Vincent, though at this stage of his career he needed this wise—this almost superhumanly wise—direction, he must not be looked upon, as the Abbé Bremond in his fine psychological study seems to look upon him, as unduly influenced by his friend. He followed Bérulle's direction up to a certain point, and that point was when he had at last discovered where his true vocation lay. From then on he stood firmly upon his own feet, maintaining indeed the old friendship as firmly as ever, but recognising that, valuable as Bérulle's advice always was, he need no longer follow it implicitly. In 1613 and for some years afterwards, however, Vincent acted always as though he were bound by a vow of religious obedience to Bérulle. Only such a spirit could have made him take up the distasteful task of acting as a chaplain and tutor in a noble household.

The Gondis were a family originally Florentine, and owed their advancement in France to that other Florentine, Catherine de' Medici. The founder of their fortunes in France was Albert de Gondi, an adroit politician, who, though he had given his consent to the Massacre on St. Bartholomew's Day, perceived (what few did perceive), that Henry of Navarre was destined to triumph over the opposition of the Catholic League, and switched accordingly—to his great advantage when Henry IV ascended the throne.

The family was duly rewarded, Albert de Gondi becoming a Marshal, and his brother Pierre, who was Bishop of Paris (only later was the see raised to the grade of an archbishopric), being created the first Cardinal de Retz. Albert's son, Philippe-Emmanuel, was appointed General of the Galleys, a position in which he was succeeded by his son, and Pierre's brother was made coadjutor bishop. In fact it may be said that these two offices were looked upon as the Gondi appanages. Paris had one Gondi after another as her bishops in unbroken line from 1570 to 1679, and the majority of these became cardinals.

All this must have been in Bérulle's mind. Knowing as he did that one of the young Gondis to whom Vincent would be tutor was practically certain in due course to become Bishop of Paris and Cardinal, and that the others were marked out for high positions in the State, he may well have thought that their training was of the utmost importance. On that side, however, we must say that he (and Vincent) suffered disappointment; the eldest boy, though he showed a marked piety, showed also an equally marked tendency to political intrigue. As for the see of Paris, when it became occupied by one of Vincent's pupils, it was held by the famous Cardinal de Retz. And he—though I confess that I have for this personage what most people will consider a deplorable weakness—was in many ways a cynical scoundrel. When Vincent went to the Gondis in 1613

John Francis Paul was not yet born (though he was to be before the year was out), and Vincent does not appear to have had much to do with his education. The young Gondi who already looked upon himself as a future cardinal, and who—dear little fellow!—used to tell his elder brother that, as such, he would take precedence over him was Henry, then about three years old, who died in 1622 from a kick of a horse and so left the ecclesiastical road open for his younger brother. The only one of the boys, therefore, whom Vincent was at the moment called upon to tutor was Pierre, the future Duc de Retz, who was eleven.

Yet their father, Philippe-Emmanuel de Gondi, Comte de Joigny, Marquis des Isles-d'Or, Baron de Montmirail and de Villepreux, and his wife, Françoise Marguerite de Silly, were notably pious people, even if their piety was not so free from worldliness as to seek no ecclesiastical advancement for their young son. But I think they may at least be credited with a wish to have little Henry—since he was to become a bishop and a cardinal—brought up in such a way as to give edification in his exalted office. For already they noticed, what was soon to be evident to everybody, that their children were far from having a naturally good disposition.

I admit that I have a greater liking for the father than for the mother. The Count, as may be seen from the print of him by Duflos, was a glorious creature, handsome of face, gallant in bearing, with curled locks and a wonderful pointed beard. There he stands for us still, beruffled and plumed, wearing over his velvet and laces and cloth of gold the cross of the Order of the Holy Ghost. As a warrior he did not perhaps have adequate opportunities, since the galleys over which he held supreme command were not a very effective naval instrument, and were mainly employed in the police work of chasing Barbary pirates, but he took his part in the naval operations during

the less famous of the sieges of La Rochelle, where he acquitted himself bravely. His celebrated son, who left so many
vivid portraits of his contemporaries in his *Memoirs*—many of
them highly malicious—says kindly of him: "I do not believe
there was a better hearted man in the world than my father,
who was truly virtuous. However, neither my duelling nor my
gallantries were sufficient to deter him from sending me into
the ecclesiastical state, though there was no one, perhaps, in
the world less suited. . . . The prospect of the archbishopric
which belonged to our house led to this determination. He did
not think so himself, and I would pledge my word that in his
heart he was urged by no other motive than the fear that any
other profession would expose my soul to great danger." To
put it in a slightly different way, as he knew his son was inclined to be wild, he imagined that an archbishopric would
induce virtue—a very dangerous supposition, as time was to
show.

Time, however, showed other things as well. After the death
of his wife, Philippe-Emmanuel de Gondi, inconsolable at the
loss of such a treasure, entered the Oratory, in which retreat,
refusing all offices and living in retirement, he survived Vincent
de Paul.

His grief over the death of Marguerite seems to me to reflect
more honour to himself than to her. For I may as well say at
once that, though Vincent's biographers in concert lavish praise
upon "this angel," "this saint" for her sweetness of character, I
cannot bring myself to like her. The fault, I know, may be
mine, but at least I am going to be honest: though I am sure
she was a very good woman, she strikes me as also a very tiresome one. Unconsciously, maybe, she was a great egotist, one of
those spiritual hypochondriacs who always need to have somebody at hand to feel their pulse. She might almost have been
the person the admirable La Bruyère had in mind when he

wrote, "If a woman should tell her father-confessor, among her other weaknesses, those which she has for her director, and the time she wastes in his company, perhaps she might be enjoined as a penance to leave him." Vincent was to discover the truth of this and, as he failed to induce her to take another spiritual director, the day came when he simply could endure it no longer and packed up and fled.

Duflos has a print of her, too, in all her finery. We see a rather pretty little blonde with that long nose and slightly sloping chin which are so often an index to inordinate self-will. Her soft and listless eyes masked the fact that she had a temper—something easy enough to forgive—and that kind of roundabout unscrupulousness in getting her own way which is not quite so easy to condone. She was given to tantrums which she thought to expiate by falling on her knees afterwards and asking pardon. I cannot help having a feeling that if she had been more even tempered, more sensible, and less exacting, that her son the future Cardinal de Retz would have turned out better than he did. There is unfortunately a type of virtuous woman that does not make virtue very attractive.

Yet let us give the Comtesse her due. She was open-handed—though it must have been partly due to her extravagance, that, despite his enormous income, her husband was always head over heels in debt. And she not only gave to the poor but, under Vincent's direction, worked among them. Her most solid title to fame and our gratitude is that it was she who established the nucleus of the fund that was many years later to endow the Congregation of the Mission. She had the intelligence to see what needed to be done for the spiritually neglected peasantry—on the Gondi estates alone there were no less than seven or eight thousand "subjects"—and it was she who gave Vincent the means he needed for doing it.

How far she was prompted in all this by Bérulle we do not

know, but the founder of the Oratory was a kind of super director of hers, to whom she appealed in special emergencies, just as she used her brother-in-law, the Bishop of Paris, whenever any intricate set of wires needed pulling.

In 1615, impressed by the holiness of her children's tutor, she conceived the idea that it would be a very convenient arrangement if she could persuade a priest who was always in the house, and who accompanied the family when it went to one or other of its numerous estates, to act as her spiritual guide. Vincent, in some alarm, declined; whereupon she promptly had recourse to Bérulle and, as usual, got what she wanted. But as Père Coste guardedly writes, "If the confessor was deeply edified by the delicacy of conscience of this chosen soul . . . he had, on the other hand, much to endure from her scrupulosity. . . . He considered that the best remedy was to divert this devout woman's attention from thinking too much about herself, to doing good to others."

As a mark of gratitude to Vincent she set the necessary wheels in motion to obtain for him a canonry at Écouis. He was still the titular Abbot of Saint-Léonard-de-Chaumes, and Curé of Clichy; but now he was provided with a second ecclesiastical sinecure. Only once did he visit Écouis, and that was only to be formally installed and to give the dinner dictated by pleasant custom to the Chapter. Neither of these benefices did he retain for more than a short time, for though the holding of them was perfectly permissible, according to the standards prevailing at the time, his conscience did not permit him to remain easy as a pluralist. His charge at Clichy was a very different matter; he went there to preach and look over his parish whenever an opportunity occurred. Moreover it is almost certain that he expected to go back to his parish and that he looked upon his stay with the Gondis as only temporary. Had he still been ambitious, now was his chance to advance. Instead he was to use the wide circle of wealthy and noble acquaintances he had made for the purposes of a charity whose sweep was still unguessed by him. By laying aside ambition he furthered the designs of Providence.

He certainly did not enjoy being in such high society. For though he made a private compact with himself to treat the Comte as though he were Jesus Christ and the Comtesse as though she were Our Lady, it was noted that he escaped from their society whenever he could and spent most of the time when he was not with his young pupils in his own room. So much was this the case that Madame de Gondi got worried lest it was a sign that Vincent was bored and unhappy. Abelly tells us that the Saint was of a naturally melancholy temperament, and Abelly should know. But the only two periods of depression we can observe in Vincent's life are those of his temptations against faith while he was with Marguerite de Valois and his first term of service with the Gondis. For the rest he strikes us as of an unusually cheerful disposition, bearing his slavery not only with courage but almost with a kind of radiance. If he seemed depressed while with the Gondis, there must have been a reason for it.

There were, I think, several reasons for it. One was that the Comtesse, for all her good qualities, was rather trying. Another was that Vincent would have far preferred being among his humble parishioners at Clichy. But another—and that this reason did exist will be shown from some excerpts which will be given later from one of the Comtesse's letters—was that Vincent found his young charges very much of a handful. Their aunt, the Marquise de Maignelay, once described them as veritable devils. And though the judgment of pious aunts on their high-spirited nephews are not always to be received at their face value, in this case it must be allowed that the phrase exactly hit them off.

Moreover, as will soon appear from one of the mother's letters, not only were they bad boys, but Vincent did not feel himself to be a suitable teacher. If he slipped away to his room, it could not have been merely because he was bored but because, after wrestling with them for a morning, he felt utterly exhausted. It is a great pity that the first two hundred and fifty pages of Cardinal de Retz's *Memoirs* got lost. Judging from the kind of things that he put into the portion that has been preserved, they probably contained an urbanely malicious account of Vincent de Paul as a teacher of young devils. De Retz had, indeed, to the end of his life a great respect for his former tutor, and to his credit it must be said that he was not addicted to the whitewashing of himself. But one somehow has a feeling that little John Francis Paul de Gondi did not have any very highly developed reverence for Monsieur Vincent in the days when he was his pupil.

Whatever motive, or group of motives, may have actuated Vincent, we know that by the summer of 1617, he had had all he could stand of the Gondis. Packing up a few things, and giving out that he was going a short journey—which probably was assumed to be one to Clichy—Vincent fled from the house.

⟨ 7. The Flight to Châtillon

SOME of Vincent's possible motives for this flight have already been indicated. Others have been suggested by some of his biographers, Bougaud, for instance, hinting that the assassination of Concini excited the Gondi household (which also was of Florentine origin), to feverish (and to Vincent, distasteful) political discussion. The suggestion does not seem to have very much point: for though Gondi may just possibly have been in Paris on the fatal 24th of April, he was certainly on duty at Marseilles in June, and he, if anyone, would have done the talking.

A much more plausible motive—though it does not appear to be the only one, despite its having been advanced by Vincent himself—is that he had begun to yearn again for doing active pastoral work. As a rule in such cases sudden action is brought about by a number of factors. Both the General of the Galleys and his wife evidently set down Vincent's unannounced departure to a desperate conviction that he could no longer cope with the boys.

However, so as to bear all factors in mind, it must be recorded that during January 1617, when the family was at their château of Folleville, an old peasant who had the reputation of being a very good man lay dying. Vincent went to see him, accompanied by Madame Gondi, and after the priest had heard a general confession, the dying man turned to the Comtesse and confided to her that he was very grateful that he had been persuaded to make a general confession, as his conscience was deeply burdened with sin. She, on leaving with Vincent, said, "If such is the case with this man, who passed as a good-living person, what is the case of others who are living an evil life?

Oh, Monsieur Vincent, how many souls are perishing! What is the remedy for this state of affairs?"

The remedy was a sermon by Vincent at Folleville the next Sunday, which happened most appropriately to be the feast of the Conversion of St. Paul; and the congregation was so stirred that everybody wanted to make a general confession. The Jesuits of Amiens had to be hastily summoned to help hear them, and they and Vincent went the rounds of the adjoining villages. In later years Vincent used to say that this sermon of January 25 was the beginning of the Mission. He also tells us that, in those days, he had only one sermon, which he used to twist a thousand ways; it was one intended to arouse the fear of God. Later his burden became that of the divine love—though of course he never was touched with the mediocrity of our time which, having smothered the love of God in sentimentality, has also ceased to fear Him.

That there was need for such general confessions became all the more evident to Madame de Gondi when she noticed that the parish priest, instead of giving her absolution by the correct formula, merely mumbled something. Investigation proved that a large proportion of priests did not know the proper formula, so the Comtesse after this took the precaution of writing it out and asking her confessor to read it. Here was a terrible revelation as to the state of both clergy and people at that period. And it began to weigh heavily on Vincent's conscience. Why should he waste his time upon three incorrigible small boys and a pious lady who—even if her scrupulosity did make her live in morbid terror lest she die with a mortal sin on her soul—was certain to go to heaven, when all around there were ignorant and often disedifying priests and a laity to match? Was there not more urgent and important work waiting for him to do?

First Vincent consulted Père Bérulle, who had sent him to the Gondis, and who in fairness ought to be told that he intended to leave. Bérulle listened sympathetically and saw that the end of the tether had been reached. Nevertheless, instead of letting Vincent go back to Clichy, he proposed something else.

A few years before two oratorians had been with the Archbishop of Lyons, Denis de Marquemont, on a visitation to the parish of Châtillon-les-Dombes in Bresse, and had observed then how deplorable was the state of affairs. Bérulle, who had heard this report, undertook to arrange with his friend the Archbishop that Vincent de Paul should take charge of the parish, and try to build it up.

Châtillon had a large church and a chapel-of-ease, but religiously and morally was in a very bad way. A large number of the people were Protestants, though they had no regular minister. As for the Catholics, their six chantry priests contented themselves with their Mass obligations and spent most of their time in the taverns. They were probably slack rather than disorderly and all of them were elderly, but, even so, the presence of young women as servants in their houses caused tongues to wag. The town had a small hospital, which was falling into ruins; the church was dirty; the services were perfunctorily performed. Such was the condition of things when Vincent, with a doctor of theology from Lyons as his assistant, set to work.

Within a few months he had brought about so extraordinary a change that the people of Châtillon used to say afterwards that this alone ought to be enough to ensure his canonization. He managed to persuade the six chantry priests to live in community and attend to their duties. He instructed the children. He preached incessantly. His confessional became besieged from morning to night. And he effected some very notable conversions.

Among these were those of several worldly young society women who were recalled to a practice of the Christian life, of John Beynier, a well-to-do Calvinist, whose name is worth recording if for no other reason that he became the procurator of Vincent's first Confraternity of Charity, and—most sensational of all—of the Comte de Rougemont, the notorious local bully.

It must be remembered that, in spite of Henry IV's edict against it, duelling was still prevalent. Every year thousands of men were slain, and in many duels each of the principals was accompanied by two, three, or even four seconds, who also fought. The slightest provocation was sufficient, and a slightly heated argument with one's dearest friend could lead to one of these bloody affairs of honour. Professional duellists numbered their victims by the score—the Chevalier d'Andrieux boasted seventy-two men slain by him—and a high-spirited gentleman almost came to feel that it was a disgrace to die except in his boots.

Cameron Rogers, in his book on Cyrano de Bergerac, gives with immense gusto, and what appears to be the fruit of learned research, some details on the *duello*. Thus he describes how, during the reign of Henry IV, six young men, all of them under twenty-five, Schomberg, Quelus, Livarot, Riberac, Maugiron and Antraguet, all close friends, decided to call one another out for a trivial point involved in a game of cup and ball. The last named alone survived, and he poignarded Quelus, whom he loved so much that he had paid his debts for him, merely because Quelus had too much pride, though lying on the ground, to surrender. The Prince de Joinville, son to the Duc de Guise, *le Balafré,* "fought four times in a morning with four private gentlemen who had seemed, only seemed, to stare a little closely at a ribbon worn by Joinville in his doublet. Joinville, afterward Duc de Chevreuse and a redoubtable swordsman, wounded all four, calling his thrusts as he fenced as a player at billiards might designate his strokes." Such famous duellists killed and were killed politely, for the mere sport of it, with,

as often as not, no hate or revenge involved. And though Richelieu severely enforced the edict against the *combat à outrance*,
and sent several offenders to the scaffold, not even he could
entirely suppress duelling, but had to content himself with
exacting the full rigour of the law only against too notorious
offenders and turned a conveniently blind eye upon duels which
were conducted without insolent ostentation.

The civil law forbade this practice; the Church of course
severely condemned it. But in the eyes of many of those of noble
or semi-noble rank, honour was superior to both religion and
law. We have an instance of this in the case of the pious Comte
de Gondi who one morning attended Mass devoutly as a preparation to crossing swords with somebody who had given him a
technical insult. Only with the greatest difficulty, and by begging
him on his knees not to go, did Vincent manage to dissuade him.

The Comte de Rougemont, of Châtillon, was a celebrated
swordsman, proud of his prowess. Life, in his eyes, without an
occasional duel, would be altogether without savour. But now,
touched by grace, he abandoned his former courses or remembered them only to say, "If I see anything that turns me away
from my sovereign good, I pray, I lop, I cut off, I get rid of the
bond; and these are my exercises." He founded a monastery and
gave away most of his possessions to the poor, and would have
given everything away had Vincent not prevented him. In the
chapel of his château the Blessed Sacrament was reserved and
adored. And one day, trying to find some last gift to offer God,
he remembered that he was wearing the sword he was never
going to use again in a duel. Following upon the impulse to
discard it, came the thought, "What! abandon this beloved
sword which has served me so well on so many occasions and
which, after God, has rescued me from a thousand perils!" He
concluded, what would he do if he were attacked unarmed?
But then he reflected that the mere carrying of this weapon

might prove a temptation if a quarrel were fastened upon him. At last he got off his horse and broke the steel blade upon a rock. On his death-bed he received the Capuchin habit.

The most important thing, however, that happened during Vincent's ministry at Châtillon was the founding of the first Confraternity of Charity.

This grain of mustard seed, from which so large a tree was to grow, was planted apparently without design and merely by accident. It happened, as Vincent was to tell his Daughters of Charity in one of his Conferences many years later, that there was a family in the town all of whose members were ill and destitute. Moved by their plight, Vincent preached about them in his sermon at Mass, and to such good effect that the parishioners held a meeting in the afternoon to see what could be done to help them. After Vespers, when Vincent went to visit the family, he met streams of people, some going to and some returning from the house of the man in question, so that upon his arrival he found that

"It snewed in his hous of mete and drynke."
The charitable people of Châtillon had overdone things. Confusion and waste were the results.

Vincent saw at once that what was needed was an organization which would at once foster and control the charitable instincts of his parishioners. One family had been helped to excess, but he knew that there were other families who also stood in need of help. He therefore summoned the parish to a meeting on August 23, when it was agreed that an association be formed for the permanent direction of charitable effort. Resolutions were passed that they should call themselves the Confraternity of Charity, that Jesus Christ should be chosen as its patron, and that its motto was to be, "Come ye blessed of my Father . . . for I was hungry and ye gave me to eat, I was sick and you visited me; for what you have done to the least of these you have done unto me." The key-note of all his later charitable enterprises was at once struck, and though experience dictated the modification of these first rules—for instance, it was found that male procurators were sometimes too inclined to arrogate too much to themselves—the main lines of charitable organization were laid down on that August day.[1]

The general idea was that those in need should be sought out, since many poor people were disinclined to ask for relief; that their cases should be investigated; and that help should be given according to their requirements. It was not a question of giving money, but of each member of the Confraternity taking it in turn to prepare and bring food. This was to be done "as if she were dealing with her own son or rather with God, Who refers to Himself whatever good she does to the poor." The quantity of food to be given was regulated, and above all, spiritual charity was to be blended with material assistance. A crucifix was to be supplied, where one was lacking, and the sick were to be prepared for confession and communion. If death occurred, the Confraternity were to attend the funeral "taking the place of mothers who accompany their children to the grave," and, if need be, pay the burial expenses.

Yet the rules were so drawn as to admit of extension in case of new needs, so that when, shortly after Vincent's departure, famine and an epidemic struck Châtillon, granaries were established and a place where medicines could be prepared. The germ of a wide-reaching scheme had been brought into existence.

It is interesting to note that all this occurred in the archdiocese of that same Denis de Marquemont whose opposition had deflected St. Francis de Sales from carrying out a somewhat similar idea with the Order of the Visitation. The archbishop

[1] The document, part of which is in Vincent's handwriting, is still at Châtillon.

had taken his stand upon the principle (or prejudice) prevalent in those days that if nuns were to be nuns they must keep their cloister. It was left to Vincent de Paul to cut that Gordian knot, though he did so unwittingly. For the Daughters of Charity, when they came into existence fifteen years later, were meant to be a group of country girls who should act as auxiliaries to the Confraternities modelled upon that of Châtillon-les-Dombes. They were not to be nuns, and indeed to this day they will tell you that they are not nuns in the ordinary sense.

We now begin to see how strange are the workings of Providence, and how unmistakable are its purposes when at last they appear. Vincent, impelled by whatever varied motives, had fled from the Gondis. And Bérulle had sent him to Châtillon. There, within a few months, he had not only reformed a disorderly parish—a great work, though one of only incidental significance—but had discovered his vocation. This being so, Providence—again operating most strangely, most strongly—removed him, and, of all things in the world, sent him back to the Gondis.

How this came about makes a story as amusing as it is instructive.

Vincent on taking French leave from the Hôtel Gondi in Paris, had not dared tell the Comtesse that he did not intend to return. He did not dare even to write to her; instead he wrote to the Comte at Marseilles, so that he might break the news gently to his wife, and gave as his reason for leaving the feeling he had of his being unsuited for the post of tutor.

Madame de Gondi, when she heard the news, had what can only be described as a fit. In the letter she wrote her husband it is clear that she regarded the reasons Vincent had given for his departure as not the real ones, and probably enough the famous feminine intuition was, up to a certain point, in this instance correct. Vincent, she said, was a coward not to have told her.

With regard to the imputation of cowardice, it might be said that there is no more discredit in a man's being afraid of a woman than of a woman's being afraid of a mouse. Both the man and the woman may still have heroic courage with regard to everything else. There is little question that Vincent was afraid of the pious Comtesse.

She, however, as has been already said, was a woman who generally managed to get her own way. Angry as she was with Vincent, her main concern was to get him to come back. She began to pull all the wires upon which she could lay her hands, and they were very many.

The Comte was of little use in this matter—husbands never are. Though we have a letter from him to Vincent, it does no more than mildly echo his wife's vehemence. Glad as he was when Vincent decided to return, it was not he who brought this about. In fact, one may surmise that, married to Madame, he had a sneaking masculine sympathy with Vincent.

Madame de Gondi's instruments were of another sort. She set a relative of hers, who lived near Châtillon, on Vincent's track. She wrote to the Cardinal of Paris and—aware of Bérulle's influence over Vincent—to Bérulle. All that Gondi did—since something had to be done to smoothe down the Comtesse's ruffled feelings—was to suggest moves that she might make to bring Vincent home. "Do everything in your power," he writes, "so that we may not lose him; for even if the motive he alleges were true, I should pay no attention to it whatsoever. . . . Tell him that even if it were true that M. Vincent could not teach youths, he could have a man under him. I passionately desire his return to my house in which he can live just as he pleases." From which it is evident that there is such a thing as masculine as well as feminine intuition.

To Père Bérulle the Comtesse writes to say that she is crying all the time and cannot eat. (Something must be done to make the soft heart of man melt at her woes!) She continues, "I bring no accusation against him; far from it." (A delightful touch, this!) "I believe he has done nothing save by God's special Providence . . . yet in truth, his flight is most strange. I confess I can make nothing of it. He knows the need I have of his guidance and . . . the sufferings I have endured through his lack of assistance;[2] and the good he did in my home and to the seven or eight thousand souls on my estates is gone forever. What! have these souls not been redeemed by the precious blood of Our Lord as well as those at Bresse?" (It is obvious that what she is really thinking of is herself and her family; the peasants on her estates are dragged in for the sake of impressing Bérulle.)

Madame's masterpiece, however, was her letter to Vincent himself: "Consider, then, whether my mind and my body can long sustain such anguish. I am in such a state that I can neither seek for nor receive any help from any other source, because you know quite well that I cannot treat of my spiritual necessities with many persons." (Her spiritual condition of course is of such a special delicacy that it calls for expert handling—which only Vincent can give.) "Once more I beseech you to show your charity towards us, for the love you bear Our Lord, to Whose will I deliver myself on this occasion, though greatly fearing I cannot persevere." (She is resigned to the will of God—only she isn't!) Then she delivers her most telling stroke, threatening Vincent with a form of spiritual blackmail: "If after all this you still refuse, I will charge you before God for all that may befall me. . . . There are very few who are capable

[2] Father Leonard translates "Mes enfants dépérissent tous les jours" as "My children are wasting away." The translation would be correct were it not for the context, and what we know of those "veritable devils." It is somehow not easy to believe that the Gondi boys, however much they may have liked their tutor, were dwindling to skin and bone because they were for the time being released from their books! I suggest as a translation, "My children grow worse and worse every day."

of assisting me. . . . I know that, as my life only serves to offend God, it is dangerous to place it in peril; but my soul should be assisted at the hour of death. Remember the state of apprehension in which you saw me in my last illness. . . . I shall probably soon be in a worse state, and the mere fear of it would cause me such pain that I think it would cause my death."

Vincent must have sighed over this revelation of "angelic" egotism and hypochondria, but he would have been hard-hearted indeed to have refused to listen to such a plea. Moreover, so as to make assurance doubly sure, the Comtesse sent her letter by Charles du Fresne—who had introduced Vincent into the household of Marguerite de Valois, and for whom Vincent had in turn obtained the position of secretary to the Gondis—and he carried a bundle of other letters. Among these were some from Cardinal de Retz, Bérulle, her children (who we may surmise wrote at their mother's dictation), and from all the ecclesiastics and religious orders in Paris who were under obligations to her. Under this avalanche Vincent fell.

He consented to consult Père Bence, the Superior of the Oratory at Lyons, who, shirking the giving of more direct advice, suggested that Vincent go back to Paris to hear what Bérulle had to say. There was nothing for it but for him to surrender.

It is interesting to note that, though he formally committed himself to no more than to ask Bérulle's advice, he understood perfectly well that, once he got to Paris, if Bérulle and the Cardinal were on Madame de Gondi's side, he had no chance. It all provides a most entertaining study of masculine and feminine psychology—a determined woman on one side overwhelming poor defenceless men with an interminable series of arguments and threats. The struggle was on unequal terms; as usual, the men had to give in. Vincent consented to ride back with Du Fresne.

He made a touching farewell to his parishioners at Châtillon, assuring them that when he came to their town it had been with the intention of staying there forever. But he knew he would never go back. So he distributed what few possessions he had among the people as mementos, even a battered old hat being fought for by several persons as though it were the relic of a saint—as indeed it was.

Paris was reached on December 23, when at once he talked over the situation with Bérulle and his other friends. The following day, Christmas Eve, Vincent rang the bell at the door of the Hôtel Gondi. He was the nicest Christmas present Madame had ever received.

⟨ 8. Extension of Work

THOUGH Vincent went back to the Gondis, it was on his own terms. The Countess had to be satisfied with having him at hand to give her the spiritual direction she so badly needed and which nobody else could give, and with her chaplain's keeping a general eye on her boys. It is reasonable to assume that he was relieved of the distasteful duties of tutorship. For though there is no positive documentary evidence that another tutor was now brought in—he probably had already been brought in during Vincent's absence—we know from the Gondis' letters that they were perfectly ready to make this concession.

There is the further fact that the future Cardinal de Retz acquired a much greater fund of knowledge than Vincent would have been able to impart. Latin Vincent could have taught him; possibly also Greek and a smattering of Italian. But the de Retz facility in these tongues, and in Spanish, German, and Hebrew—however much we may credit to subsequent studies with the Jesuits and at the Sorbonne—must have had its foundation laid down in these formative years.

But the decisive point is that Vincent was from now on too busy with other matters to have had any time to spare for the class-room. Until after the death of Comtesse de Joigny in June, 1625, Monsieur Vincent was a member of her household but was branching out more and more in work beyond it. Though he still, from time to time, felt a recurrence of his old depression, this was probably only during such periods as when the family was in Paris and he was unable to find the employment he loved. Yet like the sensible man he was, he did all he could to overcome what he called his naturally melancholy temperament, and, like the saint he was, he tells us that he turned to God and asked Him to change his cold and reserved temperament and to make him gracious. Certainly a charming graciousness became one of most striking characteristics, but it was a graciousness that was seen to be the fruit of grace. For the rest of his life there was visible upon his face not merely the good-nature of a happy disposition but the inner radiance of divine charity.

He had come rather late in life, and as a result of his five months in Châtillon-les-Dombes, to the discovery of his special vocation. From now on there was to be no hesitation. "You should not tread on the heels of Providence," he used to say; "but if Providence opens the way, you should run." Vincent ran; or if that term calls up an image which suggests precipitation, he pressed steadily and quietly forward, working unhurriedly but without ceasing until his death forty years later.

Yet two things should be noted at the outset. One is that though he showed he had organizing talents of the highest order, his work is not to be fully explained on that ground. Rather he left himself completely subject to the direction of God, living in so perfect a communion with his Creator that it was noticed that he never made even the most trivial decision without pausing a moment to seek the illumination of the Holy Spirit.

The other thing to be noted is that during the busy years of 1618-21, during which he was preaching missions and organizing Confraternities of Charity on the Gondi estates, his mind showed a suppleness which we must set down to his humility. Though the idea of establishing an association for the help of the poor had come to him at Châtillon as a sudden inspiration, and though all the later Confraternities were established upon the same general lines, he was completely without self-assertiveness or pride of opinion. He was always willing to receive suggestions, and always ready to make such modifications as later experience found advisable.

For instance: at Châtillon the work had been confined to the sick. He came to see that there were many people who were not actually sick who needed aid. Then, too, the first definition of poverty had been complete destitution; only those who had no means at all were eligible for the benefactions of the Confraternities. But that was discovered to be too rigid a means for determining eligibility. Consequently, the rule became that those who were capable of earning three-quarters of their livelihood, should have the other quarter supplied; that those who could earn half of what they needed should have the other half supplied; and that those who, because of old age or physical infirmity, could earn nothing at all should have all their wants supplied.

It must be pointed out, however, that the Confraternities did not, as a general rule, hand out money: they gave food and clothes and medicines, and offered that personal attention which was still more important. Only too well did Vincent know that there were people who would misuse alms. Moreover, in order to prevent the Confraternities from being imposed upon, a careful investigation was made of every case.

Now in all this, we have the main lines of modern charity organization—with an important difference. There were no paid workers, and so every sou collected was expended on the poor, instead of (as today) being diverted, from a fifth to a third of the amount collected, to the officials.

But there was another difference still more important: Vincent's charity was direct, individual, and animated by the love of God. Every poor man was to be treated with the veneration due to Christ Himself. There was to be none of that cold-blooded impersonality which has called forth the proverbial expression "as cold as charity," and has made most of our modern organizations stink in the nostrils of the poor.

Nor was there to be any discrimination on account of religion:

sinners and Protestants were to be helped as freely as edifying Catholics. And though nothing could have been more remote from Vincent's intention than the separation of corporal from spiritual works of mercy, there was to be no ramming of religion down anybody's throat. The members of the Confraternities were to persuade, if they could, those whom they visited to receive the priest and to make a confession, and especially were the sick to be induced to receive the Last Sacraments if they were dying; but if they refused these holy ministrations, they did not on that account disqualfiy themselves for the material assistance at the Confraternity's command. The only people disqualified were the lusty beggars who were capable of work but who refused to work. There were thousands of such cases.

These general principles, it will be seen, are of immeasurably greater significance—because of their permanent applicability—than were the details of organizations, which, however admirably they were fitted to Vincent's time, are not applicable at all points today. This nobody would have been quicker than Vincent himself to perceive and admit.

To indicate, without going into wearisome particulars, his plans in rough: it should be said that every women's Confraternity was organized with a President, a Treasurer, and a Keeper of Supplies, and (until friction arose on this account) with a male Procurator. The members—upon whom certain spiritual obligations rested, mainly those of going regularly to confession and communion—were to prepare the food themselves, in quantities specifically laid down by their rules, to visit the sick, to feed them if necessary, to pay for doctors and nurses when these were required, and to see that the dying made a good end and received Christian burial. Then a Mass for the repose of the departed soul was to be said.

The men's Confraternities, which followed in 1620, and from

which Vincent hoped more than he did even from the women (though in this he was disappointed), were expected to deal with the problem of mendicity—one which had reached alarming proportions in seventeenth century France—to establish workshops and hostels for tramps wherever circumstances called for them and to supply the necessary funds for apprenticing boys to a trade. A solemn obligation was laid upon all such apprentices of later teaching their trade gratis to others.

Further—and surely only one who had been brought up to mind livestock would have thought of this—in the country districts the Confraternities of men were encouraged to raise sheep and cattle, to be branded with the Confraternity's sign. These were to graze on the common lands and afterwards to be sold to obtain funds for the charitable enterprizes.

This, however, was only one means of raising the necessary money. Donations were to be sought from the rich, house to house canvassing was to be conducted, collections were to be made by young ladies at the church doors, and boxes for contributions were to be placed in taverns and other public places. In some cases magistrates, and those with seignorial rights, were persuaded to ear-mark tolls and similar minor taxes for the work. Obviously a great deal of money was needed, but, so far as I can discover, there was no instance of the misappropriation of funds. Under no circumstances was any money lent at interest; everything collected was to be kept intact for use as it was called for.

If the men's Confraternities never became so numerous or so flourishing as those of the women, the reason may in part be found in the fact that Vincent's main support in all this work came from the Comtesse de Joigny, and her sister-in-law, the immensely wealthy and devoted Marquise de Maignelay. But perhaps a deeper reason may be that women are, upon the whole, more compassionate and immediately responsive to concrete needs, and more practical, than men. It should at the same time be remembered that, though all Vincent's Confraternities were destroyed at the time of the Revolution, his men's groups were revived in another form in 1833 largely through the efforts of Frederic Ozanam, and are now operating in every well-organized Catholic parish as St. Vincent de Paul Societies.

The original plan of the Saint called for Confraternities of men and women working side by side, and sometimes in co-operation.[1] Thus in some places there was to be an annual meeting of the two bodies in which, after the presentation of accounts, the men were to make up any deficit. The women proved, however, to be more efficient than the men—so much so that, after a while, they rose up in arms against male procurators who, though they had done very little work, wanted to have the main say in the direction of affairs. This was a contingency not at first thought of by Vincent, and had to be corrected. In the same way it became necessary to draw up strict rules against any sort of favouritism in the distribution of offices.

In the furtherance of all this admirable enterprise great credit must be given to the Comtesse de Joigny. She still had a tendency to spiritual hypochondria and exacted from Vincent a promise that he would never leave her. But having given that promise, he applied the most salutary cure to her malady by setting her to work. And it must be allowed that she did work, up to the very limits of her somewhat fragile health. So far from being exempted from the obligations resting upon other members of the Confraternities of carrying food to the poor and of nursing

[1] So little was Vincent concerned that the Confraternities should be regarded as his own foundations, that he frequently—especially in the beginning—used one of the existing parish societies for the carrying out of his charitable purposes. If this plan was not particularly successful and had to be abandoned, it was because the organizations with which he was willing to cooperate sometimes felt a jealous suspicion that they were being absorbed into a new organization.

them with her own hands, the circumstance that she had more leisure than the others meant perhaps that she was expected, as her enthusiasm certainly impelled her, to do more. With admirable devotedness she gave herself to the needy. Whenever a Confraternity was founded, it was always her name that went down first, her purse that was opened most promptly and most widely. It did her a world of good. Though the great lady had her faults, she did by degrees develop into something resembling a saint.

Hardly less illustrious is the name of her sister-in-law. The Marquise de Maignelay, left a widow early in life when the Duc de Mayenne contrived a political assassination, would have become a Carmelite had not the Pope expressly forbidden it. She was to be of far more service to religion in the world. Therefore she gave away almost the whole of her rent-roll of three hundred and fifty thousand livres, and, wearing the plainest of clothes and driving in the shabbiest of carriages, or trudging on foot through the Paris mud, showed herself indefatigable in works of charity. Her graceless young nephew, the future Cardinal de Retz, was to write cynically but amusingly of these excursions in his *Memoirs*: "Every day I allowed my aunt to drag me into slums and garrets, and I often saw very well-dressed people, and sometimes well-known ones, who came in secret to receive alms. I did not play the pious person, because I was not certain how long I could keep it up; but I made much of them that feared the Lord, and to do so is, in their opinion, one of the chief indications of godliness." The Marquise did her best to make a good Christian of the youth, and his testimony leaves her covered with glory, even if she may have been imposed upon by his calculated hypocrisy. De Retz rather touchingly adds, "My good aunt seldom failed to tell them that they ought to remember her nephew in their prayers."

Her work, however, was mainly confined to Paris; that of

Vincent and the Comtesse de Joigny to the country. Yet admirable as it was, now and then it was opposed by the undiscerning. Though the organizers never acted without first obtaining the approbation of the Bishop, on at least one occasion a local functionary caused trouble. There is a record of delation made by the Lieutenant of Beauvais against the founding, in contravention of the royal edict against the establishment of any society, by "a certain priest named Vincent" of a "Confraternity of women without communicating with the municipal officials." The complaint was soon quashed; Vincent had friends powerful enough to see to that. It is nevertheless entertaining to notice the indignation and outraged dignity of the municipality of Beauvais.

All this while, it must be remembered, Vincent was giving missions on the Gondi estates. Indeed, Confraternities always came into being as an outcome of these missions. Vincent knew that nothing solid could be accomplished unless a quickening of religious fervour occurred first, and was followed up by steady work. Thus he visited in turn Folleville, Villepreux, Joigny (the principal Gondi estate), and Montmirail, evangelizing those country towns and the adjoining villages, and, after he had brought about an increase of the love of God in these places, established a Confraternity in each of them as a means of making divine love manifest itself in love for one's fellows. His cardinal principle was that of the First Epistle of St. John: "He that loveth not his brother whom he hath seen, how can he love God whom he hath not seen." That love, to his practical mind, had to show itself in practical action.

Nor were heretics neglected. For their conversion Vincent seems to have had a special gift. His method was not that of theological polemic, for which (though he did not lack aptitude) he had little taste, but of winning souls by gentle means. He had that kind of common sense which often counts for much more

than brilliant controversial talents. Thus we are told by himself that when one Calvinist argued that the Catholic Church,
with its hordes of ignorant priests and lazy monks could not
be of divine institution, Vincent, instead of employing the
famous argument of Boccaccio's Jew that the very corruptions
of the Church prove her divinity, since she has managed to
survive in spite of them—pointed out that, though there was
a good deal in the Calvinist's objections, the shortcomings of
individuals could not fairly be imputed to the Church herself.
When the further objection was raised that there was no virtue
in a certain image of Our Lady the Calvinist saw before him
in the church, Vincent promptly called upon a child to give the
correct answer: "It is good to have images and to pay them
the honour that is their due, not on account of the material
from which they are made, but because they represent God and
His Mother and the saints." Confuted so tellingly, the Calvinist
lived and died a Catholic.

Yet with all these highly original and valuable activities, Vincent's great life-work still remained only in germ. Here was
indeed a beginning—and a late beginning—but the full development was not to appear for many years. What we can say is that
from this point everything else that he did naturally flowed.
There was up to his death in old age a steady extension, unremitting industry, growth in personal sanctity; but already
we can see in the chaplain of the Gondis a Vincent de Paul
who has found his vocation at last.

ℂ 9. The Galley Slaves

THE fact that the Comte de Joigny was the General of the Galleys gave his chaplain access to the Conciergerie and other prisons in which the condemned were kept until such times as they could be sent to the Mediterranean ports. Vincent was appalled by the conditions as he found them to be.

It must be remembered that all prisons of the time were extremely bad, judged by modern standards. Even to our own day the French harshness in the matter of penal arrangements has been one of the scandals of the civilized world. Gondi was a very good-natured man, but, as he had not created the conditions, he—not unnaturally—did not consider that he was responsible. What is everybody's business is only too likely to be treated as nobody's business. The situation called for someone like Vincent de Paul who, so far from heaving a sigh and shrugging his shoulders, would take upon himself what needed to be done.

Political prisoners, in some instances, managed to have a fairly comfortable incarceration—so long as they were able to pay for their little comforts. But even in their case it is enough to mention the dark reputation of the Bastille to bring to mind the horrors of dank dungeon and verminous straw. Those condemned to the galleys were all poor and friendless and belonged to the most desperate type of criminal. It never occurred to society to give them any mercy—and they got none.

Vincent found them chained to the wall, in rags, with a little black bread as their food, and for the only alleviation of the monotony of their existence—and perhaps of that of their jailers—branding and the lash. If ill—and few escaped illness in such surroundings—no notice was taken of them. They were covered with lice; rats scuttled about the dark cells in which they were packed; they lived in the stench of their own ordure, loaded with manacles, cursing God for the fate that had befallen them, while waiting for the still worse fate of the galleys.

What Vincent did, as a start, was to get them transferred to better quarters in a house in the Faubourg Saint-Honoré. There they had at least cleaner cells, more light and air, and some medical attention. They did not escape their chains, but their new prison seemed to them a paradise after the old. Above all, Vincent, by going among them with kindly words, made them feel that there was somebody who cared for them. He brought in, as two assistant chaplains, Anthony Portail, who was destined to become the first of his disciples, and a priest named Belin. And the Marquise de Maignelay and other charitable ladies—among whom we may suppose was the wife of the General of the Galleys—brought clothes and food and shamed the brutal jailers into some semblance of humanity. The change that came about in a short time was the talk of all Paris.

Abelly says that Vincent began this work in 1622. Once again it is clear that he is inaccurate in his dates. For as a royal commission signed by Louis XIII on February 18, 1619, appointed Vincent Chaplain-General of the Galleys, it is safe to assume that Vincent's interest in the prisoners must have begun in the previous year. To the position, which carried with it the rank of a naval officer, an annual salary of six hundred livres was attached. He at once set about appointing chaplains to the galleys and began building a hospital at Marseilles for sick slaves. If he did not accompany any of the dolorous annual processions to the ports, this could not have been for the reason that Bougaud suggests—that it was beneath his dignity (for when did Vincent ever set store by his dignity?)—but because he did not have the time. All this while, it must be remembered, he was under an obligation to remain as much as possible with

Madame de Gondi. We know, however, that he did on at least two occasions visit Marseilles in person, and no doubt he sometimes was on board a galley when it set out to sea. But his work as Chaplain-General was one mainly of supervision.

The galleys did not make up a very effective naval force, and though they took some part at the siege of La Rochelle in 1622 (where we hear of Gondi bearing himself like the brave man he was)—they were used almost entirely for police duty in the Mediterranean against the Barbary pirates. They were indeed not built to carry enough provisions and munitions for long voyages. What they were intended for was the swift pursuit of marauders. Even so, they seldom left port during the winter months.

They were narrow, low-built vessels about a hundred and thirty feet long, carrying a couple of triangular lateen sails. For the most part, however, they relied upon their oars. On their prows they had erected a platform bearing five or six big guns, with a dozen smaller swivel guns distributed elsewhere. At their stern was the cabin where the officers lived, and above the rowers ran a half-deck called the *couroir* where the soldiers, of whom they carried about a hundred and twenty, had their stations. In the hold the soldiers slept.

Between the *couroir* and slightly below it was the gangway known as the *coursie*, where the petty officers in charge of the convicts walked, whip in hand. An overseer marked the rhythm of the stroke by blowing a whistle; the under-warders had the duty of seeing that this stroke was kept up. Sometimes the wretched convicts were obliged to row twenty-four hours on end, on which occasions they would be fed with ship's biscuit soaked in wine, put into their mouth by the guards so that there might be no cessation of their work.

Each galley had twenty-five benches on each side for the rowers, and on each bench there were five men. The strongest man, named the *passe-avant*, directed the oar, while the others, the *apostice*, the two *tercers*, down to the weakling *cague-rageole*, pulled in unison. The gang of five was called *la vogue*. They were all chained to heavy cannon-balls and slept—when they slept at all—between the benches.

Their hair (except for a tuft on the crown), their beards, and even their eye-brows were shaved; but they grew long mous-tachios—all of which made one of them who succeeded in escap-ing instantly recognisable. As if this were not enough, many of them had their ears and noses cut off by way of punishment. They wore as a rule only a pair of drawers, and a grimy red *beret*. But for cold weather at sea they were provided with coarse red jackets and overcoats. Around each man's neck went a cord on which was suspended a cork gag. When absolute silence was required at such times as the galleys were creeping up to take an enemy by surprise the order was issued, *Tap en bouche*. Then, however hard the guards laid on the lash, the rowers had to swallow their own screams and curses. As Abelly remarks, "It was a veritable picture of hell."

Under such conditions the men died like flies. Because there was never a sufficient number of rowers, magistrates looked upon it as a patriotic duty to sentence as many criminals as possible to the galleys. But as even that did not meet the de-mand, the officers were not at all scrupulous about retaining a convict, sometimes for years after his sentence had expired. Turkish slaves were also bought for the purpose in the markets of Italy, and Slavs in Constantinople. At a little later date, as a result of Richelieu's efforts to build up the fleet, volunteers were called for, and, so great was the number of destitute, volunteers were sometimes obtained. These, however, refused to be chained and had to be paid wages. It was a noble sight to see the galleys skimming out with their oars flashing and with all their flags flying; but out of sight in every one of them was the extreme of human misery.

The captain came as little into contact with the poor fellows who provided his vessel with motive power as does the captain of an Atlantic liner with the stokers. He knew they were there; he was provided with a list of their names; but he left the dirty work of driving them to the limit to his petty officers.

Vincent de Paul could hardly have undertaken a more difficult task than that of providing for the spiritual needs of these convicts—almost all of whom were consumed by a rage amounting to madness—or one that more badly needed to be done. And though he and his chaplains could not do much towards alleviating their hard physical lot, they did succeed in accomplishing miracles in the spiritual order. Under the degradation and despair of the convicts lived, as he knew, a capacity for goodness. These were souls for whom Christ had died. Sometimes they could even be brought to a wondering realization of the fact that they had a privilege in being crucified with Christ.

The most famous thing related of Vincent's association with the galley-slaves is a legend which, first put into circulation by Abelly, must be said at once to have absolutely no foundation. According to this story, Vincent once found a convict broken with dejection at having to leave his wife and children, and—in order to let the man go home to his family—took his place at the oar. Abelly, however, is rather guarded in his statement. "Although this was a most admirable act of charity," he writes, "we may say nevertheless, on still more certain evidence, that M. Vincent, by spending his time, care and possessions as he did, in the service of all the convicts, did something more advantageous to the glory of God than the pledging of his own liberty for a single individual." The only "evidence" that Abelly adduces is that once, many years later, one of the Fathers of the Mission asked Vincent what truth there was in the report, and that Vincent "answered with a smile." Obviously that is no evidence at all. We are not told how the question was framed. But even if it had been put in the most explicit terms, we do not know what kind of a smile was given in reply. There is not one of us but has given a smile which has been misinterpreted.

Yet, starting with this, the story has grown to be perhaps the best known of those told of Vincent, and all his biographers—with the honourable exception of Père Coste—have in turn further embellished it or have attempted to get round a material impossibility by means of an ingenious private hypothesis. Ulysse Maynard is perhaps the worst offender, for he takes one of the hearsay accounts given at the process of canonization (none of which, by the way, quite agrees with any of the others) and, without any warrant, makes it more circumstantial. The officer in charge, he says, would have still had his tally. If the pious fraud was discovered who would dare to condemn him? He responded, says Maynard, in tears without waiting for a more explicit authorization; Vincent put on the chains; and the young slave went home to his family. Then the Abbé falls back on Abelly's authority—without using Abelly's reserve—and says "[He] was besides a bishop of piety and learning, a pupil and friend of Saint Vincent de Paul, a personal witness of the life of his hero . . . Abelly therefore merits our full confidence, at least in the case of those anecdotes which do not arouse objections." All of which of course is to beg the question. Yet, having begged the question, he then attempts to fix the date, as though he had established his point.

He, like some of the other biographers, makes use of the Bull of Canonization as confirming the incident. To this it must be said that no historical statement in a Bull of Canonization has attaching to it the Papal infallibility which, by definition, is limited to pronouncements on faith and morals. But there is fortunately no need to make any temerarious effort to confute the Bull: it records merely "as something related" that Vincent once took the place of a slave in the galleys, but leaves one to infer that this belonged to the period of his captivity in Barbary.

What the Bull really amounts to is a rejection of the story in any of the forms in which it was told by the so-called witnesses. One of these, Charles Doustrebau, the parish priest of Fresnes in the Meaux diocese, gives the following version, one that is too much for even the Abbé Maynard to swallow: Madame de Gondi one day saw a kind-looking priest in the chain-gang and, upon discovering how he happened to be there, took him as her private chaplain. This would set the date in 1613, and of course is flatly contrary to what we positively know as to how Vincent was persuaded by Bérulle to leave the parish of Clichy to take up work as tutor in a nobleman's house. The matter is so preposterous as not to be worth arguing further.

What is much more important is the actual way that Vincent exercised his charity towards the galley-slaves. We find him, while the fleet was in Bordeaux, giving a mission. Having obtained the help of recruits gathered from various local religious communities, he put two priests on board each galley, with the result that a large number of the convicts returned to the practice of their religion, making their confessions and receiving the Communion from which they had bitterly abstained for so long. He even succeeded in converting a Turk who was among them. It is work of this sort that redounds to Vincent's eternal glory, not impossible legends, however charming they may appear to be.

After this mission was over, probably in 1623, he made a visit to his home in Pouy which, so far as we know, he had not seen for nearly twenty years. In the little village of the Landes he spent a week or ten days, edifying everybody. In the church where he had been christened he renewed his baptismal vows; he made, bare-foot, a pilgrimage to Buglose; it was noticed that he slept on straw and that he drowned in water what little wine he drank.

Nevertheless his visit must have been something of a disappointment for his family. We know that, when he commenced his studies for an ecclesiastical career, they had looked upon it as something which should incidentally prove of material benefit to them. Now that he had "arrived"—though somewhat belatedly and modestly—it was not unnaturally expected that he was about to do something for his relatives. Instead he refused to do anything at all.

It was certainly not from lack of normal human affection. Years afterwards, when speaking of this visit, he said, "Do you imagine that I have no love for my relatives? I have for them all the feelings that anyone can have for his family, and this natural love impells me sufficiently to aid them. But I must act according to the movements of grace and not those of nature; I must think of the most abandoned poor, without stopping at ties of friendship or relationship." This in itself of course might mean nothing, or even be cant. For there are instances to be found of people who are kind to outsiders and yet far from kind to their own kin. But Vincent was to relate in one of his Conferences how, after having said farewell, he walked down the road in tears—he who was so little given to weeping—turning over in his mind what he could do for this member of his family, and what for that member, until (to quote his own words) "I divided up amongst them, in thought, what I had and what I did not have." All the same, when it came to the point, he did nothing then, though, upon founding his Congregation, he made over to his family what little property he had in the neighbourhood.

He persisted in his attitude. In the last years of his life he was

appealed to for help to enable one of his grand-nephews to become a priest—and he refused. Fortunately we have the delicately expressed reasons for his refusal in a letter to the local
priest: the ecclesiastical state entails such awful responsibilities
that to enter it is temerarious; if he himself had understood
what it involved, he would have preferred to remain a tiller of
the soil. "The priests of today," he says plainly, "have great
reason to fear the judgments of God, for, in addition to their
own sins, they will have to render an account of those of their
own people." Therefore he thinks it more fitting for the boy to
follow his father's mode of life than to enter a calling "in which
eternal loss seems inevitable for those who dare to enter it without a vocation." Then he comes to the decisive point: "As I do
not see that there is any certain sign of his having been called
by God, I beg you to recommend him to strive to earn his own
living. . . . This is the best advice I can give him. Priests who
live as most priests are living at the present day, are the greatest
enemies of the Church of God." In oher words, he refuses
material charity out of spiritual charity.

Most of the biographers have either applauded Vincent's attitude towards his family as a supreme instance of his virtue
of detachment, or have passed it over in embarrassed silence.
I must take up a middle ground in the matter, candidly admitting that the facts, as they are usually stated, fail to arouse
my complete sympathy, but at the same time granting that there
may be explanations that have not been sufficiently drawn out,
or that there may be facts we do not possess.

Detachment of this extreme sort must be noted as being regarded as one of the marks of sanctity in all religions, though
honesty obliges me to add that it is one of the marks I least
admire. That, however, may well be an indication of my own
deficiency. Buddha has been almost universally praised for
deserting his wife and son. Christ's words, on the other hand,

about none being worthy to be His disciples except those who are willing to leave father and mother for His sake, are generally interpreted as meaning that, should any conflict arise between what is due to those of one's own blood and what is due to God, the divine claims are paramount. The Church does not allow any man to become a monk who has dependents upon him.

I am putting all this in a rather extreme way precisely because what strikes me as somewhat extreme statements have been made about Vincent and his family. Too many hagiographers, having got hold of the idea that saints are not as other men, twist this into meaning that inhumanity is to be praised. I do not share any part of this opinion, which seems to me to be strongly tinged with an unconscious Jansenism. And I do not believe that it can be correctly applied to Vincent's own case.

But before offering my solution, let me add that some years afterwards, when a nephew of Vincent's walked all the way from the Landes to Paris to see him and Vincent was told that a poorly dressed peasant was at the door, his first impulse—according to the story—was to avoid him, an impulse which was set down to shame. The supposititious shame (despite Vincent's profession of contrition) surely did not arise; Vincent was at that time used daily to receive beggars at his door and to invite them to sit at his right hand during a meal in the refectory. What is certain is that he went down to the young man and introduced him to the community as "one of the best specimens of his family"—and then, after entertaining him for a few days, during which time the boy was presented to many distinguished callers, the uncle dismissed him with ten crowns for the expenses for his long journey home, but nothing else. Even those ten crowns were taken not from the bursar of Saint-Lazare but were solicited from the Marquise de Maignelay.

To account for Vincent's conduct towards his family we must go back to what he often used to say about himself in later years—that it would have been better for him had he never left his original state in life. It was his definite conviction that the de Pauls could best save their souls—the all-important matter— by remaining as peasants. He knew that, though they were poor, they were not in grinding poverty. Therefore he considered that he was doing them a service in leaving them to their frugal life and in their hard-working condition. And who shall say that his judgment was not correct?

Knowing peasants as he did, he was only too well aware that they were often much richer than they seemed to be, and that their thrift was readily capable of developing into a grasping greed. On his visit to Pouy his keen eye may have recognized the first signs of this, and he may have been afraid that by bringing financial assistance—especially when it was not really needed—he would have led them on the first step of the road towards demoralization. Just because he loved them, he declined to do what was expected of him.

Immense sums came to pass through his hands, but nothing went to his relatives. Was he, who had so strictly guarded against any form of favouritism when drawing up the rules for his Confraternities, to practice nepotism, on however small a scale? To have done so would have weighed heavily on his delicate conscience; to have been known to have done so would have been likely to have destroyed that confidence in his disinterestedness which was one of the levers he had for extracting money for his charitable organizations. I leave to others more exalted considerations; the ones I have indicated strike me as being sufficient to account for his behaviour.

Nevertheless there did come a time when he brought aid to his kinsfolk. A friend (Charles du Fresne) had given him a thousand francs to use for this specific purpose. But instead of handing it on to those who were at the moment in no urgent need of it, he put the sum on one side. Then, when at the time of the distress caused by the Fronde he heard that his family had been badly hit, he wished to do something for them. But he had forgotten the thousand francs, and was troubled, since even under those circumstances, he did not wish to use the money given him for thousands who were starving for the de Pauls. At last he remembered that he had a sum he could use with a perfectly clear conscience.

Here we see a very great change from the Vincent of 1610 whose great ambition, as we learn from his letter to his mother, was to obtain a benefice in the diocese of Dax where he could live near his family and be in a position to hoist them to advancement. At the time he revisited Pouy he had even some doubts as to the advisability of going, for, as he said later, "I had seen many good ecclesiastics who had worked wonders for a time at a distance from their homes, and I had observed that after they had visited their relations, they returned quite altered and became quite useless to the public; whereas formerly they had devoted themselves only to work and were quite detached from flesh and blood. I too, am afraid . . . of becoming attached to my relations."

Here we have what I hope will suffice as an explanation that will do equal credit to the tender natural affections of Vincent de Paul and to his sanctity. It is something that needs to be dealt with without that humbug which he so detested, and to which not a few pious writers are addicted. I believe he did the perfectly right thing, and yet a thing that was by no means easy to do. With his blessing and in tears he parted from his disappointed family. Never again did he visit Pouy during the course of his long life.

❡ 10. Vincent and the Visitation

WE HAVE seen how Vincent, certainly from 1610 to 1617 and probably later, was so strongly influenced by Bérulle as to be practically dependent upon him. But though their friendship never came to an end, it is clear that Vincent, however willing he may have been to seek Bérulle's advice over special problems, and however deeply tinged he may have been with Bérulle's somewhat pessimistic brand of mysticism, came by degrees to be—not precisely independent of the great Oratorian—but to set all his dependence directly in God. Now, towards the end of 1618 or the beginning of the following year, a new friendship began which was to have an even greater effect upon Vincent. It was when Francis de Sales, after a sixteen years' absence from Paris, returned to establish a Visitation convent there. Death ended all personal association three years later, but it may be said that until Vincent's own death he was, in a certain sense and up to a certain point, a disciple of the Bishop of Geneva. Certainly from no other spiritual writer did he quote more freely in his Conferences to his Fathers and Daughters.

The two men were immediately drawn together. Despite the difference in their social rank, they had a marked affinity. The Bishop was too great an aristocrat ever to give peremptory orders—even to that valet whom many thought domineered over him. His features of classic regularity were set off by a great auburn beard. In every gesture and tone of his voice, in the very way he sat in a chair, everyone observed the charm and delicacy of his character. No wonder he had an almost irresistible power over pious women.

But Vincent, though a peasant, was an aristocrat too. If he, like Francis de Sales, added to his natural attractiveness the unmistakable benignity conferred by grace, we must remember that grace built upon a foundation of native courtesy. In this they were both very unlike the eccentric Adrian Bourdoise with his gruffness that struck many as boorish, though—in fairness to Bourdoise—we must admit the possibility that he deliberately cultivated a seeming rudeness as a cloak for his underlying sanctity. It is also possible that the man knew he was unable to change his rough exterior, and so made no pretence to be other than he was. One fears, however, that he considered his bad manners admirable.

In the case of Vincent and Francis, on the other hand, there was an exquisite politeness which bound them to one another. De Sales was a gentleman by breeding; de Paul a gentleman by instinct. Vincent's personal attractiveness is attested by all the facts of his life. From the very beginning he impressed people. In his youth he had impressed M. Comet. The old lady of Toulouse had left her small fortune to the unknown priest. The alchemist to whom he had been a slave in Barbary had offered to adopt him as a son. His subsequent owner, and his wives, had been enchanted with him. Montorio, the Papal Vice-Legate, had taken him at once under his wing. He had served acceptably in the palace of Queen Marguerite de Valois. And the Gondis, who all their lives long had lived in fashionable society, adored him. We may be sure that there was nothing uncouth about Vincent de Paul. He was not the peasant boy trying to ape the manners of his betters; he was one to whom only good manners were possible, for to his kind disposition he added that imaginative insight into the character of others that taught him what to say and do. It is necessary to insist on this point, for Vincent in his humility had a habit—almost a mania—for reminding his grand friends that he was nothing but a swineherd. It is perfectly clear that they saw nothing of the pigstye about him.

Already Vincent was, like all the well educated among the pious in France, familiar with *The Introduction to the Devout Life* and *The Treatise on the Love of God*, which had given to the seventeenth century a new concept of the Christian life by showing how all Christians, and not merely those in the cloister, were capable of sanctity. Not that all this was entirely unheard of before, or despair would have settled upon the mass of the laity; but most devotional works—even the gentle pages of the *Imitation*—were addressed primarily to those in religion. The originality of Francis de Sales was that of making Teresian mysticism applicable to everybody by shifting the emphasis from exterior mortification to interior prayer.

In this Francis parried the blow of Jansenism before it was delivered. To be continually told that we are sinful and inadequate and cold in our love for God is true—but discouraging. Psychologically it is more helpful to recall with some recent spiritual writers that, while we shall discover at that awful moment of our judgment after death that our unfaithfulness was more enormous than we have ever begun to imagine, we shall also learn to our surprise that we loved God, even if only subconsciously, much more than we ever supposed. Therefore while the consideration of the rigourists disheartens, the other consideration thrills us to devotion. As Coventry Patmore remarks, "To a great man and to God a little love is a great thing." So far from making us complacent, this inspires us to love God more, or at least prevents us from giving up loving God merely because we know that our love is not all that it ought to be.

Francis's own spiritual crisis enlightens all his writing. Like most of the people of his time he had been over preoccupied with the theological problem of predestination. At last, kneeling before the black Madonna at Saint-Etienne-des-Grés, and saying the *Memorare*, he acquiesced in his own damnation—and found release from his terrors.

This, however, must not be confused with Quietism, though Quietism was to a great extent an exaggeration and misunderstanding of his doctrine. As Father Michael Müller remarks, "Francis knew very well that the will to salvation is implanted in every man and neither should nor could be rejected. Quietism seriously preached an absolute acquiescence in one's own damnation as the peak of perfection." The Salesian idea was, on the contrary, that "Paradise would be there in the midst of all the torments of hell if the love of God were there"—an idea that Swinburne, a great filcher of ideas, has expressed in his Prelude to *Tristram and Iseult*:

> "So sweet that hell, to hell be love be given,
> Would turn to splendid and sonorous heaven."

It should be noted that Francis introduced a psychological method which anticipates the "sublimation" of the saner school of psycho-analysts of our own day. Bossuet put the whole thing in a nutshell when he said, "One cannot annihilate the passions through their opposite . . . rather one must change the object of one's passions through elevating them." And though this is no place to write an essay on Salesian mysticism, it is only proper to recall that mildness was of its essence, whether applied to life in the cloister or the world. Without adding Bremond's characteristic drop of acid when he said that some of de Sales's followers conceived the strange notion of mingling sugar with the honey of Annecy, a typical Salesian passage may be quoted here: "Even as young girls love their husbands properly, if they have one, yet do not cease greatly to love rings and trifles, or their companions, with whom they busy themselves extravagantly in playing, dancing and silliness, occupying themselves with little birds, little dogs, squirrels and such playthings—so these young novice souls have truly an affection for the sacred Lover, even when they admit with it a number of voluntary distractions and diversions: so that loving Him above all things, yet they busy themselves in many things, which they love, not according to Him but besides Him, out of Him, and without Him. In truth, though small irregularities in words, in gestures, in apparel, in pastimes and follies, are not properly speaking against the will of God, yet they are not according to it, but out of it and without it." To which, by way of balance, we may add another passage: "There are many who take no delight in divine love unless it be candied in the sugar of some sensible sweetness, and they would willingly act like little children who, if they have a little honey spread upon their bread, lick and suck off the honey, casting the bread away; for if the delight could be separated from the love, they would reject the love and take the sweetness only. Wherefore, as they follow love for the sake of its sweetness, when they find this they make no account of love."

Recognising, then, the hard core under what might seem at first sight the softness of Salesian spirituality—something that is put in a single sentence of Francis Thompson's essay "Health and Holiness": "It is clear indeed that we require an asceticism; but not so clear that the asceticism we require is the old asceticism"—it is safe to say that a good-humoured, one might almost say a humorous, indulgence in unessential matters was accorded by de Sales to those souls in the world whom he directed, even while he kept as clearly in sight as did the rigorous ascetics of the medieval school the fact that the elect few would do well to dispense with playing, dancing, and their little dogs and squirrels.[1]

His founding of the Visitation eventuated in the establishment of an order as fully devoted to contemplation as was the fiercer Carmel. It was, however, an order for those whose health would not stand the Carmelite austerities but who, lacking such a refuge, would have to abandon all idea of the cloister. Though he mitigated fasts and scourgings, and substituted comfortable beds for wooden boards on an inclined plane, he made up for this by exacting an obedience and a poverty almost absolute. The gibe that the nuns of the Visitation should be properly named those of the Descent from the Cross was even more ignorant than malicious.

At this point it should be said that, though Francis de Sales from the beginning intended the Visitation to be a contemplative order, its very name indicates that it was originally intended to unite active work among the poor to adoration. That plan was opposed by Denis de Marquemont, the Archbishop of Lyons, on the mistaken ground that there was no precedent for nuns leaving their cloister; and Francis de Sales, with his usual good temper, acquiesced, as he had previously yielded to Jane Frances de Chantal when he had wanted to put their foundation under the patronage of St. Martha. It was Vincent de Paul's intention to carry out, in an extremely novel way—one that Francis had never thought of, and which only by degrees dawned on Vincent himself—the original Salesian intention.

The meeting between these two great Saints was therefore clearly providential. Francis said that Vincent struck him as the holiest priest of the time, and Vincent used to exclaim, "My God, how good Thou art! since Thy creature, his Lord-

---

[1] He would nevertheless have probably heartily agreed with Vincent de Paul when he said, "He who makes little of exterior mortifications, saying that interior ones are much more perfect, makes one to know that he is not mortified, either interiorly or exteriorly."

ship of Geneva, is filled with so much goodness." Between such kindred spirits a perfect harmony existed.

The two Saints were before long joined in Paris by a third, who had come there to see to the founding of a house of the Visitation. The former Baroness de Chantal—a valiant woman if ever there was one—had been left a widow at the age of twenty-eight after having borne six children, two of whom had died in infancy. Her thoughts turning to the cloister, she put herself under the direction of the Bishop of Geneva who, however, kept her for some time yet in the world and deflected her from entering Carmel. He had other designs for her.

When she did at last establish the first Visitation house at Anneçy, she was thirty-seven, so there is no need to be too harrowed by the story of how her son, finding that his pleading was of no avail, threw himself across the door to prevent his mother leaving. In tears she stepped over her son's body, but she was resolute. After all, he was what would have been called in those days a full-grown man, and he was committed to the care of his wealthy grandfather. Of his three sisters, one had died; another had just been married to a husband carefully picked for her by Jane Frances herself; the third and youngest went with her mother to complete her education. Moreover, the Baroness before becoming a nun made over the whole of her property—including even her dowry—to her children, and took with her into the convent only the ten crowns she happened to have in her purse. To the end she kept affectionate and close watch upon her children and grandchildren, one of whom was to become the celebrated Madame de Sévigné.

The rule of the Visitation was that each convent, which was independent of all the others, was to be under the direct control of the local bishop. In practice this meant that the Ordinary appointed a superior. Francis and Jane Frances thoroughly concurred that no better man for the position could be found than Vincent de Paul, and the Archbishop of Paris thought so too.

There was some difficulty in getting Vincent to accept. He was already more than sufficiently busy with his work of conducting missions on the Gondi estates and organizing Confraternities of Charity, and he had had recently added to these duties that of Chaplain-General of the Galleys. But knowing that the best man to undertake a new job is he who is already overburdened with work, the two Saints persisted in their project, and Vincent yielded. He was to remain superior of the Visitation houses in Paris from 1622 until his death in 1660.[2]

It was by no means an easy task that he assumed. Francis de Sales died before the year was out, so that upon Vincent's shoulders there came to rest the spiritual direction of Jane Frances.[3] And though to her he wrote the most affectionate of all his extant letters, seeking her advice as often as she sought his, and always addressing her as his "Very dear and very honoured Mother"—though she was only about the same age as himself—they did not always see administrative details in the same light. Indeed, it is to this fact that we owe the destruction or mutilation, on the part of over-scrupulous people, of many of their letters. But how delightful are some of the letters that have escaped. Thus in one of them Vincent, after expressing his disagreement with her, adds, "But ah, my Saviour! What am I saying? In truth it seems to me that I fully acquiesce with my will, yet I am not doing so with my judgment. But good

[2] In 1646 he attempted to resign and proved obdurate even to the pleading, on behalf of the Visitandines, of the Marquise de Maignelay. Vincent suggested the names of several priests, among them that of Abelly, his future biographer, as of directors eminently capable of taking over his functions. As this did not satisfy the nuns, the Marquise appealed to her brother, the Archbishop—and Vincent yielded.

[3] The Abbé Bremond says that we have here an instance of Vincent's marvellous gift of supple assimilation, by which in his relations with Jane Frances "he assumed the very personality of Francis de Sales." It is by no means the only instance of Vincent's extraordinary pliability.

Heavens! let me do so, and that fully, in the sole view of God's good pleasure, to which I submit both my will and my judgment, never doubting for a moment, however, that it is the will of God, since it is that of our honoured Mother, who is so much my honoured Mother that she is mine alone, and whom I honour and cherish more tenderly than any child ever honoured and loved its mother since Our Lord." And he ends, "It is in this childlike spirit, my dear Mother, that I address you, and will always thank you for all the grandmother's charity you show towards your dear children, our Missionaries." In an earlier letter (written in 1639), he informs her that he is sending some of his Missionaries to Annecy, where they will be "under the shelter and direction of our worthy Mother." Could there be anything sweeter tempered or less self-assertive than this? The tone in which he wrote implied that his Fathers were to look upon her as their own Mother Superior.

Vincent was to meet Jane Frances again in 1628, 1635 and 1641. At the end of the year when she last visited Paris she died. And this was the occasion of the sole vision recorded in the life of a mystic who was so little visionary. Word had arrived of Jane Frances's death, and the next morning at Mass Vincent, thinking that he could remember that his "honoured and dear Mother" had on one occasion used words that seemed to him to be perhaps faintly tinged with venial sin, was about to pray for her soul. Just then there appeared to him a small globe of fire which rose from the earth and mingled, in the upper air, with another and a larger globe of fire, both rising upwards until they had become united to a still larger globe of infinite refulgence. He hesitated a moment, wondering whether he should trust his vision as coming from God, until he remembered that he was not "subject to visions and had never had any before." That made him sure that this was no illusion but that the soul of Jane Frances, welcomed by that of Francis de Sales, had ascended straight to Heaven.

Under Vincent's direction the Visitation houses in Paris flour-:shed, though they did not fail to have difficulties. During the first year, the sisters had to suffer extreme poverty of a kind hardly suited for women who had joined an order intended to make provision for those in fragile health. The nuns had no chairs, and so were obliged to sit on the floor; they did not have enough to eat; and they possessed only one handkerchief apiece. Even after they had moved from their temporary quarters to the magnificent Zamet mansion (upon which Francis's characteristic comment was, "in default of a fairly beautiful house we must put up with one that is too beautiful") they still were short of money for bare necessities.

Then, too, they were greatly troubled by having to take over the conduct of a house of refuge for fallen girls. And though some of these girls turned out well, and were even organized into an order of nuns, others were rebellious and reverted to their old behaviour. It was a bit too much when one of them appeared one day with a knife, threatening murder. In the end, but not until after Vincent's death, the Visitandines petitioned the Archbishop of Paris to be released from this work.

Such was the reputation for sanctity of the Visitation that the Order found many powerful friends among the pious in Paris and attracted—almost as much as did Carmel—postulants from among the nobly-born. The story of one of these Court ladies should be told here, although it falls somewhat outside a chronology which, in any event, is going to be difficult to follow strictly.

Among the most beautiful of the maids of honour of Anne of Austria was Louise-Angélique de la Fayette. The King was strongly attracted towards the girl and spent all the time he could in her company, so much so that Cardinal Richelieu's

animosity was aroused against her (for she, somewhat indiscreetly, allowed herself to be used as the tool of the party opposed to the Cardinal's policy), while she, for her part, began
to fear for her virtue, and to think that only in the cloister
would she be safe.

Her alarm was unnecessary, at any rate on that point. For
Louis—about whose strange character more will be said later
—had one mark that it is very hard to understand. Though
he had many of the signs of virility—being a brave soldier, and
a great hawker, and a man justly proud of his skill in many
handicrafts—he had an unaccountable sexual frigidity. There
was no trace in him of the kind of thing that gave out its faint
but unmistakable odour from the last of the Valois kings. But
in his case there does for once seem to be some point to the
cynical saying that the most perverse of all perversities is
chastity. He had positively to be pushed, protesting, by de
Luynes into Anne of Austria's bedroom and told that it was
high time that he fulfilled his marital obligations and his duties
towards the Crown. After that he seems to have left his wife
severely alone for many years, until his neglect became a
scandal and (though Gaston of course rejoiced in it) a danger
to the succession. Meanwhile Anne of Austria, while a virtuous
woman, had behaved only too often very indiscreetly. Platonic
love—*la belle galanterie*—had been made fashionable by the
Precieuses of the Hôtel Rambouillet, and in it the Queen became very much of an adept.

This was used with damaging effect against her by Richelieu,
whose policy it suited to keep the King from the influence of
his wife. Consequently Louis grew to be far more jealous of
Anne than Anne was ever jealous of Louis. For though she was
in many respects a silly woman, at least she had sense enough
to realise—what Louise de la Fayette did not—that the King's
affairs with ladies of the Court were all of a platonic sort. In-

deed his attraction towards any lady was generally, as in this case, on account of her piety.

There now began a most amusing little comedy. Louise, deeply distressed, took her problem to Père Caussin, the Jesuit confessor of the King. He told her, truly enough, that the friendship was perfectly harmless, and expressed the same opinion to Louis, whose strange moral constitution he was in a better position than any other person to understand. At the same time we may suspect that Caussin was not entirely disinterested in his very definite advice that the lady-in-waiting should not think of becoming a nun. He wanted her to remain at Court so that he might use her influence against Richelieu, who had entered France upon participation in the Thirty Years' War and who, by so doing, was giving aid to the German Protestant states against their Catholic Emperor. Therefore Caussin assured Louise that a secular condition of life was God's will for her.

Richelieu, on the other hand, suddenly became a great advocate of the religious life—at any rate for Louise de la Fayette. As he wanted to get rid of her, he solemnly quoted the words of St. Jerome to the effect that one must tread over the body of one's father, if need be, in order to follow the standard of the cross. This, coming from a man who had used his influence at Rome to get the Pope to order his own niece out of her Carmelite convent, was astonishing effrontery. The result was that Louise, who had some spirit, seeing through the Cardinal's designs and getting "hoity-toity," gave up for the time being all thought of becoming a nun. Richelieu had overshot the mark.

However, her scruples returned, stronger than ever. We have no record that Vincent de Paul had any hand in this matter, but, as Superior of the Visitation, he must have been consulted, and, though he may well have had sympathy with Caussin's objections to Richelieu's political projects, he was not going to

allow himself to be actuated by political considerations in judging the question of Louise's vocation. At the age of nineteen
she became a nun.

To the credit of Louis XIII it must be remembered that, as
King, he was fully empowered to forbid his friend from entering religion. But he was a deeply religious man, and once he
was convinced that Louise had a vocation and would not be
happy except in a convent he gave his consent. "I shall never see
him again!" Louise sobbed—and hurried off to the Visitandines.

She was mistaken; she was destined to see the King a good
many times. Both he and the good-natured Anne of Austria
often called at the convent to see the young nun, whose vocation was the sensation of Paris. We have pretty accounts of
the Queen and the ladies of the Court—including Madame de
Hautefort who had preceded (as she was to succeed) Louise as
Louis's pious *belle amie*—sitting with the Sisters sewing and
making artificial flowers.[4] Anne, whatever her other faults may
have been, was at least free from the vice of jealousy.

Now and then the conversations between the King and the
young nun touched upon politics, and at such times Louise
ventured to criticise Richelieu. But Louis, though he had listened to her opinions readily enough in the days when she was
at Court, was irritated by hearing her speak in the old way
now that she was in her new condition. On one occasion, when
he considered she had gone too far, he testily got up and left
the convent parlour without a word. The Cardinal, after all,
had triumphed over one whom he had described as "this child
who is thinking of spoiling my plans." As for Caussin, that
rather imprudent Jesuit was summarily dismissed from his office
as the King's confessor at the end of 1637 and sent to the house

[4] Vincent was usually very strict about not allowing outsiders to visit
the nuns, and refused permission even to the Princesse de Clarignan and
the daughter of the Duc de Bouillon. But this time he considered that the
gain from edification would outweigh all else.

of his order at Rennes.[5] His offence was that he had used Mademoiselle de la Fayette (among others) as instruments against the Cardinal.

But now comes the most astonishing detail of all, one upon which many pages of psychological speculation might be written —from which, however, with a virtuous sigh, I refrain. One day in the early part of December 1637 the King left for Saint-Maur, but stopped at the Visitation convent to see Sister de la Fayette. While he was there a raging storm broke out, and Louise begged His Majesty not to think of continuing his journey but to go to the Louvre for the night. He did so, remembering his friend's frequent admonitions—probably repeated on this occasion—that he really ought not to neglect the Queen as he was doing. As an outcome of that storm, that call upon Louise, and that visit to Anne of Austria, the child who was later to be Louis XIV was born nine months later.

The King continued to visit Louise occasionally for the rest of his life, and after his death Anne of Austria brought her two children to the convent. Then Sister de la Fayette ventured to kiss the new King, and his mother admonished the little boy, "Love this dear nun, because I owe a great deal to her." It was no more than the truth.

[5] Louise herself was in some danger of banishment from Paris. She was saved, partly because the King was angry when he heard of the plan, but also because the Cardinal was afraid of cutting a ridiculous figure should he attempt to carry it out.

⟪ 11. The Founding of the Mission

SHORTLY after Vincent's return from Châtillon-les-Dombes Madame de Gondi, impressed by the fact that the spiritual needs of the people in country districts were neglected—since their secular priests were often ignorant and the active religious orders were for the most part concentrated in the cities—set aside sixteen thousand livres for the purpose of having missions preached to them. This sum her husband raised to forty-five thousand livres, and Vincent was commissioned to find a religious community who would undertake the work. But it was in vain that he applied to the Jesuits and Oratorians; neither order felt that it fell within its special province. In the end the Gondis managed to persuade Vincent to make himself personally responsible.

At once a problem was raised. He was already doing all he could, with the aid of Louis Belin, the Gondis' chaplain at Villepreux, and such volunteers as he could secure from time to time. Moreover, since he had given the Countess a solemn promise never to leave her, he was hardly in a position to found a new order. The project, though often discussed, came to nothing for several years.

But Madame de Gondi, as we have seen, was not a woman who was ready to give up any plan she had formed; in 1624 she discovered a solution. It was that of inducing her brother-in-law, the Cardinal de Retz, Archbishop of Paris, to appoint Vincent President of the tumble-down Collège des-Bons-Enfants. Now, having a house, he would have to form a Congregation. The college, which had never been large, at this time had occupants that could be numbered on one hand—all of whom were there on a scholarship foundation for the benefit of the Pluyette family. As these only used the place as a hostel, it was easy to arrange that they should continue to reside there, and that the disgusted president retire on a pension.

A serious difficulty still remained: Vincent could assemble only two assistants—Anthony Portail, who had been a disciple of his since the pastorate at Clichy, and another priest, to whom he had to pay a salary of fifty crowns a year. But though Portail was a devoted soul, he was so shy that it was not until several years later that he could be induced to go into the pulpit. Further, as Vincent's absence from the tiny community was anything but conducive to building it up, the whole thing must have struck the ordinary observer as a hopeless undertaking.

Nevertheless the contract was signed on April 17, 1625, and under it Vincent bound himself to raise six priests (or as many as the endowment would permit) for missionary work, to send them only to country places, to make them ineligible for such benefices as would interfere with their work, to let them go only where they were invited, and never to accept any remuneration for their services. Or, as Vincent later more briefly explained his purpose: "We are the ministers of the poor; God has chosen us for them, and it is our prime object to which everything else is secondary." The Gondis, on their side, gave up all right of nominating to posts in the Congregation, but were to have Masses said in perpetuity for their souls and the souls of their descendants; and obligations were imposed of preaching a mission at least once every five years at each of the Gondi estates and of working among the galley slaves. Having signed this contract, Madame de Gondi who, it must be confessed had showed a good deal of pious egotism in insisting that Vincent remain with her, made up for it by very considerately dying a couple of months later, and the General, inconsolable at her loss, decided to enter the Oratory. Vincent at last had his hands free.

Several other priests had in the meanwhile joined them, among whom the most notable was Francis du Coudray, a doctor of the Sorbonne and a fine Hebrew scholar but a man who subsequently developed somewhat eccentric theological opinions. Vincent, it should be noted, at this time renounced in favour of his family at Pouy all that he possessed there, which was a small farm and a debt owing to him.

But though the Archbishop of Paris approved the contract—indeed it was he who made possible Vincent's taking over the Collège des-Bons-Enfants—Rome for some time refused to authorize the new Congregation. This seems to have been due to the fact that what was proposed was without precedent in canon law. Vincent indicated that he was not seeking to establish a new religious order, but to have his Missionaries remain seculars; at the same time, by wishing to have them bound by vows, he seemed to be, in effect, establishing a religious order.

Further, he wished to be free from the jurisdiction of the Ordinary in internal affairs.[1] The reason for this was that he did not consider it feasible for the Fathers to submit their accounts to the scrutiny of the Archbishop, because priests who were constantly moving from place to place could hardly keep an accurate reckoning of their expenditures. Rome, on the other hand, could not be expected to know that the Missionaries lived in the most frugal fashion, and therefore saw only the possibility of abuse.

Oddly enough, it was Bérulle, now a Cardinal, who, through his Roman agent, secretly opposed ratification. He wrote, "The design of which you inform me . . . in this matter of missions, in various and, in my opinion oblique ways, should render it

---

[1] Nevertheless Vincent was most careful not to allow any of his priests to enter a diocese unless explicit permission had been given by the bishop. But so strongly did he feel about the necessity of freedom in temporalities that he was prepared to abandon Saint-Lazare rather than yield on this point; and he told the Archbishop so.

suspect." It may be that Père Gondi had talked a little in-discreetly about the wires he could pull, but so far from Vincent having been "oblique," he instructed du Coudray, whom he had sent to plead his cause at Rome, to avoid all attempts to curry favour or make friends at court by gifts or offers of service, or to use any methods, even the most legitimate, of the kind commonly employed. "I would rather," he added emphatically, "trust the devil than attempt to attain divine ends by human means." His pertinacity eventually gained what he sought, but, even after the formal approval of the Rules of 1655, the status of the Congregation remained anomalous, as it does to this day.

Meanwhile Vincent and his little group of companions, using Paris as their headquarters, travelled about the country dis-tricts preaching, catechising and hearing confessions, founding everywhere they went Confraternities of Charity. While they were at home—where they had to do their own housework, for they had no lay-brothers until much later—they studied and prayed, in preparation for their next excursion. Then they locked up the college, though there was little enough in its barely-furnished rooms that anyone would want to steal, and left the key with a neighbour.

The fact that the Missionaries were expected to study during the intervals of preaching should be specially noted. Vincent, however strongly he insisted upon the utmost simplicity of man-ner in the pulpit, tolerated no laziness disguising itself as spon-taneity; it was a cardinal principle with him that nothing could be accomplished without thought and prayer, and that he who would save souls must first attend to his own spiritual life. "True Missionaries," as he used to say, "ought to be like Car-thusians in their houses and like apostles outside"; and "Prayer is the reservoir from which you draw the instructions you give."

Another of his principles—it was one that could not have come easily to his Gascon temperament—was to move slowly.

He was forty-five when he founded his Congregation, and after that the growth of his community was for some time almost imperceptible. "The affairs of God," as he put it, "are accomplished little by little." And again, "Moderate your ardour and weigh matters maturely in the scales of the sanctuary. Be passive rather than active. The good that God wishes is done of itself, as it were, and without our being aware of it." He was about to have a signal proof of the truth of these axioms.

Out of a clear sky there came to him some time in 1630 the offer of the Priory of Saint-Lazare, an offer so staggering that for eighteen months Vincent would not so much as entertain it, or even visit the property.

Saint-Lazare, as its name implies, was originally a leper-house, though since the decline of leprosy, following the middle ages, it had found few to house afflicted with this dreadful disease. In 1632 only one of these unfortunates was there. What it was to prove before long was a place for the cleansing of the leprosy of sin and for raising many a Lazarus from death to life; but the only definite work of mercy performed by the Priory, at the time it was offered to Vincent, was the care of a few lunatics shut up in huts in a corner of the hundred-and-thirty-acre property, and the custody of some young rakes imprisoned by their parents who, in those days, had wide legal powers over their children.

The Priory belonged to the Archbishop of Paris, but had for a long time been entrusted to the Augustinian Canons, who not unnaturally had grown accustomed to look upon themselves as owners. Their ownership, however, was not absolute, and the Order lost a law suit for the return of what it considered its property. Visitors to la Sainte-Chapelle may like to recall that, during the legal decision which was being given in the adjoining court, Vincent knelt on the stone flags of St. Louis's lovely church in prayer.

In making the offer of Saint-Lazare, its Prior, Adrian Le Bon, probably did somewhat exceed his powers. His community, which had dwindled to ten canons, was getting out of hand, so he conceived the idea that, by bringing among them Vincent's edifying Missionaries, good order might be restored. But when Le Bon made his offer he noticed that Vincent was thunderstruck.

"What is the matter with you, Sir?" he exclaimed, "You are trembling."

"Your proposal terrifies me," came the answer. "I should not even dare to think about it. We are poor priests, who live quite simply; and our whole ambition is to be of service to the poor in the country districts."

"Well," said the Prior, "I hope that is not your last word." It was not his own: being a man of persistence, he renewed his offer from time to time.

It became clear by degrees, however, that what he had in mind was an amalgamation of Vincent's community with his own. The Missionaries were to be free to go out on missions, but while they were at Saint-Lazare, Le Bon expected them to wear the dress of canons and to sing in choir. He also took it for granted that the canons and the Missionaries were to occupy the same dormitory.

At once Vincent, very courteously but very firmly, put his foot down. He had no intention of assuming canons' obligations. Still less would he tolerate the idea of sharing a dormitory with the canons. He knew—in fact, Le Bon admitted as much—that the Augustinians lived somewhat laxly, and that in particular they made little attempt to observe the rule of silence which Vincent regarded as an index to good monastic observance. So while Le Bon argued that the presence of the Missionaries would have the effect of shaming the Augustinians into reformation, Vincent feared, not without reason, that the effect would instead prove to be the demoralization of the Missionaries. Rather than that, he would absolutely refuse the well-intentioned offer.

In the end a compromise was effected, in which Cardinal de la Rochefoucauld acted in favour of Vincent's ideas. Le Bon was to retain the title of Prior and have an annuity of twenty-one hundred livres. Each of the canons was to be provided with a comfortable room and an adequate pension. But the Missionaries were to live their own life apart.

As may be imagined, the arrangement had its drawbacks, though there was also the reassuring certainty that it would endure only until the last of the canons was dead. Le Bon, who was a fussy, choleric man, full of a sense of his own importance, was quick to imagine slights, so that, as Vincent himself tells us, he was obliged to go to him at least fifty times to ask pardon on his knees for some imaginary offence. Sometimes the Prior was overheard to say that he bitterly rued the day he had surrendered Saint-Lazare to the Missionaries. It took all of Vincent's charming tact to maintain peace. He made a special point of never failing, upon entering the house, to visit Le Bon's apartments, by way of making a formal recognition of the priorial dignity. And he was always punctilious about the compliments and small attentions demanded by the situation. Eventually the short-tempered Prior was won over, and the difficulties smoothed out. The old man lived until 1651.

Strangely enough, what attracted Vincent most strongly to accept the charge of Saint-Lazare was not the value of the property. For that matter, though the grounds were extensive, the buildings were in such a condition as to call for a good deal of money to put them into repair. And though the Priory still possessed seignorial rights of high, middle and low justice (rights delegated by Vincent to a sheriff), the old glory, considered from a worldly aspect, had largely faded. The place was, indeed, an unprepossessing barracks, even if it was soon to be crowded to its last corner. The ordinary "practical man" might well have been dismayed at the prospect of accepting such a white elephant. Vincent, being a visionary, divined the great achievements in store. But the immediate attraction, for him, lay in the presence of the poor lunatics in their houses in the garden.

This will probably strike most people as an unusual taste, especially when it is remembered how badly the mentally deranged were treated in those days. The reason for Vincent's pleasure was characteristic: Christ had had a good deal to do with lunatics, and had even been Himself accused of having a devil—that is, of being insane. The Saint-Lazare lunatics therefore drew the community all the closer to Christ. Despite that, the time was to come when Vincent was obliged to rebuke very severely those in charge of these sufferers, and to insist that they were provided with fare at least as good as that received by the Fathers of the Congregation. They were, he said, his "guests." Little as he probably knew of any scientific treatment for mental disorders, at least his kindness and commonsense combined to teach him that, as he put it, "Those who are sick of mind have need of more delicate and charitable nursing than those who are ill of body."

Guests of another sort were the wild young men—spendthrifts and debauchees—kept at Saint-Lazare in a sort of private prison. Towards them, too, the fairness of Vincent's mind was shown. For one day, when a youth who had lived a somewhat fast life arrived to spend a few days at the Priory, as a way of considering how best to begin his reformation, his mother sent a message asking that he should be forcibly detained until a magistrate could commit him to the institution. Promptly and indignantly Vincent refused to be a party to such a breach of confidence. It was his joy when he or his Missionaries were successful in bringing about the conversion of any of these prisoners—some of whom were there for no worse crime than having married beneath them without their parents' consent. In not a few instances even the rakes were so deeply touched by grace as to become priests or members of religious communities; in more, they left Saint-Lazare to live decent Christian lives as laymen.

First it must be noted that, though the Congregation was founded to perform a specific work, Vincent was never tired of insisting that no work would have any value unless it was founded upon prayer. "Prayer and study," he said, "should resolve themselves into action; the light in the mind should become a fire in the heart." And again, "All other actions of the day receive their true value from prayer." This is only to put in other words the *Tradere contemplata* of the Dominicans and of all orders which aim at a union of the contemplative and active life. It was, however, necessary to emphasize this in the case of the Congregation of the Missions, because—perhaps to a greater extent than any previous religious association—it was founded to carry out activities that might have made prayer virtually impossible, had not prayer been declared indispensable to all its undertakings.

This was specially important because the Missionaries were not obligated to (though they practiced when possible) the choral saying of the Office. The prayer therefore they were urged to cultivate was that of meditation. It was an age when pious people were sometimes inclined to bind themselves to a repetition of so many set prayers. This Vincent de Paul did not encourage, as we shall see when we come to his dealings with Louise de Marillac, not because he considered that such practices had no value but because he preferred to have the mind attuned to prayer as the first action of the day, and to remain, whatever the pressure of external business might be, in the spirit of prayer, in the presence of God.

As for the general manner of life followed by the Fathers during the experimental years before any formal approval had been given by Rome to the rules of the Mission, the place where perhaps it is best set forth is in a letter written by Vincent to Jane Frances de Chantal in 1639. After telling her how his "little Company" was founded to go from village to village to give missions at their own expense and to found Confraternities of Charity to continue their work, he explains that "the greater number" of the Missionaries—but, it should be noted, not *all* of them, since there was no obligation as yet—took the three ordinary vows of poverty, chastity and obedience, together with a fourth: to devote their whole life to the service of the poor.

"We rise," he tells Jane Frances, "every morning at four o'clock, spend half an hour in dressing and making our beds, make an hour's mental prayer together in the church, and recite Prime, Terce, Sext, and None in common. We then celebrate Mass. . . . When that is over, each one goes to his room to study. At half-past ten a particular examen is made on the virtue we are trying to acquire, and we then go to the refectory, where we dine at a common table, and we have reading at meals; when that is over, we go together to adore the Blessed Sacrament and say the *Angelus*. We then have an hour's recreation together; after that each one retires to his room until two o'clock, when Vespers and Compline are recited in common. After that, each one goes back to his room until five o'clock when Matins and Lauds are recited together. We then make another particular examen, and have supper afterwards, followed by an hour's recreation; when this is over, we go to church to make a general examination, night prayers, and a reading of the points of the prayer for the following morning.

This being finished, each one goes to his room, and retires to rest at nine o'clock."

It will be observed that there is nothing very unusual in all this, unless it be the early hour of rising—something Vincent was always very particular about, as he believed that a man who got slack in this matter would get slack in carrying out the rest of the rules—and in the frequent examinations of conscience. It might be added that he expected his priests to go to confession twice a week, and that he set an example by going himself even more often.

"When we are giving missions in the country," he continues, "we act in the same way, except that we go to church at six o'clock in the morning to say Holy Mass and hear confessions; these are heard after a sermon has been given by one of the Company, who has first said Mass; confessions are heard until eleven o'clock; we then go to dinner, and return to the church at two o'clock to hear confessions until five; after that, one of us gives a catechetical instruction, and the others depart to say Matins and Lauds, and we sup at six o'clock."

Again great emphasis is laid on confession. He explains that they did not leave a village until everyone had been instructed in all that is necessary for salvation and had made a general confession. It was not a question of whirlwind preaching, but of going to the roots of sin. Which, of course, took time.

The period for the missions was from the beginning of November until the end of June: the rest of the year, being the season of the various harvests, country people were much too busy to frequent church. Each mission lasted, as a rule, for three weeks (though, as the Missionaries stayed as long as their services seemed to be needed, the work sometimes went on for as long as three months). The Fathers had intervals of eight or ten days' rest between their missions, and the autumn and winter were given to community retreats and study at Saint-Lazare.

A habit that Vincent had which struck many people as very odd was that of always disparaging his own foundation. As Bougaud remarks, "From the way he spoke one might have thought that the Congregation was composed of idiots, and that one should have lost his mind to enter it." He used to tell his Missionaries, "Each one of us should be glad to be considered as of poor and mean intellect, as a person of no virtue; we must be content to be treated as ignorant, to be insulted and contemned, to have our defects cast in our face." But there was method in this madness: he wished nobody to join who was puffed up with pride or who expected an easy life. "For," as he said, "we cannot prevail against Satan by pride, he has more than we; but through humility we can conquer him, for of that he has none." He would therefore never encourage anybody to join him, even when the man seemed to be a desirable recruit. Instead he would say, "Other Congregations are more holy; ours is the last of all."

The method may be open to question—since the majority of people are inclined to take one at one's own valuation—and is certainly not the method followed by some orders that could be mentioned. But if its effect was the loss of good material, it also had the effect of bringing in only such men about whose vocation Vincent could be reasonably sure. The practical design in all this was to discourage recruiting from among those who were ambitious; the men joining the Congregation were to understand that theirs was to be an obscure life among the poor. Once addressing his disciples and referring to the prophecy of the great Dominican, St. Vincent Ferrer, to whom he had a special devotion, to the effect that God was going to raise up a new order which would dazzle and reform the world —a prophecy which several others had appropriated to themselves—Vincent, having heard that some of his Congregation thought it applied to them, exclaimed, "The man who should imagine the Company was the one about which St. Vincent Ferrer had prophesied would be a fool!"

On the other hand, once a man had become a Lazarist, Vincent—as we may see from his letters to those who were thinking of leaving—looked upon the defection in a very serious light. Thus he writes to one of his priests, "By losing your vocation, you will deprive God of the valuable service He expects of you. You will be responsible before the throne of God for the good which you will not do, and which, nevertheless, you might have done by remaining in the state in which you now are." To another member of the Mission who was contemplating leaving Vincent wrote: "If such troublesome thoughts come from the evil spirit, you would be unwilling to accept his suggestion, which are to make you weary of the service of God, and deprive souls of the help they might receive from you; and if these difficulties come from God, you belong too much to Him to reject what He offers you, and are too well versed in the ways of grace not to know that it is to be found in tribulation." From which it is clear that he was not touchy about his Congregation but concerned only about the glory of God. Every other order he believed to be better than his; equally firmly did he believe that in no other order could a man labour so usefully for the salvation of souls.

The touchstone of the spiritual life in his eyes was humility. After remarking in one of his Conferences that in a number of convents he had got in answer to his question "What is the chief virtue?" the answer "Humility," he went on, "Whence is it, then, that so few embrace it and that still fewer practice it? Is it because they content themselves with admiring it and take no pains to acquire it? In theory it is charming, but in practice it is disagreeable to nature." Humility, and its consequence, obedience: these were what he wanted from his Missionaries. Though his life of union with God marks him out as among the company of the mystics, what is ordinarily called mysticism was allowed scant room in his scheme of spirituality. One of his sayings was "The perfection of love does not consist in ecstasies but in doing the will of God."

As Superior it was remarked that he gave, whenever this was possible, his orders in the form of hints or suggestions, and that if he had occasion to find fault it was in the same way. "I have employed," he confessed, "only three times in my life words of harshness in reprimand and correcting others, thinking I had just cause for doing so, and I have ever since repented it, because I did not succeed, and because I perceived, on the contrary, that I always obtained by meekness whatever I desired." The playful and affectionate spirit of his letter to Francis du Coudray, "my dear little Father," illustrates the point. "And how is the Company getting along?" he enquires. (He is writing from Beauvais.) "Are they all in good spirits? Is everyone gay? Are the little regulations always observed?" We may be sure people ran to serve a Superior who wrote and spoke in this tone.

We must remember in all this that, however little eagerness Vincent appeared to show in seeking for new recruits, the Congregation of the Mission was in his estimation by far the most important of all his instruments. We think of him today as the great organizer of corporal works of mercy, only too often forgetting that the spiritual works of mercy were of far more consequence. And while the Sisters of Charity—a mere offshoot from his main work—loom larger in the public eye than the Fathers of the Congregation, it was upon the Fathers and their missions that everything depended. If the tail has come, in a sense, to wag the dog, this was not of his designing. But, then, he never was tired of insisting that he had designed nothing—not even the Congregation of the Mission—but that all had been brought about by God Himself.

It was with a mere handful of men that he accomplished his life's work. During the thirty-five years between the Gondi contract and his own death, Father Leonard tells us, the total number of men who threw in their lot with him amounted, all told, to a little over four hundred, and of these many died and some left. In no one year (and then only towards the end) could he have had more than a couple of hundred belonging to his Congregation.

Yet, as we shall see, there went out from Saint-Lazare Missionaries not only to all parts of France, but to Italy, Ireland, Scotland, Poland, and Madagascar. And Saint-Lazare itself was a hive humming from morning to night, from one end of the year to the other, with most varied and novel activities destined to renovate the religious life of the seventeenth century.

In an address delivered shortly before his death he said, in part, "It is fully thirty-three years since God gave us our beginning. . . . If we had been given our Rule at the beginning and before the Company had tested it, it might have been thought that there was something human rather than divine about it, and that here was a plan of human origin, and not the work of Divine Providence. . . . I have originated nothing, and it has all developed little by little in a way I cannot explain. . . . When I contemplate the means by which it has pleased God to found this Congregation in His Church, I confess that I know not where I am, and all that I see seems like a dream. . . . It has all happened as if of itself, little by little, one thing after another."

It was how Vincent wished it to happen.

ℂ 12. The Recruitment of the Rich

WE HAVE seen that whenever Vincent de Paul or any member of his Congregation gave a mission, they considered it absolutely essential not to leave without founding a Confraternity of Charity. This was to follow up, so far as it was able, the spiritual effects of the mission, and to make those effects manifest in corporal works of mercy. In these Confraternities, as Boudignon remarks, "He created in the bosom of Catholic society a new kind of apostolate well adapted to modern needs—the Apostolate of Women."

At the beginning, there were three types of Confraternities —those for women, those for men, and (in a few instances) those for men and women together. But experience having shown that friction was only too likely to arise between the two sexes, Vincent—of all men the one most willing to learn from experience—concentrated on women's Confraternities. These were even relieved of their male procurators, for as Vincent found, the women proved themselves eminently capable of handling their own financial affairs. Though a few of the men's Confraternities continued to operate, they did so without conspicuous success, and did not really prove their worth until, in the nineteenth century, they were revived in another form as the Societies that bear St. Vincent's name.

The women's Confraternities, however, flourished better in the country than in the towns. It was in the country that the missions were given that brought them into being; in the country, too, everybody knew everybody else and so was informed as to those who needed help; above all, perhaps, it was in the country that great ladies like the Comtesse de Joigny, and the wives of professional men or prosperous shopkeepers, and peasants could be induced to work in harmony towards a common aim.

Nevertheless Confraternities did to some extent penetrate into the cities, Paris having its first foundation in 1629. But in Paris each parish seemed to wish to have its own special novelty in devotion or charity; and there, too, society being set in very definite strata, there was practically no communication between ladies of the aristocracy, the wives of the bourgeoisie, and the womenfolk of the artizans. They did not as a rule even worship in the same church; when they did, they did not know one another. Accordingly the Paris Confraternities did not—at any rate in the beginning—function very well.

Vincent perceived, however, the enormous amount of good that could be done by pious and well-born ladies of means. During his long stay in the Hôtel Gondi he had come into contact with scores of such ladies, and he knew that though they were often charitably disposed, their charity was almost always of a very disorganized character. They gave generous alms and food to such people as they encountered, but very few of them sought out the poor in the slums as did the Marquise de Maignelay. Here were immense potential resources that he could harness.

Yet it was never a question in his eyes of merely persuading these wealthy women to open their purses, but of setting them to active work. A sum of money could be handed out with hardly more real sacrifice than it cost to send a lackey with a plate of soup to a beggar at the back door of a great mansion. He wanted these ladies to get among the poor to acquaint themselves with their condition, to instruct them in religion, and (if necessary) nurse their sick. That would not only be of more benefit to the poor themselves but of more benefit to the benefactors. He, who often kissed the feet of a beggar when giving an alms, insisted that his helpers should see the face of Christ in Christ's poor and treat them, not with off-hand good-nature, but with respect and even with reverence.

Some of these ladies—notably Louise de Marillac (about whom more will be said later), Madame de Goussault and Mademoiselle de Pollalion he had already employed as visitors to the country Confraternities. And it was through Louise (later to be canonised) that the first small group of country girls had been gathered on November 29, 1633 in her house, a handful destined to grow into the immense army of the Daughters of Charity. Neither Saint had as yet the faintest inkling of what God had in store, and thought of these girls as mere auxilaries in the charitable enterprises of the Confraternities.

It was to the rich, beautiful, devout, gay-spirited widow, Madame de Goussault, that we owe the first definite organization of ladies of rank for charitable work. Probably nobody else could have accomplished what she did, for it is evident from her letters that she had not only inexhaustible vitality (and an even greater vivacity) but a way with her that the sedate and over-scrupulous Louise lacked. Her charm and charity were radiant in her face, so that wherever she went—singing and playing Backgammon (as well as games in which the forfeits were brief prayers)—all hearts were won. It was she who conceived the idea of gathering a band of ladies to visit the sick in the immense hospital known as the Hôtel-Dieu.

It has sometimes been argued by recent historians that in this she was merely used as a tool for the ubiquitous and secret society of men known as the Company of the Blessed Sacrament. It is certainly true that this society had a finger in nearly every pious pie, even though its members were careful to keep themselves out of sight, and that they were already at work —led by the admirable young Baron de Renty—at the Hospital. But it was not the Company but Madame de Goussault who brought into being the Confraternity known as the Ladies of the Hôtel-Dieu.

Only through her pertinacity was she able to accomplish her ends. For when she approached Vincent, he, remembering that some years previously another group of ladies had entered the Hospital, where they had made themselves such a nuisance to the Augustinian nuns that they had been asked to withdraw, was by no means inclined to undertake this work. In fact he definitely refused until, Madame de Goussault—using a woman's oblique methods—got at the Archbishop of Paris and won him over to her side. He virtually ordered Vincent to take charge of this undertaking. The beginning of hospital reform—however imperfect it was according to modern standards—may be said to have originated on that spring day in 1634.

That something badly needed to be done was obvious. The great hospital, where St. Louis had once tended the sick with his royal hands, was in a deplorable condition. Twenty-five thousand patients a year went into the Hôtel-Dieu, and when one hears of the conditions that prevailed there, one wonders how any of them emerged alive. Plague was sporadic, and yet patients were put three, four, and even six in the same bed, and, in order to economize space still further, the beds had between them only just sufficient space to allow a doctor or a nurse to pass. If thousands were admitted, thousands, in time of pestilence, were turned away and died in the streets—in which they were, perhaps, more fortunate than those for whom room was found. Milton's terrible description of a hospital of those times may be quoted here:

> "A place
> Before his eyes appeared, sad, noisome, dark;
> A lazar-house it seemed, wherein were laid
> Numbers of all diseased—all maladies
> Of ghastly spasm, or racking torture, qualms

Of heart-sick agony, all fevorous kinds,
Convulsions, epileptics, fierce catarrhs,
Intestine stone and ulcer, colic pangs,
Demoniac phrensy, moping melancholy,
And moon-struck madness, pining atrophy,
Marasmus and wide-wasting pestilence,
Dropsies and asthmas, and joint-racking rheums.
Dire was the tossing, deep the groans; Despair
Tended the sick, busiest from couch to couch;
And over them triumphant Death his dart
Shook, but delayed to strike, though oft invoked
With vows, as their chief good and final hope."

The hospital was under the care of Augustinian nuns, but they had no novitiate and each new-comer was assigned to an older Sister who was quite as much concerned to attach the novice to herself as to instruct her in what little she knew of nursing. The result was that the nuns were divided into factions and were relaxed and inefficient.

But they were at least no worse than the chaplains, most of whom took their duties in perfunctory style, contenting themselves with suggesting confession to the patient when he applied for admission and attending him, if the case permitted this, *in articulo mortis*. We hear of the head chaplain having to be dismissed in 1635 because of his gambling debts, and of being bastinadoed by the police.

Yet the entrance of the Ladies of Charity into the hospital created a delicate situation. They were only too likely once again to create confusion and get at loggerheads with the nuns. Very strict regulations therefore had to be laid down before Vincent would countenance their activities. They were to avoid all interference with the Sisters, and were to offer only such delicacies as the authorities approved of. Nor were they to preach officiously at the patients, but instead read to them material that Vincent had prepared for this purpose. Since the ramming of religion down people's throats would be likely to do more harm than good, the utmost tact was to be employed. Yet everything was intended to lead up to the proper disposition for a general confession, in which paramount office Vincent and his priests were to supplement the somewhat casual ministrations of the hospital chaplains.

It should be noted that here, as in all of Vincent's works of mercy, the spiritual and the corporal went hand in hand, but with the main emphasis laid on the spiritual. The soups and preserves brought by the Ladies were not offered solely for their own sake, but as a means of predisposing patients by kindness to repentance. The effectiveness of this spiritual activity may be gauged by the fact that—apart from the countless number of lax Catholics recalled to their religious obligations —in the first year alone, according to Abelly, seven hundred and sixty Protestant patients in the hospital entered the Church. All this was very different from the concept of Théophraste Renaudot, a doctor who, having made what was perhaps a political conversion from Calvinism to Catholicism, came to Paris in 1625 and opened, under the aegis of Cardinal Richelieu, an employment bureau and a free clinic. Admirable as this philanthropy was in its way, it confined itself strictly to material ends—and is now almost completely forgotten.[1] The work of Vincent, on the other hand, since it made corporal works of mercy a definitely religious exercise and one always directed to the saving of souls, has endured to this day. It is a lesson that modern philanthropy might well lay to heart.

Under the presidency of Madame de Goussault about a hundred and twenty ladies were collected whose work for the poor

[1] Indeed, if Renaudot is now remembered at all, it is as the founder in 1631 of the *Gazette*, a four-page weekly, which was the forerunner of the modern newspaper. Yet it is evident, from the variety of his enterprises, that he was a remarkable man.

was made a means of their personal sanctification. The roster of their names reads like a social directory: among them may be mentioned the Duchesse d'Aiguillon, the niece of Cardinal Richelieu; the wife of Marshal de Schomberg; the Marquise De Vigean, of whose two daughters one later became the Duchesse de Richelieu, and the other (the beloved of the Duc d'Enghien) a Carmelite nun at Vincent's instigation; Madame de Fouquet, the mother of the Minister; Madame de Villeneuve; Louise-Marie de Gonzague, soon to be married by proxy to the King of Poland; the Princesse de Condé, sister of the Montmorency executed by Richelieu and mother of the "great" Condé (at this time still d'Enghien); the Duchesses de Verneuil, Ventadour and Nemours; the Comtesse de Brienne; Madame de Miramion; and Madame President de Herse, whose husband was head of the Court of Requests. In that aristocratic, not to say snobbish, world the aid of such people had to be enlisted in order to get things done. But Vincent was also remembering that these wealthy and high-born women had souls to be saved.

In telling them and their hardly less illustrious companions that "For the last eight hundred years or so women have had no public employment in the Church," Vincent imposed the obligations of at least half an hour's mental prayer a day, weekly confession and communion, and spiritual reading in the books of Francis de Sales. He knew that piety would form a bond of union in the new Society which, without it, would have neither heart nor muscular energy.

As might be expected, in the cases of some of these aristocrats, works of charity after a time palled. It was not possible to keep out those who, however excellent their intentions may have been, showed a dainty and flowery devotion and joined the Confraternity because good works were at the moment fashionable. Yet even in these cases something valuable was accomplished, and many of those who were frivolous in the beginning developed to everybody's surprise a constancy in piety. The majority stood by Vincent with open hearts and open purses to the end.

The work begun at the Hôtel-Dieu did not end there. Vincent conceived the idea of a kind of Super-Confraternity under the presidency of Queen Anne of Austria. This group, too, was to have its religious obligations; and, since it was likely to be subject to special temptations to gossip about public affairs or to use the meetings as opportunities for asking the Queen for personal favours, it was strictly laid down that charity and religion alone were to form the subject of their discussions.

If this group never appears to have functioned to any extent, probably the fault was due to the ineptitude of that rather foolish person, Anne of Austria, whose piety, though genuine in its way, was of a rather frothy and gushing order. Something nevertheless came out of this project, for, as time went on, a number of committees were formed to look after the needs of jailbirds, prisoners for debt, foundlings, and fallen women. About these works a later chapter must be written, as something must also be said about the generous contributions of the Ladies of Charity towards the redemption of Christian slaves in Barbary, the foreign missions, and in aid of the provinces devastated during the Thirty Years' War and the Fronde. But at this stage a word or two should be given to Marie de Pollalion, a widow who, because her husband had not been of the nobility, was entitled, according to the usage of the time, only to the title of "Mademoiselle" instead of "Madame."

Her special field was work among fallen girls, and this, though she always consulted Vincent de Paul, she managed in a way peculiarly her own. This intrepid woman showed no hesitation in making her way into dens of criminals or even into brothels, where, if there was no other way of gaining entrance, she would go in disguise. Having a very wealthy son-in-law as her banker, and some fortune of her own, she rescued numbers of girls from a life of prostitution and established them in a house in which they could live virtuously. And her other benefactions were without number.

Another of Vincent's Ladies who devised a special way of working for the destitute—though it was one less dangerous than that of Madame de Pollalion—was Madeline de Lamoignon. She turned her mother's house into a kind of department store. From her friends she collected anything they chose to give from old clothes to pictures and tapestries and furniture. These she disposed of at shrewd prices to the dealers in such articles. Another room in the house looked like a grocery, so full was it of all kinds of things to eat and drink. From the Hôtel Lamoignon the poor never went empty-handed away. If her friends were often amused by her eccentricity, they nevertheless gave lavishly. The King once remarked to Madeline, "You are the only woman to whom I cannot refuse anything, for you never ask anything for yourself." And on one occasion when a niece of Cardinal Mazarin gave her some costly jewels, she got the King to buy them.

Vincent came to have great confidence in the administrative ability of his co-workers, and relied so much on their judgment that some of them reproached him with not maintaining his own opinion when one contrary to his own was advanced. His reply was "God forbid, Madame, that my ideas should prevail over those of others! I am quite content that God, in His goodness, is doing His work without me, who am quite worthless." The answer, we may surmise, was not dictated solely by humility but by his perception of the fact that these women were fully competent to manage affairs. Humble as Vincent was and little addicted to self-assertiveness, he could put his foot down firmly when the need arose.

What delighted him was to see these high-born Ladies, most of whom had up to that time filled their otherwise empty days with frivolity, so usefully employed. Work—there was nothing better for the soul than that, especially work of this character. "God," he used to say, "works with each of His creatures in particular. He works with the artizan in his workshop, with the housewife in her home, with the ant and the bee when they gather their stores." He might well have taken as his motto the words of Christ, "My father worketh hitherto, and I work." Under the infection of his example, the Ladies of Charity performed prodigies.

Another text which must often have come into his mind was that from St. Paul's Epistle to Timothy: "Charge the rich of this world to do good, to become rich in good works." That was what he was doing as no man has done it before or since. And much of the work—particularly that done in the hospital —was of a nature that can only be called heroic. For in the Hôtel-Dieu there was always, apart from the ordinary contagious diseases, the more terrible danger of plague.

The prescribed way of approaching such sufferers was in clothes soaked in disinfectants, made of a mysterious mixture of oils and powders, over which a leather overcoat was worn. A nurse dressed in this style and with goggles over the eyes and a sponge over the nose and garlic in the mouth could have been anything but a comforting sight. But the Ladies of Charity simply put on their aprons and bustled about their duties unconcernedly. They conquered their natural repulsion when Vincent told them, "What an honour it is to visit Jesus Christ! If you only look at the poor they will inspire disgust; see Jesus Christ in them, and you will be attracted and charmed." That only one or two of them died as a consequence of their work at the hospital, Vincent set down to the special protection of God.

Yet we must not expect to find in Vincent an economic program such as has been laid down in recent Papal encyclicals. If he had any ideas on the subject, he did not express them. He was no revolutionary in that field, and had he attempted to become one he would have ruined all that he was trying to do. But probably he held no theories on the subject of the unequal distribution of wealth, and so contented himself with meeting the situation as he found it. His age did not trouble itself with speculations on such matters. What he saw was that the poor needed help and that the rich could give them that help. His main preoccupation was not the social order but the saving of souls.

Nevertheless we should do him an injustice if we failed to remember that he frequently said things that contained in solution all that was needed then—or, for that matter, is needed now—to bring about a radical reconstruction of society. One of these sayings was "There is no charity that is unaccompanied by justice." And it is clear from another saying, in which he makes an application of this principle, that he set the claims of justice even above those of charity. "Yesterday," he once said, "I found myself obliged to select between two duties, one to fulfill a promise I had made, and the other to do an act of charity to one who can do us a great deal of good, or a great deal of harm, and unable to satisfy both. I left the act of charity to fulfill my promise, and the person to whom I refer is very much displeased." If Vincent failed to perceive the complete range of his principle, he cannot be blamed: nobody perceived it then, and few perceive it even now.

ℭ 13. Louise de Marillac

THE greatest of all the names associated with Vincent de Paul is without question that of St. Louise de Marillac. The Countess de Joigny has the credit of suggesting the founding of the Congregation of the Mission and of providing it with its first endowment. Madame de Goussault was the devoted and pertinacious woman who brought about the establishment of the Ladies of Charity. The Duchesse d'Aiguillon was, perhaps, the most generous of many generous benefactors of the poor. But it was Louise who was the balance-wheel even of the work done at the Hôtel-Dieu, and it was she who found and trained the first Daughters of Charity. The last work alone would be more than sufficient to cover her with glory; but there was no Confraternity in city or country which she did not visit, correct and inspire, no charitable enterprise undertaken by Vincent de Paul in which she was not constantly consulted.

Louise de Marillac came of good family, though it was not among the most exalted or wealthy, despite its frequent contribution of bishops and royal officers to France. There came, however, a moment in 1630 when the Marillacs were within an inch of supreme power: when one of Louise's uncles, Michel, was Keeper of the Seals and destined by the Queen-Mother and Anne of Austria to supplant Richelieu as First Minister, and the other was a Marshal. The family was undone by the patronage of the intriguing Marie de' Medici and by allowing itself to be used as the tool of her ambition and her spite against the Cardinal. Both the brothers fell on the "Day of Dupes," the Marshal to suffer on the scaffold and the Keeper of the Seals to die in prison.

It was Michel de Marillac, a man at once of affairs and

profound spirituality, who seems to have brought up Louise after the death of her father when she was thirteen and to have been later a kind of spiritual director to her. But already her piety had received its first impetus in what we should call today a fashionable finishing-school conducted by some Dominican nuns whose superior was a Gondi, an aunt of our friend Philippe-Emmanuel. There Louise showed a precocious interest in philosophy and learned to dabble in the water-colour painting that was to be the harmless amusement of her leisure hours during the rest of her life.

Not unnaturally her inclination was for the cloister, for which, however, her constitution was too delicate, so that, after the death of her father in 1604, her uncle Michel took charge of her upbringing and nine years later arranged her marriage to Anthony Le Gras, the principal secretary to Marie de' Medici. Again we have an inkling of how deep was the interest of the Queen Regent (as she was then) in the fortunes of the Marillacs. It was a patronage that was in the end to prove fatal to the family.

Anthony was a young man of good, though apparently no great force of character. As he was below the rank of a knight, his wife, according to the usage of the time already noted, was entitled only to be styled "Mademoiselle." It was as such that she was addressed then and during her religious work. For though she wished to assume the uniform of the Daughters of Charity she founded later, and to be called "Sister," Vincent did not permit this. Her status remained that of a Lady of Charity, and she dressed until her death in 1660 in widow's weeds.[1]

She had always been devout, in a somewhat over-scrupulous style, and, like Madame de Gondi, sought out special spiritual

[1] She has been often called "the first Daughter of Charity." In a sense the title is accurate. But it would be more accurate to think of her as the Mother of the Daughters.

directors to whom, one fears, she was a good deal of a trial. But it is no more than just to record that all of them recognised that this morbidly sensitive soul was capable of great things. Francis de Sales took her under his wing while he was in Paris in 1618-1619, and after his death she corresponded with his friend, Camus, the Bishop of Belley, the author of *The Spirit of St. Francis de Sales.*

All the tact and spiritual insight of the good Bishop (who incidentally was a connexion by marriage) was called for in this case. For when Anthony Le Gras fell ill of an incurable disease, Louise brought herself to believe that the illness was a punishment from God for her not having accepted a religious vocation. Her scrupulosity even led her to the astounding notion that she ought to separate from her husband. Camus, some of whose letters to Louise we possess, probably did not express all that was in his mind when he learned of the suggestion. It would certainly have seriously offended the sensitive soul to have been told bluntly that what she was meditating was inhuman in its cruelty; instead Camus mildly pointed out that, as she was in the married state, she should not even think of leaving Anthony. The biographers tell us that at this time she was assailed with dreadful doubts about the existence of God and the immortality of the soul. A plain man might think that this was a not unnatural consequence of the dereliction of duty she proposed, and some such thought may well have crossed the mind of her director. What Camus actually did was to permit her to take on May 4, 1623, a vow to remain a widow in the event of surviving her husband. At the same time he gave her the excellent advice that she should begin a study of the Bible in company with the ailing Anthony.

The advice bore fruit. On Whit-Sunday of that year, while at Mass, she heard an interior voice telling her to remain with her husband; and she saw a vision of a religious house in which

Sisters were coming in and going out all the time—something inconceivable in those days when nuns were always strictly cloistered. Her doubts about the Faith at once disappeared, and she took this as a sign from heaven that she was destined to belong to a new sort of community—one devoted to the service of the poor.

All this time she had often used Michel de Marillac as a kind of lay Father-Confessor. Her distinguished uncle was a man who lived, in spite of his high office, a life of extreme austerity, sleeping on the floor and wearing a hairshirt and scourging himself freely. But he was a good psychologist and his letters to his niece are full of exhortations to confidence in God. In one occurs the passage: "God is not bound by our designs and proposals, and those find Him everywhere who seek Him in the way He wishes to communicate Himself, and not in the way they imagine is useful and profitable to themselves, for often the usefulness thus imagined in our minds is merely dictated by our own feelings." In other words, Louise should conquer her scruples and remain with her husband.

Let me be perfectly candid: Louise seems to me during these years, and even for some years afterwards, to have been a very tiresome person and one who must have been something of a nuisance to her spiritual directors. She was one of those good women who confuse their hysterical sensibility with sanctity— and from such women the ordinary man flees. It called for an unusual amount of discernment to perceive the potential greatness of that tormented soul. One would think that she was about the last person in the world whom Vincent would have picked to be his right hand in the organization of charity. That he did so is the highest possible proof of his extraordinary insight.

She came under his direction towards the end of 1624 or the beginning of 1625, and probably got to know him through her

frequentation of the Visitation convent. But he, like his predecessors, had at first a good deal to contend with in the matter
of her scrupulosity. The Bishop of Belley had once written
to tell her, "You attach yourself a little too much to those who
guide you." Vincent in his turn found this to be so.

Upon the death of Anthony Le Gras at the end of 1625,
Louise took a house near the Collège des-Bons-Enfants, so as
to be nearer her spiritual director and entered her son, Michel,
now about thirteen, as a student in the seminary of Saint-
Nicholas-du-Chardonnet. Nothing would suit her except that
this rather lazy, listless and stupid youth should become a priest.
That he did not do so was due to the common-sense of Vincent
de Paul. For after the boy exploded into the protest that he
was accepting his fate only to please his mother and that he
would rather be dead than be a priest, Vincent, who had long
been aware of the true situation, advised Louise not to force
priesthood upon one who clearly had no vocation for it.[2]

Louise herself remained a problem. She was of the worrying
type, and whenever Vincent was away from Paris on one of
his missions, she was overwhelmed with despondency and dis-
couragement. Much to his disapproval, she was inclined at such
times to avoid going to Communion, though it was her usual
practice to go three times a week. In this we may perceive an incipient Jansenism which would probably have developed into
something very dangerous had Vincent not been at hand. He
insisted upon her mitigating her bodily mortifications, and when
she was troubled because she had not carried out her resolution to adore the humanity of Christ precisely thirty-three times
a day, he had to tell her that arithmetic was no essential element in devotion. "God is love and He wishes us to go to

[2] All this was due to a too anxious solicitude. As Vincent wrote to her
once, "I have never seen a mother so motherly as you; you are scarcely
a woman on any other point." He was already finding, however, a new
outlet for her maternal instincts.

Him by love," he wrote to her. "So do not consider yourself bound by all these good resolutions."

The truth would seem to be that Louise was decidedly neurotic. But it should be added that though some neurotics reach a state in which they are of no use to themselves or to anybody else, many of the world's most notable achievements have been brought about by such people. This Vincent instinctively understood. Genius has time after time anticipated the conclusions of modern psychology.

Yet Vincent, who was never in a hurry about anything, took his time. When the idea of entering the cloister recurred to Louise's mind, he held her back, advising her "To strive not to be over-eager." Like Camus, he urged her to study the New Testament and, in another letter, wrote: "Ever honour the inaction and the hidden state of the Son of God. Let that be your centre, if that is what He asks of you now, for the future, and for ever. If His divine Majesty does not let you know, and in such a way that you cannot be deceived, that He desires nothing else of you, do not think about . . . any such matter." Her acceptance of inactivity was to be the preparation for half a life-time of unremitting toil.

At last, in 1630, he found work for her, work that would take her out of herself. He needed a few women of means and leisure to travel about the country visiting the Confraternities. In selecting Louise for this, he opened for her a great life-work. It turned her from self-centered scrupulosity to sanctity. Work, as in the case of Madame de Gondi, proved the best possible medicine for the soul.

She proved herself perfectly fitted for her new duties. In every place she visited she called together the members of the Confraternities, reanimated their zeal, visited the sick and the poor in their homes, checked accounts, provided a schoolteacher whenever this was possible, and catechised the children and their mothers. We still have in her holograph an explanation of the "Our Father." Part of this reads: "We condemn ourselves, if we bear any enmity towards our neighbour and refuse to forgive him for the evil he has done us. It is just the same as if after Mary refused to give Joan some bread, she went and said to another girl, 'Give me some bread just as I have given some to Joan'; that would be just the same as if Mary asked not to be given any. Others say, 'I forgive him but I do not want ever to see him again'; now such people ask God to send them to hell, where He will never more be seen." Under the shadows that had so long terrified this morbidly sensitive mind there was a bed-rock of practicality, and it was this that Vincent perceived and employed.

There was also something else that now appeared—courage. Like many women who are absurdly fretful over trifles—Vincent once wrote to say, "I have never seen such a woman as you are for taking things tragically"—when a real tragedy occurred she met it with the most admirable fortitude. It was while she was on her visitation of the Confraternities that her uncles, the Keeper of the Seals and the Marshal, were ruined.

Marie de' Medici, whose original favour towards Cardinal Richelieu had turned into deadly hate, and Anne of Austria, thought they had at last succeeded in persuading Louis XIII to dismiss his Minister. The story is well known how the Cardinal, who somehow had got wind of what was intended, found a side-door open into the room where the royal consultation was being held and made a dramatic entry saying, "I'll wager that Your Majesties are talking about me." That same evening the King had a revulsion of feeling and sought an interview with Richelieu. The following morning—the "Day of Dupes"—the Minister was in a stronger position than ever, and Marie de' Medici fled to Flanders.

But Richelieu never failed to strike. Since there was nothing

against the Keeper of the Seals except the fact that he had been
marked out by the Queen-Mother to succeed to the position of
First Minister, he was put merely under prudential arrest.
Yet that an example might be made, the Marshal de Marillac,
who was with the army in Italy, had a charge of malversation
of funds brought against him. In this he was probably tech-
nically guilty—but then, so was every general officer of the
time, when it was an understood thing that high command permitted certain perquisites. As Marillac said, "My trial is merely
a question of hay and cheese—trifles for which a page-boy
would hardly get a whipping." But as the principle of perquisites had never been officially conceded, though it was universally winked at, Richelieu was given a chance to press his
charge against Marillac before a carefully packed court, and to
have the Marshal executed as a warning to others who might be
thinking of trying to undermine his authority.

The Keeper of the Seals went off cheerfully to prison and died
soon afterwards, when the usual accusation of poison (in this
case almost certainly unfounded) was brought. The Marshal was
not beheaded until the summer of 1632, eighteen months after
the Day of Dupes, November 11, 1630. During the intervening
September his wife, seeing what was about to come, died of
grief. She was a Medici and a cousin of the Queen-Mother.

Nothing could be done to soften the implacable Richelieu.
Anne d'Attichy, the Comtesse de Maure, the ward of Louise's
dead husband, though she was related to Richelieu through
the marriage of the Duchesse d'Auguillon, tried to get at the
Cardinal through his niece, but he would not admit of family
influence in political affairs. He would not even allow Madame
de Marillac to intercede in her husband's behalf, though, as the
Marshal said, this was something never known, even in the
case of high-treason. It was from the beginning evident that
Richelieu demanded a victim.

Yet during all this time of trouble and uncertainty Louise de Marillac was quietly going about her work. When the news came of her aunt's death Vincent wrote to comfort her. "The Son of God wept for Lazarus; why should you not weep for this dear lady? There is no harm in doing so, provided that, like the Son of God, you conform yourself to the will of His Father, and I am quite sure that you will do so." She did: she felt a natural grief; she found supernatural consolation and calm.

If we do not find in Vincent's letters to Louise that note of tender affection he so freely expressed when writing to Jane Frances de Chantal, the reason must be, not that he esteemed her less, but that he thought her case called for firmer handling. He was inclined to scold her both for her excessive scrupulosity and her excessive zeal. He was always anxious lest one whose health was frail should overwork. Thus he writes to her, "It is a ruse of the devil by which he tries to induce people to do too much so that at last they can do nothing at all." And again he tells her, "I warn you beforehand that I am going to blame you severely tomorrow for letting yourself be possessed by these idle and frivolous apprehensions. So prepare to be scolded." Yet for all that, when in 1636 he heard she was ill at Liancourt, he promised to send the King's doctor to her and begged her to spare no expense to have herself properly looked after. If he wanted to get her out of her habit of leaning on him too much, he did not fail in his solicitude when it was called for. But he knew he could develop the great gifts of her mind and heart not by coddling but by a kind of fatherly sternness.

His confidence got its reward; his method of handling her was fully justified. It was under his direction that this nervous, apprehensive and too sensitive woman became a saint, and founded the Daughters of Charity.

If she had tortured herself with scruples before Vincent had secured her release through work, she never quite got rid of her constitutional nervousness. As Vincent remarked after her death, "She was not without that shade of imperfection which even the greatest saints had. In her there was perceptible a little hastiness; but it was really nothing, since she humbled herself for it a moment afterwards." Indeed the fact that she had a somewhat difficult temperament and overcame it—or at any rate struggled against it—added to her merit. For the rest, her life was one of absolute devotion to charity. She wore the oldest of clothes, nor would she lay them aside even when they were all patched. If she was given something new, she put it aside as soon as she noticed that it was new. Even her head-dress had to come out of a second-hand store before it would satisfy her. As she was fond of telling her daughters, "We are the servants of the poor, consequently we ought to be more poor than the poor." There was, however, this difference: the girls she had gathered were—apart from a few later exceptions—accustomed to the hard lot of the peasantry; Louise was a lady of fortune and good social position, and she was all her life in very delicate health. Nothing therefore could have been more inspiring than the example that such a woman gave.

It is especially instructive to note that the partnership between the two Saints—one destined to last for nearly thirty years—was entered into, on Vincent's part, only after a delay that the highly-strung woman found hard to bear. "Wait for the hour fixed by God's Providence"—it was thus that he kept putting Louise off. Probably he had long perceived that he needed someone who could complete what he had begun, and was on the lookout for just such a woman as Louise proved to be. But he could see that she was not yet ready for her great work, and divined that God was not yet ready. Only when the providential hour at last struck did they go forward together to their original and fruitful labours.

ℂ 14. The Daughters of Charity

YET the first Daughter of Charity was discovered not by Louise but by Vincent, though it must be at once added that he did not have the slightest idea as to what was going to flow from it.

While he was conducting a mission in Suresnes he came across a girl named Margaret Naseau, whom he probably had known when she was a child. The idea had suggested itself to this poor and quite illiterate young woman not merely that she should nurse the sick, as did the other members of the local Confraternity, but that she should teach children to read. As she could not, as yet, read herself, she bought an alphabet and got the local priests to tell her what the signs stood for. While minding her cows she memorized her letters, and would ask any passer-by who looked like a person of education to help her to make out the words in a book. Having got that far, she sought Vincent's advice, and he encouraged her to continue her heroic efforts at self-education.

How lettered she became we do not know, except that she learned enough to be able to give elementary instruction to the village children in a night-school she set up. Meanwhile she saved every sou she could, often going without food, in order to assist young men who were studying to become priests. Quite of her own accord she seems to have hit upon the idea—afterwards repeatedly reiterated by Vincent—that the education of the poor was quite as much a part of the vocation of the Sister of Charity as the nursing of the sick. In the end she died—after coming to Paris—by taking a plague-stricken girl into her own bed. If that was not very wise, we may at least be sure that the devotion of her brief life received its reward in heaven.

Margaret Naseau, however, must be considered an accident.

In the ordinary course of events, she would have been a solitary case. But she gave Vincent and Louise an idea; they determined to gather other girls of the same type who would be willing to act as school teachers in the villages and make themselves generally useful to the Confraternities.

At the outset we should remember that the work begun in this casual fashion was developed only little by little, with no clear design in its early stages, by a priest of fifty—which in those days meant a much more advanced age than it would today—and a middle-aged widow, in whose case fragile health had succeeded (though without quite dissipating) mental morbidity. Vincent was still often obliged to write to her, "Do not be disturbed over things that do not matter. Withdraw your eyes a little from yourself and fix them on Jesus Christ."

The conduct of country schools in this way became part of the work of the Daughters of Charity. And sometimes this involved them in embarrassing situations. Thus we hear of the schoolmaster at Forges taking boys in need of caning to the Sisters at Serqueux near-by. His quaint notion presumably was that they would be more humiliated by being caned by the Sisters than if he thrashed them himself. Very properly the Sisters, after consulting Vincent, refused, as they also refused to subject to corporal punishment a girl brought to them by the parish priest at Chars. While the Daughters of Charity showed that they were quite ready to undertake all kinds of disagreeable tasks, there was a limit. Their work was primarily to look after the material and spiritual needs of the poor.

It should be remarked again that though Vincent and Louise always regarded spiritual works as of far greater importance than corporal works, it was from the start clearly laid down that if any poor person refused spiritual aid or even (as sometimes happened) responded with blasphemy, the secondary obligation was not on that account lessened. Whipping of naughty children, however, hardly came into this category.

The second stage in the organization of the Daughters of Charity—and it followed very closely after the free-lance efforts of the country girls—was when some of the Confraternities in Paris asked that they might have girls sent to them. Louise in her travels was every now and then coming across such girls, strong country wenches used to doing rough work and anxious to devote themselves to the service of the poor.

The plan was that these were to make themselves useful to the Ladies of Charity. Devoted as many of these Ladies were, they were not always very efficient when it came to doing what needed to be done in a house where there was a bed-ridden mother with a troop of dirty children. Besides, the aristocratic Ladies had many demands upon their time, and often were prevented, because of having to entertain a caller, from going to see those whom they had intended to visit. In such cases they would send round one of their flunkeys with a pot of soup, and it is not difficult to image the disgust of these lackeys at the service they were called upon to perform or the contemptuous way they performed it. Such charity was only too likely to arouse resentment in the heart of the recipient, and was not at all in conformity with Vincent's purpose. But the Daughters of Charity gladly undertook such menial tasks.

The third stage (which was really the first stage of definite organization) occurred when Louise de Marillac took a small group of these girls into her house to train them. Diamonds though many of them were, only too often they were diamonds very much in the rough. Coming from the country to Paris, they were sometimes inclined to hang around gossiping or even to quarrel. They had none of the refinement of well-bred ladies and were quite capable of terminating an angry argument with a blow. Well-intentioned as they were, they still had to learn how to behave. Above all they needed direction in their spiritual life. No permanent good was going to be achieved unless they based all their activity on prayer. How fully they came to do so appears in the touching story of the Sister (little Margaret Lauraine) to whom the wonders of the great city were so entrancing that she could keep her big eyes off them only by hugging her crucifix and whispering, "But You, Lord, are more beautiful than all these things!"

It was on November 29, 1633 that the first group of three girls was received under Louise de Marillac's roof near the church of Saint-Nicholas-du-Chardonnet and the Collège des-Bons-Enfants. Eight months later there were still only a dozen of them—so small and tentative were the beginnings of what was eventually to grow into the largest order—whether of women or men—in the Church. It was not until the end of 1640—after a move in the meanwhile to a house at La Chapelle in the suburbs—that the Daughters of Charity found a permanent home opposite the Priory of Saint-Lazare. And even then the community was never very large, for as soon as the girls had been trained they were sent out to work, frequently in distant parts of the country.

It must be emphasised that Vincent never looked upon himself as founding a religious order. The Daughters of Charity in his eyes constituted only a lay association that was to act as an auxiliary to the Confraternities. They were destined, indeed, to completely overshadow the Ladies of Charity, but nobody knew that as yet.

The dress they wore was not a religious habit, nor even the garb of the Sister of Charity as we know her today. Instead of the blue dress and the flapping cornette, now so familiar, the Daughters of Charity wore the rough grey dress and the white toque customary in the districts round Paris from which most of the first Sisters sprang. When postulants came from other parts of France, where the peasant girls were somewhat differently garbed, for the sake of convenience they dressed like the others. The point is that Vincent wished only a simple, modest, uniform dress for all his Daughters. Some of them, when they went into country districts, introduced little scraps of finery and tried to wear their toques coquettishly so as to show their nice little curls. Such departures from the regulations, when reported, were instantly corrected from headquarters.

As the organization developed, there was a tendency both on the part of the Sisters and the general public to regard the Daughters of Charity as nuns. Vincent would not countenance anything of the kind. He, along with everybody else of his time, held to the principle *Qui dit religieuse dit un cloître*. So he kept telling them that they were not nuns and must never allow their organization to be so classified. "Your monasteries," he told them in often-quoted words, "are the houses of the sick; your cell is a hired room; your chapel, the parish church; your cloister, the streets of the city; your enclosure, obedience; your grille, the fear of God; your veil, holy modesty." The Sisters of Charity today will still let you know that, whatever else they are, they are not nuns.

In this they are faithful to their founder. For in his Conferences to them, rather complete reports of many of which have been preserved, he kept reverting to the point: "If some mischief-making person should ever appear in your midst saying, 'We should be religious; it would be much nicer,' Oh, my dear Sisters, the Company would then be in a state to receive Extreme Unction. . . . Weep, groan, tell the Superiors about it, for whoever says 'religious' says 'cloistered' and Daughters of Charity are bound to go everywhere." Surely nothing could be more explicit.

But though they were not nuns, they were not on that account to think less highly of their vocation. "There are no nuns," he used to tell them, "of whom God demands as much as of you."[1] No Christian, he added, must fail to think of himself as called to do all he can to reach perfection. Nevertheless a modification was made in his original plan—that of completely free association—to the extent of permitting a few carefully selected Sisters, on Lady Day 1642, to take private vows. In this, however, Vincent appears to have acted against his better judgment, or without any intention of establishing a permanent rule. Certainly for at least the past two hundred years Sisters of Charity have taken only yearly vows. On March 25th each year every Daughter of St. Vincent is as free as air, to remain in the community or to go back to the world, just as she chooses.

Very few of them, all the same, avail themselves of this privilege. Before they are given the habit, their vocation is tested in a long postulancy followed by a further period in what is called the "Seminary." (They do not employ the conventual term "Novitiate.") If in Vincent's time a good many of the girls who joined Louise de Marillac had to be dismissed, or left of their own accord, this was because the selection of candidates could not always be made very carefully. Traditions, too, were still in process of formation. Therefore the defection of any of his daughters never worried him. Instead we find him writing to the over-anxious Louise, "You take the departure of your Daughters rather too much to heart. In the name of God, Mademoiselle, try to acquire grace to accept these occurrences! Our Lord shows His mercy to the Company in purging it after

---

[1] Vincent would not allow them to have any contact with nuns—though, as he put it, they were not to tell the religious so, lest they should think they were despised. What he did not consider it advisable to tell his Daughters in so many words was that, by their meeting nuns, they might hanker after becoming religious themselves, on some false understanding of the value of the contemplative life.

this manner, and this is one of the first things He will reveal to you in Heaven. You must be quite certain that none of those whom Our Lord has really summoned into the Company will fail in her vocation. Why should you trouble about the others? Let them go; we shall not lack for Daughters."

In all this Vincent shows at once his magnificent common-sense and his confidence in God. He was well aware that the anomalous position in which he put his Daughters had disadvantages as well as advantages. The fact that they were not religious and without vows left them without the protection of the civil power. Yet they were obliged to go into disreputable city slums; and later incurred still greater dangers when they worked among the badly disciplined armies during the civil wars. But he accepted, and asked them to accept, all these dangers rather than bind them in such a way as would have made their distinctive work altogether impossible. If they had become nuns, they would have indeed received a recognised status; but they would have ceased to be Daughters of Charity.

It is necessary to stress the point, because in our time canon law makes all the required distinctions. There are now many communities who have adopted the Vincentian innovation, and the Sisters of Charity are not alone in their work among the poor. But in Vincent's time the innovation was startling. He had succeeded where Francis de Sales had failed.

What is interesting to note is the way Vincent, at any rate in the beginning, used to address his Daughters. The title of "Sister" gradually crept in, but at first he used to refer to them and address them merely by their Christian names, the title of "Mademoiselle" being reserved exclusively for Louise de Marillac. Thus, writing in 1636 to Louise, he says, "Your Daughters of the General Hospital are all doing well, except Henrietta, who is constantly depressed; Mary says it is on account of your absence. This prevented her from going to Saint-Nicholas, and Barbara from going to Saint-Sulpice. Isabella is getting better." In conversation it was simply "Jeanne" or "Barbara"—or, when there were two girls of the same name, he differentiated between them as "little Jeanne" and "big Jeanne," or as "Barbara of this parish" and "Barbara of the other parish." As his Daughters, they were treated with affectionate familiarity.

If later the "Sister" came into use, this was partly due to the fact that, though not nuns, they acquired a quasi religious status, and was probably also due, in part, to the fact that a few high-born ladies joined them, who could hardly be called merely by their Christian names. As Vincent could permit no distinction in treatment between his aristocratic and his rustic Daughters, the "Sister" was a way out of the difficulty. Let us hear what he has to say: "If you desire to be true, good Daughters of Charity, you must be temperate, you must not be looking for highly seasoned dishes, neither those of you who are widows of great rank nor those who are just simple village girls. There is no distinction, my Daughters, no difference whatever when one is a real Daughter of Charity."

In the beginning they were not looked upon as a body really separate from the Confraternities; in fact, only by degrees did it dawn upon Vincent and Louise just what they were. It might even be said that this did not become perfectly clear until shortly before the death of their Founders. For Vincent debated within himself a long while what he should do in the event of the death of "Mademoiselle," and his original intention appears to have been to place them under the President of the Ladies of Charity at the Hôtel-Dieu, or at any rate under the control of one of the members of that Confraternity. When at last he did decide that Louise ought to be succeeded, not by someone whom he now saw would be an outsider, but by a Daughter of Charity, it was agreed that her title should not be "Superior" but "Sister Servant." That custom still prevails.

The Sisters' manner of life was marked by no great bodily mortifications or singularities of any kind, but was sufficiently austere. At first, while experience was still lacking and while rules were not definitely set, a good deal more liberty was accorded than was later found to be advisable. For instance, the girls were allowed to go home on special occasions, such as family weddings, something later forbidden to the Sisters. In the same way, during the first year or so, there was no rule of silence. But from the start it was made clear that the servants of the poor ought to live at least as frugally as the poor they served. Their houses lacked the substantial dignity of convents; their food was plain and meagre; they were not allowed any wine. Yet in all this there was no intention of imposing special hardships; the Sisters, being with few exceptions peasants, had the standard of living to which they were accustomed. About all that they added was a greater amount of prayer.

Since, however, their vocation was one of work, their devotional exercises were crowded into the early morning hours. After the first years, during which their day began at half-past five, they had to rise at four to attend Mass and make their meditation. And this meditation was always of a practical sort, upon the Christian virtues rather than upon the Christian mysteries. No wise Mother Superior or spiritual director looks with anything but suspicion on tales of ecstasies and visions; Vincent positively discountenanced anything of the sort. His Daughters were to love God, and to try to remain all day in His presence; but they were to express their love through their love of the poor. That is why Vincent told them, "The Daughters of Charity will remember that they must always prefer the service of the poor before the practice of devotion, when necessity or obedience requires this. In doing so, let them picture to themselves that they are quitting God for God."

Few of these simple country girls would, of course, have been likely to have been attracted by the contemplative life; but Vincent recalled how Louise de Marillac had with difficulty been drawn from it. His was to be an active order even though, as Abelly remarks, his ideal was the union of the functions of Mary and Martha. It was enough for these Sisters to remember, "Love God and then you will indeed be learned." It was all the learning, except just enough for the running of village schools, that he asked of them. All the same, as he said in one of his Conferences, "How do you know but that God wishes to make St. Teresas of you?" And lest they should undervalue their vocation (of *themselves* he wished them to think lightly), he told them: "Just think! When God chose you, there were plenty of other people in the world—and yet he chose you,— you, Anne, Mary, Margaret and all the rest of you . . . how indebted you are to God."

Used as these girls were to heavy work, many of them must nevertheless at times have found the unending drudgery difficult to endure. Moreover, when they were sent out on service in groups of twos and threes into country districts, it was inevitable that they should come to feel very isolated, and, at the same time, find it hard to keep up a community life. In such cases it was not at all easy to direct them from Paris, and yet many problems cropped up in which they needed direction. Even when their devotion could be counted upon, the event sometimes proved—how could it be otherwise?—that the Sisters lacked judgment. They had many demands made upon them from which nuns living in the shelter of a convent were happily free. It speaks volumes that very rarely were Vincent and Louise disappointed.

But when Louise personally undertook the formation of each of the Daughters of Charity, she did so only under Vincent's keen eye and wise supervision. Her own tendency, as we have seen, was to be somewhat too severe. Though she managed to curb her worrying disposition and her scrupulosity, she never quite lost a spirit which, had Vincent not been at hand to check it, would have proved disastrous. She was, indeed, far more rigorous with herself than with others, and this extract from her private meditations will indicate the tenour of her mind: "We have no knowledge of our way unless we follow Jesus, always working and always suffering. Again, He could not have led us unless His own resolve had taken Him as far as death on the Cross." So far, so good. But she adds, "Consider, then, whether we do well to spare ourselves, lest we lose whatever we have gained hitherto. When we have laboured forty-nine years, if we have relaxed in the fiftieth, and it is then that God calls us, the whole of life will have availed nothing." Logically or theologically, indeed, that cannot be cavilled at; there *is* always that awful possibility; but to be too preoccupied with such considerations is not very helpful or healthy.

Fortunately Vincent instituted weekly Conferences for the Sisters in Paris, when they would gather in the Mother-House from all the various parishes. On such occasions Vincent was always at his best, for, instead of lecturing to his Daughters, he would chat with them in the most intimate and fatherly fashion. He would draw them out, calling upon this Sister and that in turn, always listening intently to what they said and giving praise freely. His homely humour and powers of mimicry were very useful in these little gatherings, and it is still possible to get an impression of their effect. This incident, of those that have come down to us, is typical. One of the Sisters naïvely asked one day whether it would be permissible for any of them to use a little perfume. Instead of exclaiming, "My dear child, what *are* you thinking of!" his only reply was to assume an attitude of silent astonishment. One can imagine the gales of merriment that followed.

It is upon the voluminous notes taken at some of these Conferences that the spiritual life of the Sisters of Charity is still largely nourished. But though the doctrine is there, the kind voice and the deep-set twinkling eyes are no longer present. Something of the open-hearted charm remains; we can still reconstruct a picture from these fragments of the old priest talking to "Mademoiselle" and the Sisters. But much has vanished. And it is a pity that not until recently have the Conferences been made available for the general public.

These Conferences to the Sisters form volumes nine and ten of the documents edited by Père Coste, and though we have a hundred and twenty of them, covering more than fourteen hundred pages, many have been lost. Some of the earlier ones are in the handwriting of Louise de Marillac herself—presumably because she was the member of the group best (or perhaps the only one) fitted to act as stenographer. Later reports are made by Sisters Hellot and Mathurine Guérin, as others are in a handwriting that cannot be identified. In general we may say that they are far more full and accurate than the reports kept of the Friday evening Conferences given to the Missionaries, for these, until the last years of Vincent's life, when Brother Ducournau set diligently to work to preserve his words, are usually no more than extracts or summaries.[2]

The subjects are always of an extremely practical sort—on

---

[2] Except for one conference, Brother Ducournau's MSS have been lost, but fortunately two copies of it are in existence. He did not make stenographic reports, any more than the Sisters did—for Vincent's humility would not have permitted this—but he wrote out afterwards, no doubt with the help of some of the Fathers, what he could remember. It is clear that he had an excellent memory—as most people had in the days before brains were turned to paper and ink—and, from being all day long in Vincent's society as secretary, he contrived to catch the Saint's tone as well as reproduce his matter.

vocation, fidelity to the rule, reconciliation, mutual respect, obedience, love of work, the service of the sick, perseverance, and the like. And we find Vincent coming back frequently to the same topic, sometimes because he has a great deal more to say upon it, sometimes (we may suppose) because the group in Paris was continually getting new members to replace those sent out to work elsewhere, but also no doubt because Vincent saw the pedagogical value of repetition.

Rarely can what he says be considered a formal lecture; when it is, we may note that he has carefully prepared himself in advance and arranges his material in a remarkably orderly fashion. More often he spends his time—especially after April 26, 1643, when he announced a new method—in asking the Sisters questions, or inviting questions from them. It would seem that they were always free, as in a class-room, to interrupt him. Yet his tone is never professorial but paternal. His personal manner, almost the very tone of his voice, have been captured for us in these full and intimate reports. Vincent makes no attempt to be brilliant, for it was clearly his intention to put the Sisters at their ease and to draw them out. Even Louise de Marillac (though in her case it was probably only to keep the bashful from feeling humiliated, for she spoke readily enough when a question was put to her), handed in her comments or her questions in writing. And when stupidity or ignorance was displayed, as now and then happened, Vincent's exquisite tact came to the rescue. Then (as we may see from the report of the conference held on January 22, 1646) he managed to re-state what the Sister had said, on the kind assumption that this was what she had meant to say, and so made it appear passably intelligent. The surprising thing, however, is how well these country girls answered his questions, and what spiritual insight they often showed. Few teachers can have been more

successful in developing the minds of his pupils than was
Vincent.

He does not attempt to talk theology—at any rate not theology of the speculative sort—but keeps inculcating obedience
and humility. In one Conference he quotes Clement VIII as
saying, "Show me anyone who has lived in perfect observance
of the rule, and I will canonize him without any other miracle."
In another he tells them, "It is impossible for a Daughter of
Charity who is careless about the rule to be happy." He wants
to know exactly how good the observance is, and puts pointed
questions:

"À Saint-Paul, ma soeur, se lève-t-on à quatre heures?"
Or (this was on the same day towards the end of 1658):

"Anne, soeur de Saint-Germain-de-l'Auxerrois, ma fille, faites-
vous l'oraison mentale tous les matins?"
Or (and this comes in the last Conference he ever gave):

"Je vous dirai, mes soeurs"—he is telling them what alone
can sustain their Company—"que c'est l'humilité. Et quoi en-
core? L'humilité,"—so reminding us of a famous if very different remark to be made nearly a century and a half later
by Danton.

If he talks about the love of God it is still with the practical
object in view. He is delighted when, in answer to his question,
a Sister says the love of God is best shown by the keeping of
His commandments; and equally delighted when another Sister
suggests a further mark of the love of God—that of walking
always in His presence. They should, he tells them, ask God
for the ability to pray, and ask it incessantly. "It is an alms
that you ask. It is not possible that He will refuse you if you
persevere."

Now and then it happens that a Conference is devoted to
saying farewell and giving final instructions to Sisters who
are leaving for work elsewhere. And when a Sister has just

died Vincent uses the occasion, not to pronounce a panegyric, but to ask each of those present to speak in turn and say what she has noticed about the virtues of the departed. From this they may all learn something—as we may too. For one realises that, though not all who joined the Company proved satisfactory, all who remained seem to have become saints. Not only the stars in the crown of the dead shine on these occasions, but the living—speaking in the accents of simple sincerity— unconsciously reveal their own holiness.

Sometimes there are touches of humour, and sometimes there are tears. It was noted that Vincent's eyes when he spoke of the love of God were always wet. And in the first of the two conferences on Louise de Marillac, just after her death and just before Vincent's, one Sister, when called upon to speak, broke down in her emotion. But she pulled herself together and said, "Father, if you think it well that I should speak, I will try to do so." To which he answered, "It *would* please me, my daughter." Then, while she spoke, he was unable to keep back his own tears. One can understand why the Sisters of Charity have for such a long time tried to keep these Conferences for themselves. Their appearance in French, and now their new translation into English for the general public, will, however, put within the reach of thousands of people a Saint seen at very close quarters and under conditions where his natural as well as his supernatural qualities are most completely revealed.

Let us take one sample, that from the Conference of November 15, 1654. "The malice of scandal," Vincent said, "may be compared to the malice of a person who would dig a deep and wide ditch in the middle of a great thoroughfare that the passers-by might fall into it, and, the better to prevent them being on their guard, would cover the ditch so as to hide it from their view. Scandal is something far worse, because the malice of that person tends to precipitate only bodies into the ditch, whereas the malice of scandal tends to precipitate souls into hell." It reminds one of the penance of St. Philip Neri imposed on a woman who said she had been speaking evil of her neighbours. She was given the impossible task of walking from her house to the church scattering the feathers from a pillow and of then gathering them up again. Vincent's way was perhaps less striking but not less effective. He never attempted to be clever or to put what he had to say in sparkling epigrams, and for this reason his reported speech sometimes appears to be rather wordy. But at least nobody can deny that there is never any possibility of mistaking his meaning—as there might have been had he indulged in epigrams—and he is always very practical and to the point.

After all, he would have lost much of his effectiveness if he had not sacrificed style to simplicity (which is another sort of style). Just as Father Damien's most thrilling sermon was the one in which he quietly opened with "We lepers . . . ," so a great part of Vincent's hold upon his Daughters was the fact that he was never the superior person, but on the contrary kept reminding them that he, too, was a peasant. They, as he put it in a letter to Louise, "From being poor girls, they will become great queens in Heaven."

His simplicity permitted him to make no designs of his own, but to wait for the guidance of God. This and the experience of many years were needed before at last a rule was drawn up. Then he called the Sisters together and said, "Who would have thought that there would have been Daughters of Charity when the first girls came to some parishes in Paris? Oh no, my Daughters, I did not think of it; nor did your Sister Servant either, Mlle Le Gras, nor Father Portail. God was thinking about it for you. It is He, my Daughters, who may be called the author of your Company; He is more truly and really so than anyone else."

One fact bears this out all the more fully because it lets us see, for once, how Vincent's judgment was at fault and yet providentially overruled. On November 20, 1646 the Archbishop of Paris gave his approbation to the Company but reserved control of it to himself. He had no intention of interfering, but this was no guarantee that a subsequent Archbishop might not take it upon himself to make fundamental changes in the rules. Even Vincent's position was purely personal; any priest could be appointed after his death. But the document got mislaid— so much to Louise's delight that some people, aware of what wiles women are capable, have suggested that she may have had something to do with the disappearance of the Act of 1646. There is, however, not a particle of evidence for this. What we do know is that, when in 1655 the exiled Cardinal de Retz signed a new document, the control of the Daughters of Charity was permanently invested in the Superior of the Congregation of the Mission and his successors.

The loss of this document reminds one of the providential mistake that happened in the case of the Visitation Order. Though Francis de Sales had wished it to be known by that name he was overruled and the name "Presentation" substituted. Yet when the document arrived it was seen that an altogether unaccountable series of clerical errors had occurred, and that the word "Visitation" had been written in in every place. God, it seems, can make a blundering official as good an instrument as any other for His purposes.

Steadily the group of Daughters of Charity grew. There were only three girls when Louise de Marillac took them into her house on November 29, 1633. By July 31st of the following year (when we have the first of Vincent's Conferences) they had increased to a dozen. At the end of his life there were often close to a hundred who attended these weekly gatherings, which meant that there were several hundreds more in the provinces.

In spite of hardships (or, shall we not say, because of them?) they flourished, and were all the sturdier for being utterly unpretentious. Poverty and hard work indeed perhaps were not even looked upon as hardships. Misunderstandings and calumny (coming as these did sometimes from quite unexpected quarters) were another matter. Even when the stories were patently preposterous—as that a plan was on foot to gather country girls and ship them to Canada so that they might marry Red Indians and propagate the Faith—these had their serious as well as their comic aspects. Yet in spite of it all the Daughters of Charity went quietly on with the task in hand and increased in numbers from year to year.

Vincent dreamed of sending some of them to the missions in Madagascar, but except for the few he let the Queen of Poland have, none during his lifetime went beyond the borders of France. Nevertheless there was nothing narrowly French about any of Vincent's enterprises; his charity at least in intention embraced all mankind. In the Daughters of Charity he created what has proved to be among the most flexible instruments for the furthering of spiritual and corporal mercy under any conditions in any part of the world.

ℂ 15. The Renewal of the Priesthood

LIKE all of Vincent de Paul's labours, the one he undertook for the reformation of the clergy was forced upon him by circumstances. Even so he would not have admitted he was attempting anything so ambitious as all that but only a few small projects which might, indeed, contribute to such an end as details in the larger process. Nevertheless it was due to him more than to any other man that the French priesthood began to be lifted from the deplorable condition into which it had fallen until it became, as we see it now, the glory of the Catholic world.

In the Gondi contract of 1625 no mention appears of this work. It was initiated, however, because it was in perfect conformity with the intention of that contract. Vincent soon discovered that it was even essential, if the missions preached by himself and the members of his Congregation were to bear any permanent fruit, for there was little use in raising a parish to temporary fervour if afterwards it was to be left to the ministrations of pastors who were slothful, ignorant and (in a good many cases) vicious.

Even so, Vincent advanced slowly, step by step, towards a goal which grew clear only as he advanced; and the first step came as the result of an apparent accident. In July 1628 he had been discussing the state of the clergy with Augustin Potier, the Bishop of Beauvais,[1] and had only reached the

---

[1] Even at the risk of appearing unkind, I cannot refrain from quoting Cardinal de Retz's judgment on him: "A greater idiot than anyone whom you ever knew," "The Bishop of Beauvais proved a mitred ass." Though de Retz's *Memoirs* are to be received with caution, there is no doubt that he excelled in portraiture. The sentence on Potier might seem, standing alone, merely abusive, but is thrown off in passing, over his shoulder.

disheartening conclusion that the older priests were, for the most part, too settled in their bad habits to be changed. Then, in the coach in which the two friends were travelling, the Bishop fell asleep. Actually he was only according himself—like the Judge in *Pickwick*, and many other gentlemen of high position —the privilege of thinking with his eyes shut. When at last he opened them he made a suggestion—that he gather the young clerics preparing to take Holy Orders into his house and have them instructed in the obligations of their calling. He asked Vincent to undertake this work.

Augustin Potier was later to show himself a Jansenist partizan, so it is a little curious that one who was to be ranged on the

---

As against this compare his wonderful page on Richelieu. De Retz confesses that in his youth he was twice implicated in plots to assassinate the Cardinal, and twice escaped undetected. So he evidently hated the man. Yet here, as elsewhere, he shows a malice perfectly detached and even good-humoured. "He was true to his word, except when some considerable interest induced him to the contrary, and then he did what in him lay to keep up the appearance of an upright man. He was not liberal, but he gave more than he promised, and he seasoned his gifts admirably. He carried his love for glory a great deal further than morality allows, but it must be allowed that though he gave way even in excess to his ambition, the ill use he made of it never went further than he was able to support by his own merit. Neither his heart nor his mind was superior to danger, but neither sank under it; though it is certain that he prevented more dangers by his prudence than he overcame by his courage. He was a good friend, and I may even say that he would have been glad to have gained the public love. But though he neither wanted civility, nor many other qualities fit for that purpose, he always lacked that indefinable something which is more requisite in this case than any other. . . Nobody in the world was better able than he to distinguish between what is ill and what is worse, what is good and what is better . . . He was too impatient in small matters, which are a prelude to greater; but that defect, which proceeds from a sublimity of the mind, is always accompanied by a clearness of understanding which makes amends for it. His stock of religion was sufficient for this world. He was led to do good, either by his own good sense, or by his inclination, wherever his inclination did not lead him a contrary way." The Bishop of Beauvais was no doubt not a very intelligent man, but he was a well-meaning one, and we find him, in this case, initiating, if only by accident, something of the highest importance. Yet no doubt it would have happened sooner or later in any event.

opposite side taken by Vincent in that famous controversy should have started what was in many ways the most important, though perhaps not the best remembered, of all of Vincent's enterprises.

The state of the French clergy at that time was indeed terribly bad. "Yes," Vincent used to say, "we are the cause of the desolation that afflicts the Church, of that falling away which she has suffered in so many places. . . . It is the clerics . . . that have brought this catastrophe on the Church." France had an enormous number of monks and secular priests—perhaps even an excessive number—and though not all religious communities were relaxed and not all the parochial clergy had degenerated into mere ecclesiastical functionaries, ignorant, drunken and immoral, such was only too often the situation. The best educated priests were those in the cities, and many of these were really learned men. But such disdained as a rule to waste their gifts on the brutish peasantry, and not a few of them comported themselves as fashionable men of the world. These swaggered about in civilian or even military dress, with long curled locks and luxuriant beards, and the country priests, for their part, often administered the sacraments in leather jerkins or frieze overcoats under their vestments. The clerical cassock was abandoned.

It was not, however, merely a question of dress; the cowl does not always make the monk. Even today one may come across clerics who go about in a slovenly fashion in slippers and unbuttoned soutane, and yet are very good priests. All the same one may say that attention to significant externals is usually not only a general index to interior dispositions but has a definite interior effect. The modern army realises the psychological importance of the well-kept uniform. For though a soldier does not fight with his well-polished buttons, his trimness is understood to be part of good discipline. In the same way the sloppiness of the village curé and the perfumed finery of the fashionable abbé were equally signs that the clergy were not living just as they should. Serious disorders were rampant among them, and even of those who lived well some had hardly more than enough qualification for their office than the ability to say Mass. As we have already seen, Madame de Gondi and Vincent had already discovered that many a confessor did not know so much as the correct formula for absolution. And instead of following the prescribed rubrics, each priest made up his own to suit himself.

All this did not of course come about without cause. And the immediate cause was the lack of ecclesiastical seminaries. Vincent himself—though he had obtained a degree of Bachelor of Theology from Toulouse and had somehow found time later to obtain a degree in canon law in Paris—had never gone through a seminary. But he thoroughly grasped the fact that it was not enough that a candidate for the priesthood should have theological knowledge; he needed also that formation in habits of piety which a seminary provides.

The vast majority of priests, however, did not have even the necessary education. They became priests because it was the easiest of all professions, one that offered a peasant who had picked up a little Latin a better living than he could obtain on his father's farm, and to those with a university diploma or powerful friends to push their fortunes, fat somnolent benefices.

If seminaries had not been established in accordance with the rulings of the Council of Trent, this was because France at the beginning of the seventeenth century was still suffering from the effects of the religious wars. Cardinal Gasquet has shown that the Reformation was, at least in part, brought about by the Black Death having made it necessary for bishops not to enquire too closely into the qualifications of those who were to fill the ranks of a depleted priesthood. Much the same thing had happened during this period in France. So long as a man could say Mass, bishops often asked very little else of him. Enquiry was not closely pressed as to whether he had reached the canonical age for ordination—Vincent's own case was one in point—and, what was much worse, character standards were lowered to vanishing-point.

A few seminaries were indeed established, but most of these were very short-lived. Even the best of them, that conducted by the Jesuits at Rheims, accomplished little, so that the seminarians there came to be regarded as lackeys and train-bearers to the Canons. "In twenty years," Père Coste records, "the seminary of Rouen produced only six priests. The Seminary of Limoges during this time did not produce even one."

The reason for this state of affairs was partly the poor selection of both instructors and students, and partly the seminaries' being full of boys who did not have the slightest intention of ever becoming priests but took this opportunity of obtaining a cheap education. So insoluble did the problem seem that most bishops—especially those who had on their hands the pressing obligations of building up a ravaged diocese—did not so much as make any attempt to solve it. As Francis de Sales put it, "I know there is nothing more necessary for the Church, but after having striven seventeen years to train merely three priests to assist me to reform the clergy of my diocese, I was able to produce only one and a half."

The majority of the bishops, however, were indifferent. Half the sees in France were either vacant or held *in commendam* by a layman or a child—sometimes the abbeys were actually held by Huguenots[2]—and of those that did have bishops, a good many suffered from absenteeship. The bishopric of Metz, for example, was held for more than fifty years by one of

[2] Vincent's own Abbey of St.-Léonard-de-Chaumes had been so held; that of Fontgombault had been in Huguenot hands for nearly a hundred years.

Henry IV's bastards, who never meant to receive consecration and who, in old age, married. Bishops who did receive consecration were only too often appointed merely because of their influence at Court, and though such appointments occasionally proved providential—the worldly abbé turning into a zealous prelate—as a general rule the system worked further disaster.

Again, a reforming bishop was only too likely to have his efforts thwarted. His clergy could appeal to the local Parlement or the Governor of the province who might, for any one of a number of reasons, take the side against the ecclesiastical superior. In face of such a complexus of difficulties it looked as though nothing could be done. Well intentioned men thought it not worth trying.

Yet a great deal was done, and in a surprisingly short time. And we must date the first effectual move perhaps to the retreat Vincent was persuaded to give in 1628 to the ordinands of Beauvais. With characteristic humility he brought down two doctors of the Sorbonne to give the main instructions, reserving for himself merely a series of expositions of the Ten Commandments. But so successful was he that not only did all the candidates for ordination make a general confession, the doctors themselves were moved to seek for a complete clearing of their consciences in confession.

The Beauvais retreat, however, successful as it was, could only be considered as being better than nothing; it did not touch the heart of the problem even in that diocese. There still remained the question as to what could be done to obtain a steady succession of good priests all over the country.

Vincent probably understood the situation better than anybody else in France because of his having travelled about so much giving missions. He saw that, however great a fire could be kindled in a parish in two or three weeks by a zealous missionary, it would soon die unless there was somebody left behind to tend it. Only too well did he know that the curé was generally useless for this purpose.

Nothing, he decided, could be done for the older men; they were almost literally past praying for. The sole chance the Church in France had was that of securing in the new generation of priests a clergy of a higher type. And for the development of such a clergy, retreats of the kind given in Beauvais, although they might do temporary good or even permanent good in individual cases, were altogether inadequate. More and more Vincent pondered the problem.

Fortunately he was not alone in this. The matter had been frequently discussed by the group of ardent souls who gathered round Bérulle, and in varying ways several of these were about to act, since the bishops were shirking their duty. Being freelances, they could not be expected to agree on all points as to method; they did, however, all perceive that nothing would serve except the establishment of seminaries, private seminaries as there were no diocesan ones.

But before Vincent had reached that point, he came to extend the Beauvais plan to Paris. In the transfer that had occurred of the Priory of Saint-Lazare to Vincent and his Missionaries, the Archbishop of Paris had stipulated that his young clerics should be housed and boarded and instructed there for the two weeks preceding their ordination. As he made no financial provision for their support we must suppose that he looked upon this service as a kind of rent. It was one Vincent was very willing to pay. Yet it was still very far from achieving the goal of a seminary.

Once again we find Vincent allowing himself to be guided by circumstances and making no effort to reach what he was after in a single stride. "In the beginning," he confessed later, "we did not think at all of serving the clergy; we thought simply of ourselves and the poor." By which he meant that he found that he could not serve the poor in any solid fashion unless he did something for the clergy. So Vincent accepted the obligation imposed upon him, though he must have wondered where the money was to come from for taking in guests in groups of about a hundred five or six times a year. Or he would have wondered had he not had so perfect a confidence in the providence of God. Madame de Herse immediately came forward with an offer to pay the costs for the first five years—which involved about a thousand livres for each retreat—and long before that time was up, Anne of Austria, having attended one of the sessions, was so deeply impressed that she offered to pay for the next five years. The Ladies of Charity, especially the Marquise de Maignelay, afterwards provided what Vincent needed for this and his other projects.

It should be noted, however, that just before he moved from the Collège des-Bons-Enfants, when the Archbishop of Paris suggested that he give a retreat there to ordinands, Vincent had demurred. This was on the ground that his Congregation had been founded with the special object of preaching missions in rural districts; retreats in Paris accordingly, he argued, hardly fell into its scope. He did not, however, maintain this position for long, and that for reasons already indicated. So far from raising further objections to giving retreats, he was soon considering what more he could do along the same lines. By 1636, therefore, we find him opening a seminary at the Bons-Enfants.

But first let us cast an eye upon similar efforts, all of them begun about this time. That of St. John Eudes—though he, too, was one of Bérulle's group—need not concern us, as it was outside Paris. Within Paris there arose in rapid succession four seminaries, each of a distinct type.

Adrian Bourdoise's scheme was for the establishment of communities of secular priests to train the clergy in the actual duties of their office. Bourdoise does not seem to have been concerned about giving theological instruction, nor did even the development of spirituality loom very large in his plans. His idea was the simple and practical one of teaching clerics—those already ordained, or about to be ordained—how to perform the offices of the Church in a fitting manner, and how to administer the sacraments. Without bothering himself with imparting moral theology, he showed, by a form of object-lesson in which one of his group would act the part of the penitent and another the part of the priest, how confessions ought to be heard. How to baptise and to give communion were taught in the same way. The system would now be regarded as rather ludicrous, but at the time it served its purpose—that of providing an intensive course in pastoral practice.[3]

Father de Condren at the Oratory (Cardinal Bérulle had died in 1629) did not receive men before they had reached the sub-diaconate. His methods were less rough and ready than those of Bourdoise, and he usually got a higher type of students, many of whom became Oratorians. What he had was almost as much a novitiate as a seminary. Unfortunately the Oratory soon became deeply infected with Jansenism, so it was providential that the Oratorian seminaries declined.

The most brilliant of all the plans was that of Jean-Jacques Olier. He was about fifteen years younger than Vincent and was of good family. In his early days as a priest, though there was no flaw in his moral conduct, he was a great frequenter of society, in which he was very popular. Vincent soon perceived under the dashing exterior solid spiritual gifts, and tried to have him made a bishop, insisting so strongly upon this that for a

[3] Vincent himself rated Bourdoise's practical methods as superior to those of Olier and the Oratory. And though he had been opposed to establishing houses of the Congregation in cities—Saint-Lazare and the Bons-Enfants were necessary exceptions—he came to wish for churches in large parishes in order that the seminarians might learn a priest's duties by watching them done and practising them prior to ordination.

while there was a coolness between the two men. But Olier knew where his true vocation lay, and after a brief experiment at Vaugirard, accepted in 1642 the pastoral charge of the great church of Saint-Sulpice. The parish, though it contained some stately mansions, was full of disreputable houses, and frail ladies were even accustomed to use his church for the making of assignations.

With impetuous intrepidity the new Curé cleansed the Augean stables and established a seminary which, like that of Saint-Nicholas-du-Chardonnet gave practical instruction in the performance of priestly offices, but added to this a rigorous spiritual training and solid instruction in theology. His work has lasted and has gathered strength down to our own day; the Society he founded has only one function, that of conducting theological seminaries.

Olier's work was different from Vincent's in one important respect: Saint-Sulpice accepted only students already in theology, not those who had to be educated in the humanities. Vincent, on the other hand, after a period during which he learned by the process of trial and error and had to suffer some disappointments, carried out the instructions of the Council of Trent by gathering together boys who would remain in the *petit séminaire* (as it is now called) before proceeding to the major seminary. In other words, it was Vincent who provided the model that is now universally adopted.

Some early mistakes were made but were soon rectified. Vincent discovered that it would not do to keep in one group boys still occupied with their Latin grammar, and young men getting ready for ordination. That they were under the same roof was of little consequence; what did matter was that the two groups should be separated. As his seminary grew in numbers, he found it advisable to keep the older students at the Collège des-Bons-Enfants and to build, for the boys, the Collège de

Saint-Charles at the back of the grounds of Saint-Lazare. But so far from treating his institutions as a nursery and a novitiate for the Congregation of the Mission, his purpose was merely that of moulding worthy parish priests. If some of his students did join the Congregation, that was in face of his habit of depreciating his own foundation. Had he wished to do so, he could easily have greatly increased the recruiting of his Missionaries. His perfect disinterestedness is amply proved by the fact that their numbers remained small. He accepted only those who insisted upon joining him.

The efforts of all these founders of seminaries left something to be desired, in the sense that their foundations would not compare very favourably with those of our own time. But with them at least the process began, and all honour is due to the courage of those who worked so hard in the face of almost insuperable difficulties. According to modern ideas Saint-Nicholas-du-Chardonnet was not, properly speaking, a seminary at all. But Vincent's tribute was deserved when he said, "Good Monsieur Bourdoise was the first person whom God inspired to set up a seminary in which men should be taught how to administer the sacraments and carry out the rubrics; before him, men scarcely knew what a seminary meant; there was no special place in which these things were taught; a man after his theology, his philosophy, his minor studies, and a little Latin, went to a parish and administered the sacraments there just as he fancied." In the same way the curriculum of the Bons-Enfants, when the major seminary was opened in 1642, was rather rudimentary, Vincent contenting himself with providing a minimum of instruction (he could hardly do more with the professors at his disposal) and laying the main emphasis upon developing virtue among his students. Nevertheless from these modest objects and small beginnings flowed the rejuvenation of the Church in France, so that at the time of the Revolution the Congregation of the Mission had under its charge fifty-three major and nine minor seminaries, or more than a third of those existing in the entire country. And though today ecclesiastical seminaries are for the most part diocesan and conducted by secular priests, the Vincentian division of students everywhere prevails, long after the Congregation of the Mission has ceased to be very conspicuous in this particular work. Without in the least wishing to detract from the glory due to Olier's name, it must be added that the Sulpicians themselves have fully accepted the type invented by the splendid common-sense of Vincent de Paul.[4]

The founding of Vincent's ecclesiastical seminaries did not, however, mean the abandoning of the retreats for the ordinands. On the contrary, that movement expanded side by side with the other work. The majority of clerical students still went to no seminary, and the men who did—such as those at Saint-Nicholas-du-Chardonnet and Saint-Sulpice—rounded out their training with a fortnight at Saint-Lazare. Bishops of dioceses near Paris sent their candidates to Vincent, and those in distant parts of the country begged him to send priests who would conduct retreats for clerics about to receive Holy Orders. And other communities now felt impelled to assist in so excellent and badly needed a work.

Among the men who had Vincent's mark put upon them were about eighty priests who afterwards became bishops, and men so varied and illustrious as Bossuet, who at twelve had preached his first sermon standing on a chair before the admiring salon of the Hôtel Rambouillet; Rancé, the future reformer of La Trappe (at that time an elegant young abbé with an ecclesias-

---

[4] It is worth noting that all these independent efforts, with the exception of that at Saint-Nicholas-du-Chardonnet, received financial support from Richelieu, Vincent's first thousand crowns for the establishment of a seminary coming from that source. Even Bourdoise would no doubt have obtained a contribution from the Cardinal had he not shown his boorishness towards the Duchesse d'Aiguillon. But unfortunately Bourdoise belonged to that type of person who imagines that there must be some connexion between honesty and bad manners.

tical sinecure of fifteen thousand livres, who according to his own description "preached like an angel and hunted like the devil," quite unsuspecting the austerities of his future life); and Jean-Jacques Olier himself.

No doubt in many instances the effect of the retreat was not lasting; we could not expect it to have such solid results as a seminary training. But something could be and was done. Instructions were given with a view to inducing the ordinands to realise that the life of a priest should be one of spirituality, and they were taught how to make interior prayer. A course in rubrics was added, to make sure that Mass was said with reverence and without private eccentricities. But perhaps most important of all was the contact the ordinands had with the Missionaries and especially with Vincent himself. They got a new insight into the sacerdotal vocation, and when they saw that the conferences on prayer and the Christian virtues were not mere talk, but that the humility of the Superior of Saint-Lazare was such that it led him to get up early in the morning to help the servants clean the young gentlemen's boots, they could not fail to perceive that this was the real thing.

"Behold our mission!" Vincent said to his Fathers. "But who are we that this ministry should be committed to us? We are only miserable creatures, poor labourers and peasants; what fitness is there in such as we for so holy, so exalted and so celestial an employment? Yet it is to us that God has entrusted so great a grace as that of contributing to the reform of the clergy. To this end God did not turn to wise doctors, or to the many communities and religious houses, which are full of sanctity and learning; but He has chosen to employ this poor, mean, and pitiable Company, the last and most unworthy of all. . . . God of His own free will has made choice of a set of poor, miserable beings to labour to repair the breaches in the kingdom of His Son and in the ecclesiastical state. O gentlemen, let us take care not to lose the grace which God has bestowed upon us."

C 16. The Tuesday Conferences

LET me open this chapter by quoting one of the most appallingly cynical passages ever written. It comes from the *Memoirs* of Cardinal de Retz and describes his attendance at an ordination retreat. Not all of those who attended could have been brought to conversion, but this is surely an extreme case. Yet it should be noticed that John Francis Paul de Gondi, while writing with unblushing candour, admits that he might have been a still worse man had he not gone to Saint-Lazare. To prevent evil occurring is an act almost as meritorious as to stimulate good. Now for de Retz:

"As I was obliged to take Orders, I made a retreat at Saint-Lazare where I behaved in the usual fashion, so far as externals are concerned, but inwardly my mind was much and deeply preoccupied with the line of conduct I should adopt in future. It was very difficult. I saw the archbishopric of Paris degraded in the sight of the world by the baseness of my uncle, and rendered desolate in the sight of God by his negligence and incapacity. I foresaw infinite difficulties in its re-establishment, and was not so blind as to recognise that the greatest and most insurmountable obstacle was myself. . . . I felt that I was incapable of it, and that all the obstacles I could oppose to a disorderly life, such as a sense of duty and a desire for renown, would prove to be very uncertain barriers. After six days' reflection, I made up my mind to do evil with my eyes open, which is, without comparison, the most criminal of all things in the eyes of God, but doubtless wisest in the eyes of the world; for when a man acts thus, he always takes precautions for partial concealment and so avoids the most dangerous form of ridicule that can be met with in our profession, namely, an unseasonable mingling of sin and devotion. Such was the holy disposition in which I left Saint-Lazare. Nevertheless it was not wholly or completely bad; for I made a firm resolution to carry out exactly all the duties of my profession and to be as good for the salvation of others as I was bad for my own." In his extenuation it should be remembered that young de Gondi had done his best to escape from a clerical career for which he knew he was not fitted, even to the extent of making it impossible by an elopement and marriage. There was much good in the scamp, and Vincent's comment that, though he lacked piety, he was not far from the kingdom of heaven was discerning as well as charitable. On the other hand, de Retz records the reason which finally decided him to accept Holy Orders: "Cardinal Richelieu declined daily in his health, and the archbishopric of Paris began to flatter my ambition."

I confess to a certain shame-faced liking for the fellow, this snub-nosed gallant, this bandy-legged duellist, this unworthy Cardinal. And it is clear that my liking was enthusiastically shared by the populace of Paris in the sixteen forties. I infinitely prefer him to the smooth and supple Mazarin, his great enemy; and I think I may add that Vincent de Paul had the same preference.

De Retz not only attended a retreat at Saint-Lazare before his own ordination—for that was obligatory—but afterwards of his own free-will was for a time associated with the next important activity begun by Vincent, that of the weekly conferences for a select group of priests; and in his capacity as coadjutor and, later, titular Archbishop of Paris showed himself a firm supporter of the work of the Congregation of the Mission.

It was in June 1633 that Vincent, taking a suggestion as usual from somebody else (one hitherto supposed to have been Olier, but shown by Père Coste not to have been that gifted young abbé), decided to start a kind of clerical guild which should be composed of the élite of the Parisian priesthood and act as an auxiliary to the Missionary Fathers. This auxiliary aspect of the association, however, would not appear to have been part of Vincent's original intention—which was directed merely to the formation in virtue of the best of the men who had passed through his hands—but to have been a natural outcome of the weekly gathering of this group for a discussion of the problems peculiar to their state in life.

There were in Paris at this time several "Academies" which met for a survey of various scientific and literary questions. Père Mersenne had founded one in 1635 for the promotion of philosophy, and about the same time Richelieu established the French Academy. Adrian Bourdoise had introduced as early as 1615 an ecclesiastical conference at Paris and had established branches in other dioceses. But Bourdoise's idea, as might be expected, was somewhat restricted in its scope and made no notable mark upon the religious life of France. It was quite otherwise with Vincent's famous "Tuesday Conference."

The number of those admitted was small—only about two hundred and fifty in the course of over twenty years—but only first-class men were allowed to join, and they had an effect quite disproportionate to their numbers. From among them arose Bossuet and Olier, and nearly thirty of their members became bishops.

Before he was accepted by what had something of the nature of a club, something of the nature of a guild, and something of the nature of a religious order, the candidate's credentials were carefully scrutinised. Upon being passed as satisfactory he had to make an eight-day retreat at Saint-Lazare. And after he was admitted to the Conference he was obligated to attend regularly, so much so that, if illness or pressure of business prevented this, he was expected to send in writing his observations upon the topic to be discussed, which was always announced before-hand in order that the members could come prepared.

In view of all this, it is somewhat surprising to find that the Abbé de Buzay—the future Cardinal de Retz—was allowed to join. His, however, was an exceptional case. His father and mother had given the first endowment to the Congregation; he was (as everybody knew) destined to become the Archbishop of Paris; and Vincent, always hopeful of the good that lay at the bottom of that cynical heart, no doubt counted upon the Tuesday Conferences to develop his virtue. About his ability there was of course no question at all.

Again we can turn to the Cardinal's *Memoirs*: "I began to lead a more regular life, at least in appearance. I lived in great retirement and no longer let the choice of a profession seem problematical. I studied a great deal and carefully established contact with learned persons; I almost turned my rooms into an Academy and began, without affectation, to treat with respect the canons and parish priests I naturally met at my uncle's [the Archbishop of Paris]. I did not play the devout, because I could not feel sure that I should be able to keep it up for long, but I did esteem devout persons very highly; and that, in their eyes, is one of the great marks of piety." That last sentence repeats almost word for word what he wrote about the time when he used to go about with his aunt, the Marquise de Maignelay, in her slumming expeditions. The comment must be admitted to have its grain of bitter truth.

In general the main feature of the meetings was a discussion, in a spirit of the utmost humility and simplicity, of the Christian virtues, and in particular those that were most necessary to the priesthood. Oratory, in the ordinary sense, was severely discouraged, though many of the members were men of learning and eloquence. The moving spirit of the gathering, though he kept as far as possible in the background, and as a rule did not do more than bring the assembly to a close with a summary of what the members had said, was Vincent himself. Bossuet has remarked, "He was its founder and its soul. We listened to him with the utmost eagerness, clearly recognising that in him was realised the words of the Apostle, 'If any man speak, let his words be as the words of God.' " And he goes on to record that on one occasion, when several bishops were present, Vincent modestly kept silence, until one of them pressed him with, "M. Vincent, you must not, in your humility, deprive the Company of the good thoughts God has communicated to you on the subject with which we have been dealing. There is an inexpressible unction of the Holy Spirit in your words which touches each of us, and therefore, all these gentlemen beg you to let them share your thoughts, for one word from your lips will produce more effect than all that we could say." Only then, and squirming at hearing himself publicly praised, could Vincent be induced to speak.

His own attitude is indicated by his words: "What is there in us to attract all these gentlemen, the ordinands, the theologians, the bachelors and licentiates of the Sorbonne and Navarre, who come here? It is not the learning or the doctrine which we offer them, for they have more than we. No; it is the humility and simplicity in which, by the grace of God, we act towards them. They come here only to learn virtue; when they see its light grow dim in us they will withdraw."

The light did not grow dim, and the influence of the Tuesday Conferences steadily increased. Cardinal Richelieu, who was genuinely interested in the promotion of religion—however little he let religious considerations interfere with his politics —highly approved of what was being done and supported it in every possible way, just as he had given the first donation of a thousand crowns towards the establishment of the seminary at the Bons-Enfants. He attended several of the meetings and was so deeply impressed by all he heard and saw that he sent

for Vincent afterwards and asked him to make a list of names
of the members of the Conference who were, in his opinion, fit
to be appointed to bishoprics.

This of course at once created a delicate situation. If it became known that membership of the Tuesday Conference was
likely to lead to ecclesiastical promotion, there was a danger
that ambitious priests would try to join for the sake of advancement. On the other hand, Vincent knew that the Church
in France needed bishops of the type of the men he was training. Tactfully he solved the problem by furnishing the Cardinal
with the desired list, but pledged him to absolute secrecy. It
must never be known that he had any part in the bestowal of
benefices. And to the members he spoke so often of the perils
of ambition that when bishops were drawn from among them
they either, as in the case of Olier, gave a determined refusal,
or, as in the case of Pavillon, accepted with the greatest reluctance. In Vincent's opinion, the only proper person to be
elevated to a bishopric was one who said (and meant it) *Nolo
episcopari.*

The work he employed his guild of priests upon was that of
supplementing what the Fathers of the Congregation were
doing. On innumerable occasions his Missionaries were accompanied into the country by one or more of the priests of his
auxiliary organization. And since the Congregation of the Mission was founded for the express purpose of evangelizing the
neglected peasantry, Vincent was able to employ the members
of the Conference for missions in Paris and other cities. This
was how the famous mission at Metz, which lasted two and a
half months, was carried out.

In the same way we hear of the Tuesday Conference giving
missions that included one to the workmen of Paris during
their dinner hour, and another at Saint Germain-en-Laye, which
the Court attended. It was on this occasion that Louis XIII

was inspired to place France under the patronage of the Blessed Virgin.

But the members of the Conference did not confine themselves to missions. They conducted such retreats for ordinands, either at Saint-Lazare or in the provinces, as the Fathers of the Congregation were unable to give themselves. They were encouraged to give their spare time to teaching catechism, to visiting the poor and the prisoners, and to hearing confessions in the Hôtel-Dieu. In fact there was hardly any work performed by the priests of the Congregation in which the priests of the Conference were not invaluable assistants. For Vincent expected to see in their case, too, the life of prayer manifest itself in practical works of spiritual and corporal charity.

One wonders how Vincent—with his duties as Superior of Saint-Lazare and his supervision of the seminary and the activities of the Ladies and the Daughters of Charity—could have had any time, now that he had established the Tuesday Conferences, for any other work. Yet somehow he found time, and though all these enterprises were steadily increasing and going further afield, he continued to the end to branch out in new projects. There surely was never a life more crowded with activity than that of this saint.

It was not enough for him to open Saint-Lazare to the ordinands and the members of the Conference, he felt he had to do something for the spiritual life of laymen and priests who had no connexion with any of his organizations. So that as Père Coste remarks, "There was not a single day in all the year when at least twenty externs . . . might not be seen on retreat at Saint-Lazare." And as Abelly, who must often have been there, says, "It was a wonderful and edifying sight to see in the same refectory, lords, viscounts, marquises, barristers, judges, merchants, soldiers, artisans, and even footmen. All were welcome to make their retreat in this great hospice of charity." Vincent definitely discouraged social visits, however; it was not easy for anyone to obtain admission to Saint-Lazare unless he went there for a specific spiritual purpose.

One notable feature of all this was that, so far from any charge being made, even voluntary contributions were refused. For voluntary contributions have a way of becoming customary, and then many a man of little means would stay away to avoid embarrassment. Everything was to be entirely free. This generosity was all the more remarkable when we recall that the Ladies of Charity, usually such open-handed supporters of Vincent's enterprises, remained decidedly cold to this one.

Often the procurator was at his wits' end as to how to pay for the cost of entertainment. Often he had to tell his Superior that there was not another room vacant in the house. At such news Vincent would merely beam delightedly. As for the money, God would send it; if there was no other room, let them use his own. One day, when the poor procurator moaned that it was absolutely impossible to accommodate the crowd that was applying for admission, Vincent said, "Very well, I'll see them and make a selection." The number admitted that day was the largest on record.[1] If, as sometimes happened, one of those on retreat fell ill, he was kept at Saint-Lazare until he got well. And there were many occasions when Vincent, having discovered that one of his guests was destitute, gave him a substantial alms on farewell, just as it sometimes happened that a newly-received convert, being friendless, was boarded at the Priory for as long as a year or two after having been received into the Church.

[1] On the other hand, Vincent showed a careful concern about unnecessary expenditure. His peasant upbringing made him abominate anything like waste, and he would often look into the smallest details concerning the management of the various farms owned by Saint-Lazare, and even into the lay-brothers' petty-cash-book. He preserved always a nice balance between the niggardly and the prodigal.

Sometimes of course Vincent's good-nature was imposed upon: doubtless there were men who went to Saint-Lazare out of curiosity or to get a week's free board and lodging. But Vincent was a shrewd judge of character and there were limits even to his generosity. Thus he tells us of a woman who had come begging on the plea that she had once been a servant to "Madame, Monsieur's mother," only to be informed that his mother had never had a servant and had been only a poor peasant woman. Yet, though he was quick to see through frivolity and pretence, he always hoped for the best; one could never tell what good a retreat might not do.

Only on one occasion do we hear of positive abuse of his hospitality. This was when a young German arrived, and decamped with some clothing. He was caught by the police, and turned out to be a Lutheran. Immediately upon hearing this, Vincent went to the magistrates to secure the man's release. Such was the Saint's charity, that sometimes he had on either hand in the refectory, instead of the customary old men from his alms-house, a couple of newly-released jailbirds. Only too well did he know how easy it is for the poor to get into trouble with the police.

That he was well aware that many odd characters turned up in his priory is shown by his referring to Saint-Lazare humorously, according to Abelly, as a "kind of Noah's Ark where all sorts of animals, great and small, were received." In their own house in the grounds was his small collection of lunatics; as likely as not he thought that some of his retreatants were eccentric enough to be put among them. But he went serenely on his way, knowing that tares will always be found among the wheat, that the fisherman's net will drag bad fish as well as good to land.

To have preached all the retreats himself would have been a physical impossibility. And as the Fathers on hand were few, and all busy in one way or another, we must suppose that he often had to draw upon the members of his Tuesday Conferences for this work. But, whoever the official retreat-master might be, Vincent met all the visitors who came. A few minutes conversation with the holy old man with the twinkling eyes and beaming face often left a deeper impression than the formal exercises of devotion. Thousands of men in all ranks of society owed their first real impulse to the spiritual life, or its deepening, to a retreat at Saint-Lazare.

The women, too, were not forgotten. They were accommodated by Louise de Marillac in her house on the opposite side of the street. Great ladies, wives of artizans, actresses, and girls who wished to prepare themselves for marriage all entered there. If their numbers were not so great as those of the men, this was mainly because the establishment of the Daughters of Charity was small. All the same they made further demands on Vincent's time and energy, since he had to provide a priest to direct their devotions. In one way or another Saint-Lazare had become the spiritual centre of Paris.

But as is usually the case, the best way of stating the situation is in Vincent's own words: "This house once served as a place for lepers; they were admitted here and not one of them was cured. At present it serves as a place of retreat for sinners who are sick men, covered with the leprosy of sin; but they, by God's grace, are healed. We may go even further and say that they are dead men restored to life." And again, more specifically, he explained the purpose that a man should have in making a retreat at Saint-Lazare: "It is to become a perfect Christian, perfect also in one's vocation in life: a perfect student, if one is a student; a perfect soldier, if one is a soldier; a perfect lawyer, if one is a lawyer; and a perfect ecclesiastic, like St. Charles Borromeo, if one is a priest."

ℂ 17. "The Little Method"

IN THE work of preaching missions and retreats or giving conferences to his Fathers or to the Daughters of Charity, Vincent consistently employed what he was fond of describing as the "Little Method." It was that of speaking with an absolute simplicity.

Perhaps one of the best illustrations of what the "Little Method" was comes from Francis de Sales, though we hear about it from Vincent. The famous Bishop of Geneva, after a long absence in Paris, had arrived there towards the end of 1618, when his first public appearance was to preach on Saint Martin at the Oratory. A large and fashionable congregation, including the King and Queen, had assembled, and the preacher found the place so crowded that he had to climb in by a window. Then, instead of delivering the discourse he had prepared, de Sales, actuated by a sudden motive of humility, decided to speak extemporaneously. Vincent records (he must have got this detail from Francis) that there was present a young lady of the Court who afterwards became a nun who said to her companion, "How vilely this mountaineer preaches! Was it really necessary for him to come such a distance to try the patience of so many people?"

That, however, deserves some comment. Francis de Sales was to a certain extent addicted to a flowery style, at any rate to giving a good deal of care to the fashioning of his sentences. And it seems to me that a congregation is entitled to receive some amount of consideration from a preacher. Far too many men go up into the pulpit without knowing what they are going to say and proceed to ramble, to nobody's spiritual profit. Such exhibitions are due not to humility but to laziness. They are not instances of the "Little Method."

Vincent, however, never recommended his Missionaries to preach without preparation, and we know that, though his Conferences have the air of intimate chats, he never failed to jot down the main points he wanted to make and to follow a logical order. Moreover, it was part of the rule of his Congregation that the autumn and winter should be spent by his Fathers in getting ready their sermons. He was not a man to countenance slovenliness in any form.

We may surmise that when Francis de Sales put his prepared sermon into his pocket and preached according to the "Little Method" he gave his distinguished audience something well worth listening to, even if it was not quite what they expected. The young lady's criticism should be accepted in this light; she was merely expressing the taste that a great many people had in those days for the ornate and florid in oratory. Probably the spontaneous address was actually better than the set discourse. For if Francis de Sales was a saint, he was also an artist. I cannot imagine that he would have thought it fair to choose that particular moment for the exercise of "humility,"—if it was to be at other people's expense. He once advised a friend to write "affectively" instead of in an oratorical or "affected" vein; and the advice was a piece of sound literary criticism. So also was it when Vincent de Paul, writing to Robert de Sergis in 1639 remarks, "St. Vincent Ferrer says that there is no means of making preaching avail unless we preach with the bowels of compassion." Therefore, while it is perfectly true that all three saints detested posing in the pulpit, they were thinking of avoiding the oratorical vice which—whether in the pulpit or on the platform—ruins the effectiveness of the spoken word. It is not a question of one's making a fool of oneself to show that one is humble.

The broad rule in the matter is merely that of being natural. If a man has an ingenious cast of mind—as had that heart-shaking preacher, John Donne—let him preach in the way he is constituted, so long as he keeps a certain guard upon himself and does not strain for effect. If a man is learned or profound, these qualities will appear (and very properly) when he speaks. Only such a man would do well to remember that he may find what he is saying going over the heads of his audience. The only things really to be condemned are an ostentatious parade of learning, merely literary affectations. In other words: intellectual snobbishness and bad taste.

Samuel Taylor Coleridge's erudite but rather simple-minded old father was accustomed we are told to quote the Scriptures in his pulpit of Ottery St. Mary's on the ground that this was "the actual language of the Holy Ghost." It was no doubt not a good method; it must have astounded his rustic congregation; but at least it was partially redeemed by the childlike innocence of the Vicar. In a very different spirit was Sidney Smith's confession that he always quoted Greek—when he was sure that nobody was present who could understand it. But the seeming cynicism of the saying has another side: the Reverend Mr. Smith probably was afraid of being caught out in a false quantity. Besides, he was far too clever a man to have "shown off" in the pulpit; he was merely making a joke which he intended nobody to take too seriously.

Naturalness—remembering that what is natural to one man is not always natural to another—we may take as the first element in good public speaking. For if he is natural, a man will always manage to hold his audience. But to move them he must feel deeply what he is saying. And upon this point no rule can be laid down. All we can say is that a man speaking with conviction, and able to impart it, speaks powerfully. The classic example is that of Lincoln's Gettysburg Address, which everybody remembers though it was only a brief postscript to the long-forgotten orotund periods of Edward Everett.

The secret of true as distinguished from artificial oratory, therefore, is incommunicable. And yet it is simple enough— to those who know how to manage it. About the only suggestion one can offer here is that a man should speak *to* instead of *before* his audience. A golden voice, originality of idea, coherence of presentation—all these are valuable gifts; but the great thing is that the preacher or speaker should contrive somehow to establish personal connection with every person whom he is addressing. "Mummy, why did that man speak to *me* all the time?" asked a little boy who had been taken to hear Charles Haddon Spurgeon. It is what a real orator must make every member of his audience feel.

Of course not every priest of the Congregation of the Mission was a great preacher, and no doubt many of them were not even very good ones. Poor Portail, for example, was so shy that it took until 1630 before he could be induced to go into the pulpit. But Vincent believed, and with justice, that practically everybody can be taught to speak in public with a reasonable degree of effectiveness so long as he can be brought to realise that deep learning and the usual bag of oratorical tricks are of little value when compared with simplicity and earnestness.

The early seventeenth century was a time when it was specially important that such a lesson should be thoroughly learned. For one of the consequences of the Renaissance and the classical education it brought into vogue was to make both writers and speakers cultivate a ridiculous ornateness. As the Abbé Bremond has said, "College rhetoric had taught them to chisel and adorn their phrases in a thousand dainty ways, since whatever one loves to do is well done, and they loved such pastimes." The carving of gems, or even of cherry-stones, has its rightful place in literature. Merely because we think that Dryden and Swift wrote extremely well is no reason for denying that Sir Thomas

Browne wrote equally well, or perhaps even better, in another mode. Nevertheless there can be little question that, upon the whole, the straightforward style is to be preferred in the public speaker (or, for that matter, the writer) than the involved, over-loaded and artificial style then in fashion. It is at all events more practical, and Vincent was an eminently practical man. Hence the "Little Method."

Yet his own style both in speaking and writing has, in my opinion, been overpraised. De Broglie claims for him a high place among the authors of the seventeenth century, and Coste (rather more cautiously) says much the same thing.[1] The truth is that he paid no attention to style and was almost always too discursive and repetitious. But he was admirably lucid; there is no mistaking his meaning—and that is a great literary merit. In addition, though the last thing in the world he was aiming at was the exhibition of his own personal qualities, those qualities appear in a delightfully intimate fashion in many of his utterances. In this, too, there is a merit that far more accomplished writers might well envy. In short, Vincent de Paul was not a conscious artist, but an artist in spite of himself, by virtue of a genius which, though not of the literary order, nevertheless had (simply because it was genius) some affinity with other creative modes. That is a good deal to claim for him; to claim more would be utterly absurd.

The "Little Method" was badly needed as a corrective, and may still be usefully studied by orators who imagine that a finical or roaring flamboyance serves any good purpose. La Bruyère, writing only a generation later, sadly remarks, "Declaimers will

[1] Coste's later comment (Vol. III, p. 348 of Father Leonard's translation) admits, however, "A rather monotonous and involved style, due, perhaps, to want of imagination or, possibly, to the fact that he deliberately eliminated it." Here Coste is commenting on Vincent's letters; the Saint's Conferences are racier and livelier and more personal, though in them too there is apparent an indifference to stylistic finish. He never wrote a book.

attract large congregations until that man returns who, in a style based on the Holy Scriptures, shall explain to the people the Word of God in a simple and familiar manner." The "Little Method" had at least started a reaction in preaching.

Père Coste gives a good many samples of the pulpit manner of the time—many of which are selected from Camus, the Bishop of Belley, who was a friend of Francis de Sales, Louise de Marillac, and Vincent himself. Poor Camus, I cannot help feeling, is not quite fairly treated. All he was doing was to preach in the style then generally taken for granted, and even expected, by a cultivated audience. So while Bougaud is witty when he says, "In order to preach so badly it was necessary to know a great deal," he, too, is not altogether just. Many of these "learned" preachers preached well in their own way and cannot be doubted to have moved and enlightened such congregations as had the capacity to understand what they were talking about. The trouble is that it was not the kind of preaching that was the slightest use in Vincent's missions to peasants. They would merely have sat and gaped, and not understood a word. The Missionary, according to Vincent, "Will speak to convert and not to be esteemed, and if men are to be converted they must understand what is said." The opposite method he described as a playing of the peacock: "It is to preach oneself and not Jesus Christ."

It would, however, be going altogether too far to claim that the reaction against the over-elaborate began with Vincent de Paul. It was rather that he joined a general movement. Molière was about to satirise the *Précieuses Ridicules*, Bossuet to found the classical school of French oratory. The magnificent lucidity of French prose was already coming into being. Already Malherbe had initiated a departure from the "rules" of the Renaissance. And though he, and even Racine and Corneille, will seem somewhat stilted to most English readers, it must not be forgotten that their work was strongly in favour of sobriety in poetry. Even the style of language in vogue among the *Précieuses* made for precision and clarity, and it was upon this style that Vaugelas tried to codify French.

So also in the matter of the spoken word, a great change was already coming into effect, and Vincent gleefully records, "Would you believe it, that actors, recognising the beauty of simplicity, have changed their manner of speaking, and no longer recite their parts in a high tone, as they did formerly, but speak in a medium voice and familiarly to audiences? One of them told me so a few days ago. Now, if in order the better to please the world, actors have changed their method, what a subject of confusion to the preachers of Jesus Christ if their love and zeal for souls do not make them change theirs."

Therefore if Vincent was an innovator in the matter of the style of preaching, it was only that his genius and commonsense united to bring about, within the scope of his own influence, a change that would have occurred even without him. The age of the Renaissance was about over; that of the *Grand Siècle* was about to begin. Vincent deserves, indeed, credit for his contribution to the reform of preaching; but to read some of his biographers one would imagine that it was all his own little idea.

What Vincent saw, however—and this is much more to the point—is that the "Little Method" was good not only for congregations of peasants (in *their* case it was absolutely necessary) but good for practically all purposes. Thus when a group of priests from his Tuesday Conference undertook to preach a mission in the Faubourg Saint-Germain, they asked him whether they should not adopt another style, since this was to be before a city audience. His answer was prompt: "Hold fast to the simplicity which you have found so successful in other missions. The spirit of the world, with which this district is saturated, can neither be fought nor conquered save by the spirit of Jesus Christ." It was the answer of a saint; it was also the answer of a sensible man. Even when Pavillon and his confrères went to preach at the Court at Saint-Germain-en-Laye Vincent told them that the "Little Method" would be good for the King and his courtiers. If it failed at all in effectiveness, this was because Pavillon used it rather too bluntly in his references to the low-necked dresses of the ladies. Such was not Vincent's way.

The Vincentian mildness appears especially clearly in his instructions about the best way of handling Huguenots, who were numerous in many of the districts visited by his missionaries. The tolerance of his attitude is all the more remarkable when we consider the lurking bitterness left by the religious wars, and the fact that everywhere Catholics could still see images in their churches that had been defaced by Calvinist fanaticism. But Vincent was aware that Catholics had been almost equally violent—and that all violence in the cause of religion is futile. Francis de Sales had already said, "Whoever preaches with love, preaches sufficiently against heretics, though he may never say a controversial word."

In the same spirit Vincent writes to his Missionaries that adherents of the "so-called reformed religion" were to be taught "gently and humbly, so that it may be seen that what is said proceeds from a compassionate, charitable, and not a bitter, heart." The Protestant ministers were on no account to be challenged to debate—since that might cause acrimony—nor were they to be dealt with roughly in the pulpit. "It should not be said, save in a spirit of humility and compassion, that they cannot point out any passage in their articles of faith in Holy Scripture. . . . Our Lord Himself had to predispose, by His love, those whom He wished to believe in Him. . . . If you act likewise, God will bless your efforts; if not, you will do nothing but make a noise, blow your own trumpet, and do no good." And again, "Bitterness has never served any other purpose than to embitter." The best method of Catholic controversy, then as now, was not to refute Protestant calumnies but to expound Catholic truth.

He seems to have attached more importance to the simpler method of giving catechetical lessons than to formal sermons. For by the interchange of questions and answers the Missionaries would be best able to discover how firmly the people were grounded in their faith, and upon what points they needed fuller instruction. Without this, Vincent felt that a preacher was only too likely to go into the pulpit and waste much of his time. But with it, he could deal much more usefully with such subjects upon which further enlightenment was most badly needed. He was well aware that the peasantry, having such pastors as were then so common, were in many instances almost completely ignorant of even elementary Christian doctrine.

In all this we may discern a deep psychology. Vincent's methods were as novel as they were unpretentious. The antics of "Little Father Andrew," the Provincial of the Augustinians and the Billy Sunday of the times, may now and then have been effective. But one cannot reflect with pleasure upon the good manners of a man who, preaching upon Mary Magdalen's sinful life, stopped short and said, "Ha! I see a woman down there like her; I'm going to throw my handkerchief at her head." When a number of women, very naturally, "ducked" their heads, he shouted, "Oh, ho! I thought there was only one; and now I see that there are a hundred!" That sort of "psychology" was very cheap—and very different from Vincent's.

But if Vincent de Paul was always simple in his manner of speaking, and sometimes perhaps a little too neglectful of style, he could, on occasion, rise to heights of oratory which will compare favourably with any specimens of eloquence. Two examples of this must suffice. It might be noted that they both come from speeches delivered when he was seventy, at which age all a man's powers are in decline. Probably therefore still better speeches—of which no report exists—were given in his prime.

Vincent had sent a group of his missionaries to Madagascar under Toussaint Bourdaise, and, as it was some time since he had heard from them, he wondered what was their fate. To the Fathers of the Congregation, assembled in Conference in Paris, he broke out with this apostrophe: "M. Bourdaise, my brethren, M. Bourdaise who is so far away and all alone and who, as you know, has won to Jesus Christ, with so much pain and anxiety, a great number of the natives of the country where he now is—let us also pray for him. M. Bourdaise, are you still alive, or are you dead? If alive, May God be pleased to preserve your life; if you are in heaven, pray for us."

Could anything be more natural? Could anything be more thrilling?

If in the second speech he was not quite seventy (it was delivered in 1647) he was close to it. The Foundling Hospital which he had established, and about which there will be more in a subsequent chapter, had proved a very costly undertaking and, as times were bad, it seemed that the Ladies of Charity might have to abandon this work. But Vincent, after having put the situation squarely before them, concludes with this peroration: "So now, Ladies, sympathy and charity led you to adopt these little creatures as your children. You have been their mothers according to grace, ever since their mothers according to nature abandoned them; reflect now whether you, too, intend to abandon them. Cease to be their mothers and now become their judges. Their life and death are in your hands. I am now about to collect your opinions and votes; the time has come to pronounce their sentence and to see if you still have desire to have mercy on them. They will live if you continue to take charitable care of them; on the contrary, they will most certainly die if you abandon them; experience does not allow you to think otherwise."

If it is hard to read that passage even now without having the tears come into one's eyes, surely the Ladies of Charity were in tears on hearing the words spoken by one whom they all revered as a saint. What *could* the Ladies do after such an appeal except decide to continue the work at any sacrifice?

Having given these two samples of Vincent's oratory, I find myself unable to resist giving a third. It is from the address he gave to the Fathers at Saint-Sulpice after the death of Olier, who had himself been, in some sense, Vincent's son. There is not here that rolling thunder that made the *Oraisons Funèbres* of Bossuet so famous.[2] But, I for one, confess to feeling often a little ill at ease at the praise lavished by the great Bishop of Meaux on doubtful characters. Vincent, however great his charity, could not, I think, have done it; Olier deserved his praise, which is indeed not so much panegyric as consolation and encouragement to those left behind to continue his work. Here is the passage:

"I should have wished, my dear Brethren, when I see the grief into which you are plunged by the death of your dear Father, to restore him to you that he might wipe away your tears. But, as I cannot restore his body to you in the flesh, I thought I should set his spirit before you, for it is the better part of him. Earth holds his body, and heaven his soul—his spirit is for you; and if God has judged him worthy of a place in Paradise beside His angels, you should not consider him unworthy of a dwelling-place in your hearts. He will gladly have left his body, if his spirit abides in you. Such was his life-long wish and desire: now that he is dead, it is in your power to make

[2] It should be added that the early sermons of Bossuet follow the "Little Method" rather strictly, and though later his soaring genius refused to be bound by it, his indebtedness to Vincent de Paul remained considerable.

him happy. It was said in the Law that if a brother died without children, another should *suscitare semen*. Your Father, whom I may also call your brother (bearing in mind his age), has died, so to speak, without children, seeing how greatly he desired to convert the entire world and to sanctify the clergy. He has left you his Spouse, which is this holy house, acquired by his blood and his death, for he died to self in his desire to give you life. Raise up children to him, by making Jesus Christ known; and, if you can, assure him as many servants as there are men in existence, and supply him with as many holy sacrifices as there are priests in the Church. *Fac secundum exemplar quod tibi in monte monstratum est.*"[3]

[3] We must remember, however, that we do not possess a single address of Vincent's, or an absolutely reliable report of any of his Conferences to judge from. What we have are only specimens reconstructed from memory on the framework of notes. On the other hand these reports, being written by men and women who lived intimately with Vincent, do enable us often to catch the very tone of his voice. Though many different people made them, Vincent is to be recognised in them all. Even when we cannot be sure that the precise phrasing used is the one recorded, we may be sure that every effort was made to reproduce Vincent's meaning exactly.

❡ 18. The Jansenist Miasma

WHEN the average modern man of education—that is, the man who knows much more about literature than theology—thinks of the Jansenist controversy he is likely to do so in terms of Pascal's *Provincial Letters*. The personality of Pascal is so appealing and what he wrote has such charm that his book lives, and will continue to live, on account of its beautiful style, even though its thesis is quite unsound and though Pascal was not very well read in Escobar and the Jesuit casuists against whom he used his delicately devastating satire.

The wicked Jesuits, though from the beginning they were strongly opposed to Jansenism and later shouldered the brunt of the defence of the orthodox position, had nevertheless relatively little to do with the controversy in its early stages. The man who was mainly instrumental in securing the condemnation by Rome of the famous five propositions found in Jansen's *Augustinus* was Vincent de Paul. As he had been at one time a close friend of the first Jansenists, the later Jansenists not unnaturally regarded him as a kind of Judas to their cause, though, at the same time, the circumstance that Vincent continued to remain on friendly terms with some leading Jansenists after their condemnation made him also a little suspect in certain Catholic quarters. A careful examination of his connexion with the matter, however, cannot fail to reveal at once his intellectual acumen and his Christian charity.

The usual Jansenist attack upon Vincent—and it has created a tradition which has lasted to our own days—was that he was a kindly and simple man who was woefully ignorant of theology. At this stage all that needs be said upon that point is that the Jansenists themselves refute it, since they moved heaven and earth to draw Vincent into their camp. If they really considered him so poor a theologian why were they so eager to get him on their side?

Probably the very fact that Vincent was not a doctor of theology, like Saint-Cyran and Arnauld, was in some ways an advantage to him. Because all except the very finest sort of speculative intelligences are only too likely to go astray, seeking intellectual novelties, and entangling themselves in pride. Great wits *are* sure to madness near allied—deny it as we may. And the leading Jansenists of those days, while no doubt cleverer, or more ingenious, men than Vincent, lacked his sane balance. By using his shrewd common-sense and a mind that, we should never forget, was, after all, trained in the dialectic of the schools, he cut at once through the Jansenist sophistries. We must not take too seriously his constant belittling of his own educational achievements; these were solid even if not sensational. There were a great many men more learned than Vincent in the France of that time; there were a number of them in the Congregation of the Mission who were only too glad to be his disciples. What the age needed was precisely the kind of man he was. Charity alone would, in this controversy, not have sufficed; simplicity would not have sufficed; humility would not have sufficed— though all conferred an advantage on their possessor, and in all of these attributes Vincent was richly endowed. What was needed was a man of good clear unpretentious intelligence, with enough theological learning to have read the authorities upon whom the "new theologians" relied, and enough cold logic to be able to recognise the misuse of those authorities. Vincent was just such a man.

On the other hand, let us candidly admit certain things about the Jansenists. They were, as a group, distinguished both for their learning and their piety. Further, the orthodox contro- versialists in many cases displayed a venomous acrimony—as

commonly happens in theological controversy. Charges have
even been brought that some of the engravings made from the
contemporary paintings of Vincent were deliberately falsified
so as to belittle him. Another charge is that the deposition made
by Vincent in favor of Saint-Cyran after his arrest (which I
shall put in evidence later) was a Jansenist forgery. There is
no foundation for such puerile nonsense. Nobody, I believe, will
accuse me of having any Jansenist leanings if, to clear the air,
I say that, whatever bitterness came into the quarrel, the
Jansenists were at least above such dirty tricks. They were
men of high character, and though they were grievously in
error, and angry with Vincent (with good reason as they supposed), there is no need to call names or throw mud.

Further, by way of attempting to clarify the issue, let it be
said that Jansenism is two things—a doctrine and a spirit. Now
that doctrine (which alone is condemned by the Church) repre-
sents the impact of Calvinism upon Catholicism. Even Father
Leonard remarks, "It may . . . be admitted that [Vincent] had
a certain amount of sympathy with a number of their ascetic
and moral ideas." But the spirit (which can hardly be ex-
plicitly condemned, since it takes all sorts of people to make a
Church), may be called that of "Catholic Puritanism"—a very
unCatholic thing, though it is to be found today among thousands of Catholics whose formal orthodoxy is irreproachable. I
hope that without offence I may add that it is most frequently
to be encountered in France and in Ireland—in Ireland because
many of the early Maynooth professors were French exiles.
But it is by no means absent from the other English-speaking
countries, since the Catholics in these live in a Protestant at-
mosphere. In all kinds of subtle ways the Jansenist miasma has
a way of penetrating. Its rigorism, like the vaguer sentimental-
ism of modern Protestantism, remains a real danger to the
Catholic spirit.

It should be said that, if there may be recognized in Vincent a tinge of "Catholic Puritanism," this was almost inevitable in one whose rôle of reformer set him in opposition to the glaring abuses prevalent in the Church during the seventeenth century, and who could see for himself how lax many Catholics were in their lives. There was also to be found in some of the noblest spirits of the time—in Bérulle for example—a pessimism which suggests Jansenism, though it did not always go to the Jansenist extreme. From the beginning, however, Vincent was perfectly and clearly orthodox in all matters of doctrine. As he was a reformer, the Jansenists thought they were going to secure him; as he was a theologian, he not only escaped them but became the most redoubtable of their opponents. In later life he used to talk as though he had had a narrow escape. But in all probability he had never been in any serious danger. Not only his sound theological training but his profound humility saved him. Whatever other good qualities the Jansenists may have had, humility was assuredly not among them.

Vincent's contact with Jansenism began about 1621, when it was only in its incipient stage. At that time he got to be very intimate with Jean du Vergier de Hauranne, better known as the Abbé de Saint-Cyran, who was Jansen's great friend and a man of the same age as Vincent de Paul. Saint-Cyran frequented the Bérulle circle and edified everyone by his piety, as he aroused in everyone admiration for his brilliance and learning. There is no wonder that Vincent was powerfully attracted towards him.

Moreover Saint-Cyran did Vincent several services in connexion with the founding of the Collège des-Bons-Enfants, and on the strength of these he felt he was entitled to advise his friend about the conduct of the Congregation of the Mission. The man was undoubtedly gifted, but he was inclined to take offence easily when his advice was not followed. Yet in spite of

a certain coolness that sprang up between himself and Vincent
on this account, the two men continued to meet frequently up to
about 1634, and occasionally even afterwards.

What shocked Vincent was the theological opinions Saint-
Cyran was beginning to express in conversation. Nevertheless
Vincent continued to make allowances; Saint-Cyran was of an
impetuous choleric disposition and given to the making of ex-
travagant paradoxes. These the sober-minded Vincent did not
take too seriously. How could one take seriously a man who
used to say that there had been no Church for five hundred
years or that the essence of Calvin's doctrine was sound, only
he had defended it badly: *bene sensit, male locutus est!*

Saint-Cyran would brook no contradiction. When Vincent
mildly reminded him that the definition of the Church was "The
congregation of the faithful under our Holy Father the Pope,"
Saint-Cyran retorted, "You know as little about the matter as
you do about high Dutch." Another time, when Vincent did not
show himself submissive to Saint-Cyran's advice regarding the
affairs of the Mission, the fiery man burst out with, "You are
simply an ignoramus. I'm astonished that your Congregation
tolerates you as its Superior." To which Vincent good-
humouredly replied, "You are not so astonished at it as I am,
for I'm even more ignorant than you imagine."[1]

Another day he told Vincent—and this was something that
he also told others—that the Holy Scriptures were more luminous
in his mind than they were in themselves. It is rather amusing
to record that these conversations prompted the Abbé to com-
pose for Vincent's benefit a little treatise on humility.

---

[1] Here we have the well-born and brilliant Saint-Cyran showing himself a boor (and an obtuse one), while the rustic Vincent appears as the
urbane gentleman. The Abbé clearly was about as perfect a specimen of
the intellectual snob as one can discover. But Saint-Cyran, even in rage,
could hardly have taken leave of his senses to make such a remark, had
Vincent not actually been (as compared with himself) lacking in book-
learning.

The truth of the matter—and it is the most charitable explanation to offer—would seem to be that Saint-Cyran was afflicted with paranoia. His long and astounding letter to Vincent, dated November 20, 1637 cannot be accounted for on any other ground. Though it is hardly possible to quote it here in its entirety, a few characteristic excerpts may be given. The Abbé reproaches Vincent for having turned against him "because I wished to render you and your house a great service." Yet he writes, "[I] excuse you for having abandoned me when I was being persecuted," and adds, "Although I might have expected sympathy from you, you have on that account and against your own inclination and custom, taken it upon yourself with extraordinary boldness to unite with others to crush me." He continues, "As far as your house is concerned, you thought you had acted wisely because you prevented me from doing it the good turn I had wished to render it. So far am I from being vexed on that account, that I thank you most heartily for having relieved me of the trouble, without perhaps thereby having diminished God's good pleasure in my regard for the desire He had given me to serve you in both spiritual and temporal matters." Then he charges Vincent with harbouring animosity because of "services of which you had so little esteem that you took the simple proposal I made you on this matter as a proof of the four things of which you accused me." He concludes, "Nevertheless, I will be patient with you as God is in letting you go your own way, and I will be just as ready to be of service to you in the future as I have shown myself to be in the past, out of kindness, even if I cannot give my entire approval, putting aside the title of master for that of your very humble and obedient servant."

One can read that only with pity. It is from beginning to end a scream of wounded vanity and offended affection. So far from Vincent having persecuted him, it was Vincent who was about to save him from the scaffold. For Cardinal Richelieu, having got wind of Saint-Cyran's eccentric theological opinions, had him imprisoned, and finding a copy of this letter among his papers, sent for Vincent to question him. The Cardinal was a great stickler for orthodoxy and would not tolerate anything that might cause disunion in the Church. He was ready to make an example of Saint-Cyran.

Richelieu got very little out of Vincent, and nothing at all that would serve as the basis for a charge of heresy. Indeed, he was so annoyed at his lack of success that he showed his displeasure in his usual way, by scratching his head at the end of the interview.

He had not quite done, however. On three successive days Vincent's evidence was taken, after which it was signed. And this document was so little incriminating that the Abbé Maynard, and indeed most of the biographers until Père Coste, contested its authenticity. Coste, while admitting that it raises some difficulties, unhesitatingly accepts it, for the reason (among others) that it gives correctly Vincent's age, about which all the earlier biographers were mistaken, and which the Jansenists would not have known.

The main difficulty is in squaring the moderate tone and the frequent answer "I do not remember" with the letters Vincent wrote to John Dehorgny in 1648 when that Missionary was showing some disposition to defend Jansenism. Had Vincent related the same things to Richelieu, there is no question but that Saint-Cyran would have been executed. As Vincent said afterwards, he had in making his deposition two objects—"first, to say nothing contrary to the truth, and second, to say nothing that could injure the accused."

Very skilfully he achieved his purpose. Did Saint-Cyran ever say that the Popes and the majority of the bishops do not constitute the true Church? "Oh, no; except that he had said

that many bishops had no vocation. . . . Yet I have never
seen anyone who had a greater esteem for the episcopate than
he." Did Saint-Cyran ever say that God had destroyed the
Church for the last five or six hundred years? "Well, yes;
but I suppose that he intended it in the sense in which it is
related that Pope Clement VIII used to weep because it seemed
to him that, whilst the Church was extending to the Indies, it
was being destroyed at home." Had he spoken against the
Jesuits? "Yes, he had censured some of their opinions regarding
grace . . . But I have also heard him speak in the highest terms
of the first members of their Order." Saint-Cyran had, indeed,
much to thank Vincent for.

Père Coste offers as explanation of the discrepancy between
this document and some of the later letters: "In the first case,
he wanted to save a man; in the second to preserve the faithful
from the errors which that man had propagated. In the first
case the kindest interpretation was put on Saint-Cyran's remarks; in the second, it was his duty to expose the danger, such
as it actually was, without minimizing it. Again, in the first
case he was not actually obliged to say all that he knew; he
might even pay no attention to what was known solely from
private letters or from strictly private conversations."

It may be my ignorance of the niceties of moral theology that
leads me to question the validity of the argument contained in
that last phrase. But to my plain mind it seems that Vincent's
examination was precisely about what he knew from letters
and private conversations. He would have been within his rights
in refusing to answer; he would not have been justified in giving
false answers.

I offer the explanation that Vincent was well aware that
Saint-Cyran was, to say the least, unbalanced, and so did not
take all his remarks seriously. He knew that a man of this
temperament often says things provocatively without really

meaning them. But after the Jansenist storm had broken, Vincent perhaps swung to the other extreme and came to take Saint-Cyran's remarks too seriously and to read into them more than was ever intended. He apparently considered, however, in the official examination of 1637, that it would have been unfair to quote *obiter dicta* of this fantastic kind. In later years he was, on the other hand, perhaps unconsciously unfair in attaching too much importance to them. A man may be unconsciously unfair, however, and yet perfectly honest. Unless we are going to say, as M. Raoul Allier does, that Vincent had misunderstood Saint-Cyran, I do not see how he can be completely acquitted of some degree of disingenuousness (to put it mildly) except on the supposition I advance. I do not like to think that Vincent felt that he could with a good conscience "pay no attention to what was known solely from private letters or from strictly private conversations." Rather than that, it would make things easier for us if we could continue to consider the deposition apocryphal.

The upshot of the affair was that, though Richelieu was unable to bring Saint-Cyran to trial, he kept him in custody until his own death, upon which Louis XIII released the Jansenist leader, who died from an apopleptic stroke a few months later. With this there ended what may be considered the first phase of the great Jansenist controversy.

The second stage began with the publication in the same year as that in which Saint-Cyran died of Antoine Arnauld's book *On Frequent Communion*. Yet as this work cannot be properly understood except in relation to the posthumous *Augustinus* of Jansen, Bishop of Ypres, we must go back to that for a moment. Jansen had given to St. Augustine an interpretation decidedly Calvinistic, but his book remained hardly more than a thesis to be debated by the contending factions of the universities of Louvain and Paris until Arnauld's great polemical and popularising ability suddenly made theology a subject for fashionable discussion. The lucidity with which he presented his case gave everybody the delightful illusion of being learned. And this—especially since it took Jansen's ideas out of the merely speculative field and put them to practical application—forced the issue. When at last condemnation came from Rome, however, Arnauld himself was passed over; it was Jansen, deep in his grave before the controversy began, who suffered.

Antoine Arnauld was one of the brothers of that very noble and gifted woman, Mother Angélique, who in 1608 had been appointed superior of the relaxed Cistercian abbey of Port-Royal. He had passed through Vincent de Paul's hands, at any rate to the extent of having made his ordination retreat at the Bons-Enfants. And he had a high opinion of Vincent, just as had Saint-Cyran, who was at that time the spiritual director of Port-Royal.

In this connexion it is curious to note that Angélique Arnauld had been a friend of Francis de Sales, and that he had directed her earlier spiritual life. As far as that goes, Saint-Cyran himself used to talk of the Bishop of Geneva in the highest terms, privately canonizing him before the Church did. Nevertheless Jansenism was, from some aspects, a reaction against the Salesian system. As the Abbé Bremond puts it, "The difference here was that while the book of Francis de Sales aimed through fervour and attractiveness at conciliating the world to religion, that of Arnauld recalled it to remembrance of severity and justice." There ought to be a fear of God, but it is seldom felt by wicked men. This holy fear is rather the fruit of love—the fear of losing God, or of doing something contrary to love. But Port-Royal tended to accentuate this fear until it became a shuddering terror, or tended to become such.

Further, although a thirst for the heroic and a hatred for the mediocre are good in themselves, they are liable to lead to pride. Christians are, indeed, called to be perfect, yet God is willing to accept a little instead of the all to which He is entitled. The Jansenist rigour, while it may have proved of spiritual benefit—as Vincent admitted—to a few choice spirits, was terribly depressing to the majority of people. Upon the logical French mind it easily led to the conclusion that those who were predestined to Heaven need not bother to lead good lives, while, on the other hand, it induced among those who could not bring themselves to believe they were of the "elect" the idea that they might as well give up all attempt to practice virtue. The cynic, for his part, was encouraged to believe that, when he failed to go to the sacraments at all he was no worse—and perhaps in some respects better—than the "hypocrites" (as he too easily called them) who went to Communion regularly. For Arnauld's powerful book, which was supported by many quotations from the Fathers and Saints of the Church, and endorsed by no less than fifteen French bishops and twenty doctors of the Sorbonne, definitely discouraged Communion on the ground that virtually nobody was worthy to receive it.

It was this practical conclusion that stirred Vincent most deeply. To purely speculative issues he could not be, in this instance, indifferent, for he knew that thought must inevitably have its effect upon action; and when he saw that almost every Church in Paris was losing a very high proportion of its communicants, he realised that something had to be done, and done at once.

We should note, however, that the frequency of communion of modern times dates only from the pontificate of Pius X. During the seventeenth century only the exceptionally pious went as often as once a week, we might say once even a month. To go two or three times a week, one had to get express permission from one's spiritual director. So on that point Arnauld had in his favour a rigour much greater than prevails today.

But what his argument led to was this: a spirit of penance and humility should make people very cautious about approaching the Holy Table. Indeed, it would almost seem that they would do well to abstain altogether. In the same way, absolution from sins should not be given before but after penance, and this ought to be (as in the early Church) prolonged and public. Had Arnauld's ideas prevailed it would have meant that the faithful—with a few chosen exceptions—would have been altogether deprived of the sacraments which, according to the teaching of the Church, are the medicines of the soul. Rigour could have led only to ruin.

Note how Vincent disposes of the thesis. He did not engage in public controversy, and the following passage appears in his letter written in 1648 to Dehorgny, one of the Missionaries at Rome who had been attracted by the new doctrines: "It is obvious that a man cannot maintain that these maxims are certainly true without, at the same time, feeling strictly bound to abstain from frequenting the Sacraments. As for myself, I frankly confess that, if I had as high an opinion of M. Arnauld's book as you have, not only would I renounce forever, in a spirit of humility, Holy Mass and Communion, but I should have a horror of the Sacrament, if what he maintains is true in regard to those who go to Communion in the usual dispositions approved of by the Church. . . . And even if one were to close one's eyes to every other consideration, and confine one's attention solely to his remarks in several places on the admirable dispositions without which he does not wish persons to receive Holy Communion, can any man be found on this earth with such a high opinion of his own virtue as to think he is in a fit state to receive Holy Communion worthily? That appertains to M. Arnauld alone who, after having pushed these dispositions to such a height that a St. Paul would be afraid to communicate, does not cease from boasting . . . that he himself says Mass every day! In this, his humility is as much to be admired as his charity is to be esteemed, and not only his charity, but his high opinion of so many wise spiritual guides, both secular and religious, and so many virtuous penitents who practice this devotion, both of whom are as a rule the butts of his habitual reserve."

To read such a passage, so full of irony and indignation and clear common-sense, makes one regret that Vincent did not take up the cudgels of controversy. Even the clever skull of M. Arnauld would have got cracked by such as blow as that. Only that was not Vincent's way; distressed as he was, he would not appear in the public lists. He writes as he does only because Dehorgny is in danger of becoming a Jansenist, and he wants to save him.

What Vincent did—along with other people—was something else. They picked out from Jansen's *Augustinus* five propositions which they thought deserved condemnation. The chief of these were Jansen's assertions that grace was irresistible—thereby removing free will—and that Christ did not shed his blood for all men but only for the elect. Then Vincent took the lead in writing to the bishops in France inviting them to sign a petition asking Rome to consider whether or not the five propositions deserved censure.

The bishops, like the rest of the clergy, proved to be divided on the subject. Eventually, Vincent managed to get eighty-eight signatures, or those of about three quarters of the bishops, but a group of fifteen sent a counter-petition to Rome, and a third group (most of whom were concealed Jansenist sympathisers) took the attitude that it would be better not to raise the question at all so as to avoid strife. Among this last group was Pavillon, the Bishop of Alet, one of Vincent's protegés who, so long as Vincent lived, kept denying that he was a Jansenist, but afterwards came out in his true colours. As M. Boulenger says, "He was a man of stern and austere virtue, who had the confidence of a heretic in his own logic, and the temperament of a Calvinist." The commission sent to Rome to present the orthodox side of the case were given hospitality in the house of the Congregation of the Mission there.

Again Vincent's skill in dialectic appears. To the hedging Pavillon he writes: "When the Lutheran and Calvinist heresies made their first appearance, if the Church had waited to condemn them until the members of those sects seemed prepared to submit and to be reunited, then those heresies would have been matters of indifference that could either be followed or not as the case might be, and they would have infected more persons than they actually have done." If Pavillon refused to listen to such reasoning, Rome did not. On May 31, 1653 the Bull of Condemnation, *Cum Occasione,* was issued.

Now we see the great charity of Vincent towards his defeated opponents. His first act was to call on all those who had worked against Jansenism to beg them to refrain from making a public display of delight at their victory and to do everything possible to soften the blow for the condemned party. Not content with that, Vincent then called on the Jansenist theologians of the University—where the Irish students for some reason were specially attracted by the new heresy—and on the solitaries of Port-Royal. To all these he talked at length and most affectionately, and left under the impression that they intended to submit and that the controversy was over.

The ingenious M. Arnauld, however, soon concocted a theory to cover the case. Even if Jansen was condemned, he argued, he himself was not. But *was* Jansen, he went on, really condemned? Were the five propositions actually contained in the *Augustinus?* That they were not there in a form textually identical with the Bull left him free to maintain that Rome had misunderstood Jansen's sense, and that the infallibility of the Pope did not extend to matters of fact. To which Bossuet replied that all this was thoroughly disingenuous, for the propositions were certainly in the *Augustinus* in substance. Such an instance of special pleading on the part of Arnauld would of course have appeared highly "jesuitical" to the author of the *Provincial Letters* had the Jesuits employed it. But the great polemic skill of Arnauld kept the controversy alive to trouble the Church for another century, and indeed, though it would today be hard to find open profession of Jansenism, it would not be at all hard to find a sneaking sympathy for it still in some Catholic quarters. The snake has been scotched but not quite killed. Its venom and fetid breath may even today be encountered.

But at least it was destroyed as far as the Congregation of the Mission was concerned. The Oratorians were deeply infected, as were several other religious orders to varying degrees; and numbers of the secular clergy and their bishops were either open or secret adherents of Jansenism. Vincent, however, managed to keep the institutions over which he had control free from the virus. Some of the Ladies of Charity had Jansenist sympathies, and Vincent was afraid that they might lead the Daughters of Charity astray. The Visitation nuns, with their aristocratic connexions, were particularly exposed. All the same, Vincent contrived to save them. To Père Dehorgny Vincent had sent, at the end of his long argument, a warning, "In case anyone should not wish to defer, it would be better for him to withdraw from the Company, and for the Company to request him to do so." About fifteen men—among whom Dehorgny was not numbered—did leave the Congregation of the Mission on this account.

Vincent said afterwards that all his life he had expected to see the rise of a new heresy, and added that he had been afraid of finding himself enmeshed in the errors of some new doctrine before he noticed it. That is what always happens to the heretic: he thinks a certain doctrine exciting or attractive, and is edified by the zeal of its adherents. There had been much that was speciously pleasing about Jansenism. The Jansenists were zealous in an age when many of the orthodox were lax, learned where the majority of the orthodox were otherwise ignorant, and reformers in an age during which reform was badly needed. The trouble was that these gifted and devoted men and women did not have the mind of the Church or the spirit of Christ. It was the profound Catholicism of Vincent that kept him secure, his prompt action that prevented the triumph of Jansenism in France at the moment when it seemed as though it was about to sweep everything before it.

ℭ 19. At Court

VINCENT in 1610 had grown acquainted in the magnificent palace of Marguerite de Valois with what was a small edition of the King's Court. That he was appointed to a position there at all and that he stayed a year and a half is sufficient proof that this peasant—this "swineherd," as he was fond of calling himself in his humility—was no country boor but a natural gentleman and a man of parts. If further proof of this is needed, we have his long stay—on his own terms during his second period—in the princely household of the Gondis. The traditional picture of Vincent as nothing but a kindly simple old priest is badly in need of revision. That he *was* this, is true enough; but he must have been a good deal more. Great nobles do not flock to put themselves under the direction of one who, however virtuous, lacks distinction of mind and manners.

Some time during the sixteen-thirties he had begun to frequent the Court. Most, if not all, of the Ladies of Charity moved in very high circles, and from them both Louis and Anne of Austria must often have heard of Vincent, whom they are likely also to have encountered at the Visitation convent. We have already seen how the Queen paid at least one visit to the retreats for ordinands and was so impressed that she undertook to pay the expenses for five years. And Vincent had been led to project—either at the instigation of the Queen herself or at that of the noble ladies of his Confraternity—the formation of a kind of super-committee, to be divided into various sub-committees, that would manage and finance his charities. If the scheme never seems to have come to anything, this must have been due to the incurable ineptitude of Anne herself; the kernel of the idea was nevertheless retained and the Ladies of

Charity did group themselves into departments, each one of which made itself responsible for one or other of the phases of Vincent's charitable work.

But when Vincent went to Court, he did so reluctantly. Only too well did he grasp the significance, or soon came to, of La Bruyère's aphorism, "The most honourable thing we can say of a man is, that he does not understand the Court; there is scarcely a virtue which we do not imply when saying this." If Vincent understood well enough the shallowness and chicanery of most of the courtiers, it was to ignore people of this stamp; he went as rarely as he could, and only under royal command, and then to use in the service of God the piety of the King and Queen and that of the more virtuous of the people by whom they were surrounded. For, as Matthew Arnold paraphrased Marcus Aurelius, "Even in a palace, life may be led well."

The biographers are fond of dilating upon the "patched cassock" in which Vincent used to appear. The only bit of evidence I can find in support of his shabby appearance (at any rate when he went to Court) is that Mazarin, who did not like him, one day made a somewhat spiteful remark about Vincent's frayed cassock-band. I think, however, it is safe to assume that, though he was very far from dressing himself up like one of the fashionable abbés—many of whom did not wear cassocks at all—he was polite enough to put on the best clothes he could find for such occasions. In any event, he was not invited there as a sort of clerical fashion-plate.

Moreover, other people besides himself were welcomed in the royal circles for what they were rather than for what they wore. Not yet had the punctilious and elaborate ceremonial of the Court of the *Grand Monarque* been made *de rigueur*, even if it was already to some extent in the process of development. Thus we hear of Madame de Miramion once being stopped by a soldier when she was about to enter the Queen's apartments because she was not sufficiently well dressed. On that occasion the Duchesse d'Aiguillon spoke sharply to the man, saying, "What do you think you are doing? The Queen would rather see this lady as she is than any of us in our finery."

Vincent was much more at home trudging about the muddy city streets, which—despite the spaciousness indicated in Turgot's pictorial *Plan de Paris*—were so narrow that when two of the huge, gilded, velvet-upholstered, leather-curtained, heraldically-emblazoned coaches of the rich appeared, with three or four footmen on the running-boards, there was nearly always a long argument about precedence before one of the coachmen could be induced to draw up at a turning to allow the other to pass. Pedestrians of course were splashed with mud and the filth of the gutters. If Vincent did occasionally visit any of his Ladies of Charity in one of those new mansions of an age which, disdaining the delicate grace of Gothic, were built in a style of gloomy ostentation, he made such calls only under the pressure of urgent business, and then accompanied by a *socius*. That was the rule he had imposed upon himself. When any of the Ladies called upon him, it was his habit to leave the door of the parlour at Saint-Lazare open all the time —something that may strike the modern reader as an excess of caution, unless he remembers the manners of the time and the propensity of tongues to wag. Much more frequently was Vincent to be found in one of the notorious *Cours des Miracles*, where thieves and beggars had their squalid hiding places, than in the sumptuous salons of royalty and nobility.

Yet, for all his love of personal obscurity, he did frequent the palaces in Paris and Saint-Germain. That he did so, as we shall see, resulted in very important services rendered by him to the Church. It was only because of what he hoped to accomplish for God that he went at all.

He had known Marie de' Medici in the days when she called

(ostensibly out of good-nature, but more probably out of insolence) upon ex-Queen Marguerite. No doubt he took the measure then of that heavy, foolish, meddlesome woman, and sympathised with Richelieu's having got rid of one who had an itch to govern precisely because she had no capacity to govern. The Day of Dupes had brought about her downfall before Vincent began to attend the Court. Perhaps his charity would have put Saint-Simon's verdict a little more mildly, but his judgment of character must have seen the justice in the description of her: "Imperious, jealous, stupid to a degree, ruled at all times by the dregs of the Court and of the people she had brought with her from Italy, she was the cause of wretchedness to Henry IV, to her son, and to herself as well, though she might have been the happiest woman in Europe at the cost of abstaining from giving way to her temper and her servants."

But if she was no longer there, Vincent must have sometimes encountered the foppish poltroon Gaston, even if it was only to bow low in passing to that unworthy heir-presumptive to the throne of France, who was always whistling, hands in his pockets, and with his hat tilted over his head. Vincent would hardly have said, as de Retz did, that Gaston "wanted everything without exception that distinguishes a great man"; but for all that he probably thought it.

With his insight into human make-up he must have weighed accurately the curious character of the Queen, however much his charity may have hoped from the genuine, if unstable, goodness in her. Anne of Austria was a fine, fresh, buxom woman, one obviously fitted by nature to be the mother of a large family, and yet a wife strangely neglected. If her normal good temper now and then changed into sudden fits of furious anger, when her voice grew shrill and strident, the poor woman had her excuse. Her life might have been actually easier had her husband done as his father before him and taken mistresses.

But we know her neglect was of a more positive sort, and, being due to Louis's indifference, was all the harder to bear. She liked admiration and considered she was entitled to receive it. Therefore, though strictly virtuous in practice, she often allowed herself to be put in compromising positions. Her famous flirtation with the Duke of Buckingham—though entirely innocent on her side, despite legends to the contrary—was, it is to be feared, encouraged by her enemy, Richelieu, who then promptly put the worst construction on it and so brought about a further estrangement between the royal couple. As likely as not she had the idea of winning her husband by making him slightly jealous—a very dangerous game for anybody to play. It exactly suited the Cardinal's book. Vincent must have pitied the unfortunate Queen, however clearly he perceived her silliness and lack of fibre. Concerning that, however, we can do no more than guess; he was always extremely discreet about what he said of people. De Retz was less kind when he wrote of Anne as she was a little later, in the days of her regency: "Persecution to persons in that high rank stands them instead of eminent virtue. People were willing to imagine that she had borne her sufferings with patience, the appearance of which indolence often assumes. . . . The most godly had already forgotten her coquetries." And in a later page he gives a more complete analysis: "The Queen had an unequalled genius for concealing from others that she was a fool. . . . Her intention towards piety was greater than her piety; she had more of obstinacy than of firmness; and more incapacity than all the rest which I have mentioned before." Like every etching it is made with acid.

Louis XIII, her husband, was one of the most virtuous men —in the sense of being free from positive vice—that ever sat upon the throne of France, and also one of the most complex and baffling characters. The early historians almost unanimously

underrated his capacity, but the process began with Marie de'
Medici, who spread the report that her son was a half-wit. He
was, however, nothing of the kind; he merely showed in his
boyhood a stubborn refusal to study. On the other hand, he
had abundant good sense and was extremely brave, so much
so that modern historical criticism—veering in the opposite direction—has sometimes been inclined to suppose that, had
Richelieu allowed him adequate scope for his military qualities, he would have made a first-class general officer.

Here again there is a false estimate, though of a different
sort; he was without that concentration and quickness of grasp
necessary to take in complicated operations at a glance. In the
same way, about politics he knew, and pretended to know,
nothing; but he recognised that what that extraordinary man
the Cardinal planned generally brought the desired results, and
so was willing to leave the conduct of affairs to transcendent
genius. He chafed and grumbled, but wisely concurred, knowing
as he did his own limitations. It was quite the best—indeed, it
was the only thing he could have done under the circumstances.

By being set free from the preoccupations of politics, the
King was able to devote himself to the hawking to which he
was so passionately addicted, and to his queer hobbies. His
versatility in the trivial was really immense. That he composed
music and sang and painted tolerably well was sufficiently
within the royal tradition.[1] That he enjoyed pottering about
his garden and working in wood or leather or iron was certainly
not contemptible. What was surprising and was considered un-
dignified was the delight he took in larding meat and in poach-

---

[1] Even on his death-bed we hear of his gathering a few of his nobles
and singing with them some metrical versions of the Psalms (possibly
Clément Marot's) that he had set to music of his own composing. His satis-
faction with the performance was such that an immediate improvement was
noticed in his condition, so that the Court began to think that he was going
to recover after all.

ing eggs and in shoeing horses; and he was even more proud of his manual dexterity than he was of his artistic talents. The most singular of all his accomplishments was his ability as a barber. Nothing pleased him better than to be allowed to shave his courtiers; if they submitted, they jeered at him for it: he, not they, paid the bill.

He was decidedly not liked, for not only was he without his father's jovial temperament, but he was morose and given to not altogether unaccountable fits of jealousy. The odd thing about this was that they should have been shown by a man who was notoriously cold sexually. If he had "affairs" they were invariably platonic, and it generally needed a very pious lady to attract him at all. His friendship with Louise de la Fayette, which has already been related, was typical. His incongruous qualities did not arouse respect, but it would be a serious error to think of him as he has been represented in romantic fiction as a wholly negligible person, dominated by the mesmeric power of his First Minister.

Richelieu died in December 1642; at the end of February of the following year the King, whose health had never been very good—though he had accustomed himself to bear fatigue—was stricken with what he knew was to prove a fatal illness. He had always been devout and regular in the practice of his religion; now as he lay dying he made an exemplary preparation for his end.[2]

Anne of Austria, in whom there now flickered up affection and compassion for her dying husband, was very anxious that the King should be attended in his last moments by Monsieur Vincent. Indeed, she assembled a little army of priests to assist the Jesuit, Père Dinet, who was the King's confessor; she meant

[2] He did not, however, escape the malicious wit of the makers of epigrams. Tallement des Réaux said of him, "No man ever loved God less than the King—or feared the devil more."

to make sure that Louis did not leave the world without all the consolations of religion.

We have from several different sources a full account of the royal passing. Vincent used to say afterwards, "Never have I seen anyone die a more Christian death," but some of the details supplied by Abelly strike one as slightly surprising. We are told, for instance, that the man who never opened a book if he could help it answered patly to Vincent's exordium, *"Timenti Deum bene erit in extremis," "Et in die defunctionis suae benedicetur."* However, perhaps the King remembered the proper response from oral repetition.

Other details seem to be more likely. Thus we hear that Louis said, "Monsieur Vincent, if I recover I shall appoint nobody to a bishopric who has not been three years with you"—that is, as a member of the Tuesday Conference. After all, we know that Richelieu had already asked Vincent to supply a list of names of those suitable for the episcopal dignity. And it is pathetic to know that Louis lifted his wasted arm and asked, "Is that a King's?" and of his requesting that the window be opened so that he might see his last resting-place in the Abbey of Saint-Denis. Just before the end, so the story goes, the dying man in clairvoyant vision foretold the victory of Rocroi.

There can be no doubt that Louis died a very good death. His main fear was that at the supreme moment he might succumb to an assault upon his faith. To this Père Dinet, who knew that at least his faith was strong, replied that it was much more likely that some ancient resentment would well up in him. In saying so he had reason. Though a reconciliation had been effected between Louis and the Queen, which had resulted in their having lived together as husband and wife since the end of 1637, it could never have been easy for the King to forgive Anne for having often forgotten her duties as Queen of France and for having carried on, as a Spanish Infanta, a correspond-

ence with the nation's enemies. This she had sworn upon the
Blessed Sacrament she had never done, until Cardinal Richelieu
confronted her with the proofs. It is hardly to be wondered
at that Louis on his death-bed said of her suspected implication
in the conspiracy of Chalais, "It is my duty to forgive her; but
I am not bound to believe her." He could hardly accept her
facile protestations after what had happened. It was not without cause that he feared lest his last moments be overwhelmed
with personal bitterness.

"If that should happen," the King asked, "what shall I do?"
It was agreed that if he should find himself suffering this
temptation, he was to make a sign with his hand and that the
confessor was then to call out "Charity!" He managed, as it
turned out, to die with forgiveness in his heart—even towards
a wife whom he had treated badly, and Vincent was able to
say of this death, "Never have I seen greater nobility of soul,
greater tranquility, greater dread of the slightest atoms that
seemed sinful, greater kindness or sounder judgment in a person in this state." One wonders whether he thought it necessary
to confess among his sins the latitude he had given to Richelieu
in the prosecution of his devious political aims. Probably not;
the King's grasp of politics was slight, and it is likely that what
he did in this line was with a good conscience. Only a few
months earlier the dying Cardinal, when asked whether he forgave his enemies, was able to answer that he had never had
any enemies, except those of the State.

After the King's death, when France passed under the regency
of the Queen-Mother, Vincent was more than ever at Court.
This was because Anne of Austria, stricken with some obscure
compunction, induced him to become her spiritual director and
appointed him, much against his will, to the Council in charge of
ecclesiastical affairs. About the latter office—concerning which
in the nature of things we know vastly more than we do about

the former—the next chapter will be concerned. All that needs to be said regarding Vincent in his capacity as the Queen's confessor is that his duties, though probably not very onerous, may have been somewhat embarrassing. The frivolous Anne no longer had the dreadful eyes of the Cardinal, which had seen everything and had let nobody guess anything as to his own thoughts, to observe her doings, or his cruel lips to report them to the King. And although there is absolutely no reason to suppose that at any time Anne had been worse than coquettish, Vincent, who was so particular about avoiding even the appearance of evil, must have needed all his tact to warn the lady not to give occasion to malicious tongues to gossip about her.

One of these pieces of gossip—though vigorously denied by Vincent, who ought to have been in the position to know—was that her relations with Mazarin exceeded the limits of the favour accorded a First Minister by his Sovereign. The report was spread, and is still believed by a good many historians, that she ended by marrying the Cardinal—something that is not materially impossible in view of the fact that he was only in Minor Orders. I believe that she was in love with the handsome Sicilian, as she was certainly under his complete domination. I express no opinion about the clandestine marriage, however, except to say that it has never been proved, but that Vincent's denial, on the other hand, would at best only suffice to set it after and not before 1652—which was when he finally ceased to attend Court. At all events, the relationship between the Queen and the Cardinal—whatever its nature may really have been—caused France in the years to come a great deal of suffering, and Vincent many years of difficulty.

ℂ 20. The Council of Conscience

WE HAVE already seen how Cardinal Richelieu consulted Vincent de Paul about the appointment of bishops, and how Louis XIII upon his death-bed said that, if he lived, he would never elevate anybody to the episcopate who had not passed through Vincent's hands. One of the first acts of Anne of Austria during her regency for Louis XIV was to set up a committee for the control of ecclesiastical affairs. That she did so is very much to her credit, for it showed her sincere desire to bring about reform in the Church. The wisest of her appointments to this body was that of Vincent de Paul.

When he heard of his new duty he was filled with consternation. He urged the Queen to remember that he already was weighed down by numerous affairs, and he protested his unfitness. It was no good; Anne had made up her obstinate little mind: she insisted that he take office. Vincent's own feelings about the matter are expressed to one of his Missionaries in Rome: "I never have been more worthy of compassion than I am now, nor have I stood in greater need of prayers than at present in the new office which I hold: I hope it will not last long." If Mazarin had had his way, Vincent would never have held it at all; the Cardinal would have much preferred that all such matters had come under his untramelled control. But as yet he had not established his domination over the Queen. For nine years therefore Vincent was able, with whatever distaste he had for his duties, to retain a position in which he was able to effect a great deal in the way of improving by degrees the condition of the French Church.

We need not, however, ascribe Vincent's reluctance to take a position in which he (in concert with others) had to act under the royal name as due to any special political enlightenment; it was merely that in his humilty he shrank from all personal honours. The current theory of the relation between Church and State was no doubt accepted by him, though he must have seen that it was by no means consistently applied. The coöperation of the civil and ecclesiastical functions, and the establishment of the Church, is still—at least officially—the Catholic ideal.[1] But it must be admitted to be one which is perhaps impossible of attainment except under exceptional conditions and (such is the tendency of all things human to corruption) only for short periods of time. At the bottom of all of Dante's concepts lies this ideal—which is why he is continually denouncing, and in the fiercest terms, the encroachment of the papal upon the imperial power. In the sixteenth and seventeenth centuries the drag was all in the other direction. The radical Erastianism of Henry VIII developed by degrees into the more moderate Erastianism of Elizabeth (though this became coupled with a much more drastic Protestantism). In the Germanies we had the principle of *cujus regio, ejus religio*. In France a middle position was reached under which the royal power, while it made no attempt to tamper with doctrine (and indeed upheld a strict orthodoxy) had a good deal to say about ecclesiastical government,—and this developed into Gallicanism. Vincent, therefore, acted for the Crown, but was hampered by the very fact of being a royal functionary from doing all he would have liked to have done for the Church. It was an exceedingly difficult position for any really spiritual man to be in.

The range of his duties was considerable and many of them

[1] Father Leonard believes Vincent de Paul to have had a clearer idea as to the theory of the relations between Church and State, and even a better grasp of secular politics, than he has been credited with in these pages. Certainly Vincent was a close friend of André Duval, the author of what was (for those days) a good book on political philosophy. That fact may be taken for what it is worth.

must have been disagreeable. Among minor matters there was
the reaffirmation and enforcement of the edicts against blasphemy and duelling. For after Richelieu's death many hot-
spirited men took advantage of the passing of the Cardinal
who was not to be trifled with—though even he had been obliged
to wink at cases which were not too flagrant—and began to re-
vive the custom of the *combat à outrance*. Vincent's method
was that of inducing all the marshals of France and many
prominent nobles to sign a pledge that under no circumstances
would they fight a duel. Something of the sort was badly needed.
How little the royal edicts were observed is indicated by the
fact recorded by de Grammont that nine hundred men died
in such combats during Anne's regency, which means that the
number of the more or less seriously wounded must have been
enormous.

The laws against blasphemy were naturally rather more difficult to enforce, as the crime was not always a simple one to
define or to detect. Vincent seems also to have taken the lead
in putting down customs that had arisen in many places of
turning carnivals and even religious processions into opportunities for unseemly horse-play that often verged upon indecency.
It must be remembered at the same time that he was not responsible for the making of these laws, but had merely the
obligation of trying to see that they were observed.

Though he was punctilious in carrying out the duties he had
been so reluctant to accept, he was, whenever this was possible,
very mild. The latter from which the following quotation comes
was, it is true, written before Vincent's membership of the
Council of Conscience, but it may be taken as an expression
of his general attitude to the fulminations some of the bishops
were only too ready to employ. Writing to Abelly in 1640—
when his future biographer was Vicar-General of Bayonne—
he says: "Just as a priest should be more perfect than a mem-

ber of a religious order, so, and much more so, should a bishop. And then, after having preached to them by way of example (Our Lord preached in that fashion for thirty years), he should deal with them graciously and charitably and, in the end, firmly, without however making use of suspensions, interdicts, and excommunications. . . . This, Sir, is how Our Lord acted. Now, I am firmly convinced that a prelate who acts in this manner will do more good to such persons than all ecclesiastical censures put together."

The tolerance and fairness of his mind appear in a letter dated 1644 giving directions as to the treatment of Protestants. Under the Edict of Nantes the Huguenots had certain privileges guaranteed to them. But inevitably it happened that cases were continually cropping up in which complaints were made that they were over-reaching their rights, or, on the other hand, that the local Governors were not acting fairly towards them. It was Vincent's practice to enquire carefully into the merits of every case and to hold the scales even. Justice as well as charity demanded as much. "How do you know," he writes, "if the Catholic has a really just claim to what he demands? There is a wide difference between being a Catholic and an honest man. Again, even if you were quite certain that he has a just claim, why do you not take into account that the Governor and the magistrates will judge the matter conscientiously? Is a Catholic less subject to justice because he is a Catholic?—Yes, but the judges are Huguenots.—It is true, but they are also lawyers, and judge according to the laws, customs and ordinances; and, apart from their consciences, they profess to be men of honour. . . . The Governor is far more clear-sighted about the duties of his office than you or I." Even if his confidence in the inherent justice of all magistrates was perhaps more generous than well-founded, it at least shows how scrupulous he

was about not using his influence against duly constituted
authority.

But business of this sort, though it probably occupied most
of the time of the Council of Conscience, was of course of much
less importance than other issues. These concerned the appointment of new bishops, the bestowal of important benefices, and
the reform of such religious communities as needed it. The good
estate of the Church in France depended to a very large extent
upon the right decisions being made: how necessary it was to
have worthy occupants of episcopal sees and abbacies may be
seen from the fact that there were something like a hundred
thousand secular priests, eighty-five thousand monks of various
orders, and eighty thousand nuns—all of whom were going to be
affected for good or for ill by their superiors.

Indeed the task was so vast that only a beginning could be
made. Except for positive heresy it was not possible to remove
an unworthy prelate. All one could do was to wait until death
took him. We have already seen how Vincent in his conversations with Potier, the Bishop of Beauvais (now one of his confrères on the Council, though a Jansenist), reached the melancholy conclusion that the older members of the secular clergy
were in many cases so hardened in their bad habits that it was
no use wasting time upon them. The only chance the Church
had was in creating in its younger clergy a better generation.
And now the problem had been complicated by the fact that
a large number of the more zealous and learned priests had
turned to the false reform of Jansenism.

Vincent had already contributed towards the renovation of
the priesthood by starting retreats for ordinands, by establishing his Tuesday Conferences, and by setting up—at the same
time that others were inspired with the same idea—seminaries
where clerics could be trained. Now his position on the Coun-

cil of Conscience gave him the opportunity for doing something towards raising the standard of the higher clergy.

The abuses up to this time were so deeply rooted in custom that it was necessary for even the most ardent reformer to proceed with caution. The bishoprics and the greater benefices had come to be looked upon by the nobility as a convenient means for making provision for their younger sons. In the larger and richer convents a system had developed under which an abbess arranged matters in such a way that a niece or some other relative was made her coadjutor with the right of succession. While it must be confessed that this form of nepotism sometimes worked tolerably well in practice—as nepotism commonly does—it was entirely false in principle (especially where spiritual authority was concerned) and only too often deplorable in its effects.

Yet it would not have been so bad if those appointed to offices in the Church made some attempt to perform the duties entrusted to them. Unfortunately they sometimes never so much as pretended to carry out their functions, or were even capable of doing so. The bishoprics—especially the wealthier bishoprics —were in many instances held by men who, though consecrated, never went near their dioceses. Still worse, there were bishoprics held by soldiers, royal bastards, or courtiers, who considered that they did enough by drawing the revenues and by appointing a Vicar General to do the actual work.

This was the device known as *in commendam*. The twindevice of holding a benefice "in confidence" was equally vicious. Under this a child in the cradle could be made an abbot, with the formal understanding that, after he had reached a certain age, he was either to resign or to enter the ecclesiastical state. But that obligation was easily disposed of by his appointing, when the time arrived, another ecclesiastic who, in consideration of a salary, bound himself to hand over the revenues to the lay beneficiary.

This corrupt system had arisen from the Concordat Francis I had made with the Holy See in 1516, or to a free interpretation of the terms of that agreement. It had served to prevent the great nobles of France—unlike those of England and Germany—from throwing in their lot with the Reformers in order to loot the Church. For there was no need for them to become Protestants when it was possible to remain good Catholics and still batten on the fat of sacrilege. It therefore eventuated in the Huguenots' gradually losing all their powerful leaders among the nobility and declining into insignificance.

But at what a cost had the safety of the Church been maintained! As an institution it was intact, but was slowly rotting. That it did not die the most ignoble of all deaths is due only to the providence of God. Perhaps one of the most striking signs of that providence was the Revolution which, in plundering the Church, gave it a new lease of life. Just at the moment when the corpse was about to be carried out to burial, it sat up.

It should, however, not be forgotten that in the seventeenth century a reform was initiated which, however much hampered in achieving its full results by the stubborn persistence of nepotism, at least checked some of the abuses. In this work of reform Vincent was the leader.

He had always seen clearly that the most crying need was for bishops worthy of their office. During Richelieu's administration he had been instrumental in getting several zealous priests elevated to the episcopate. But though at that time he had been exceedingly careful not to let it be known that he had any influence, now, as a member of the Council of Conscience, he could no longer conceal the fact that his recommendations had great weight with the Queen.

The result, as may easily be imagined, was that he was besieged by ambitious clerics. Very tactfully, very gently, with a profuse distribution of compliments, he contrived to excuse himself so effectually that it began to dawn on the more intelligent of these gentlemen that the most certain way of *not* getting a bishopric was to ask Vincent to take the matter in hand. They found it better to go direct to Mazarin himself, who was little troubled by the Vincentian scruples.

We have, for example, a letter written by Vincent during his term of office to a member of a religious order who had asked Vincent to recommend him. He explained that he was not actuated by ambition—oh no; but that he was getting old and his health had suffered from the strenuous work he had done as a preacher. A bishopric would provide a nice comfortable retirement for his declining days.

Vincent's reply was delicious. "I have no doubt," he wrote, "that your Reverence would work wonders in the episcopacy if you were called to it by God but, as He has let you see it is His will that you should carry out the duties of the state in which you now are, by the great success He has bestowed on your employments and ministrations, there is no indication that He wishes to remove you from them.

"If His providence called you to the episcopacy, it would not have recourse to yourself that you might seek it, but would rather inspire those in whom resides the power of appointment to ecclesiastical charges . . . without your making any advance whatever. . . . It seems there might be something to be said against your putting yourself forward, and that you would have no reason to hope for God's blessing on such a charge, which cannot be either sought after, or desired, by a really humble soul, such as yours.

"Moreover, Reverend Father, what an injury you would inflict on your holy Order by depriving it of one of its chief pillars, a man who sustains and brings it credit by his teaching

and example! . . . If you would attend to me, you would abandon preaching for some time, in order to re-establish your
health. You can still render great service to God and your
Order, which is one of the holiest and most edifying in the
Church of Jesus Christ."

If such a good man destroyed his chance for promotion precisely by asking for it, what chance had those who sought a
bishopric for less worthy motives? Even to Molé, the President of the Paris Parlement, Vincent advised the withdrawal
of the candidature of his son, to get from the father the frank
if pathetic confession: "I am an old man, and I am not rich,
and I have a large family. It is my duty to put my children
in good positions before I die. If my son lacks the qualities
for governing a diocese, he will always have some experienced
ecclesiastics to advise him." As that bishopric was, in fact, bestowed, we may be sure that it was because Molé was able to
work upon other members of the Council. Mazarin in particular
wanted to placate him.

We hear stories of benefice-hunters offering large bribes or of
threatening Vincent with physical violence. The most diverting
of these is one that the Abbé Maynard put into circulation and
which has found a place in most of the subsequent biographies,
though Père Coste assigns it a place among the legends. It is of a
Duchess who so far forgot herself in her rage when a bishopric
was refused her son as to throw a footstool at Vincent's head.
According to this account, Vincent merely wiped the blood off
his face and retired in good order murmuring, "What a wonderful thing is mother-love!"

Probably the genesis of this engaging anecdote is the fact
that many people were angry when their ambitions were
thwarted. Much more likely is the circumstantial incident related by Abelly of how the Comtesse de Chavigny—whose husband was then one of the Secretaries of State—asked and was

refused a couple of abbeys for her five-year-old son. Chavigny, however, who was more sensible than his wife, told Vincent that, so far from having any ill-will towards him on this account, he thought all the better of him. But then, of course, Chavigny was in a position to understand how useless such an application was.

For Vincent had induced his colleagues on the Council of Conscience to agree to certain regulations. Among these were that no pension was to be drawn from an episcopal see except in case of a bishop who had resigned because of ill-health or old age; that laymen should not have the revenues of any benefice; that before a man could be made a bishop he must have been a priest for at least eighteen months; that the position of coadjutor abbess should be restricted to nuns who were at least twenty-three years old and had been in religion for five years.

This was about as far as he found he could go. Those nominated "in confidence" to a benefice were to be at least eighteen in the case of abbeys, sixteen in the case of priories and canonries, and fourteen in the case of collegiate churches. Vincent found himself unable to remove ancient abuses entirely, but he managed to restrict them somewhat. If even these moderate regulations had been faithfully carried out a great deal of good could have been accomplished. But Vincent always had to contend with the wily Mazarin, to say nothing of some of the more worldly of the members of the Council. And to gain his ends —which were always political rather than religious—the Cardinal adopted the ingenious expedient of failing to notify Vincent as to the date when the Council was to meet.

There was another matter that fell within the province of this body: it was that of the reform of the religious orders. Richelieu had been sincerely anxious to effect this, and by way of doing so had appointed himself titular abbot of some of the greatest houses in France, using the *in commendam* system for once to a good purpose. But after his death, relaxation occurred again, so that, as Vincent put it, many an Order was really a disorder, "a body without any consistency or head, in which the members live without any government or common bond . . . a refuge for unruly or dissolute religious."

As it is only too easy for certain minds to picture bad conditions as being much worse than they actually were, perhaps Vincent's letter of 1652 to Cardinal Barberini had better be quoted; it relates to a community of nuns which had been driven away from their convent by the civil war and had come to Paris, where, says Vincent, "Many of them are leading scandalous lives." He specifies: "They spend their days in the houses of citizens, where they go visiting, and are shut up alone with men in their rooms; and when the Abbess was informed, by a very pious ecclesiastic, of the scandal given by these nuns she told him she could not remedy it, and begged him to speak to them himself, which he did; he told me that they answered as dissolutely as abandoned women would have done." Now of course that sounds very bad, but when Vincent talks about "scandalous lives" he is clearly meaning scandalous according to the standards of the religious life, not of the world. That these nuns could not have been guilty of anything worse than frivolous behaviour may be inferred from the horror with which Vincent tells Barberini, "There are several nuns who are not modest in their attire and, in the parlour, wear gloves, combs with rosettes of ribbons, or scarlet-coloured streamers, and gold watches and, when reprimanded for doing so by the Abbess, they said the Father Provincial had given them permission."

I am not trying to suggest that nothing worse was ever to be found among religious orders of men and women of the time than the breaking of enclosure and the wearing of gold watches and ribbons; no doubt there was. It could hardly be otherwise during a time when many men became monks for the sake of an easy life, and when many a girl—especially of good family—was put into the cloister by her parents for no other reason than that a husband had not been found for her. Having no vocation, such religious inevitably did not always submit easily to the restrictions of the monastic life. But the terms "scandalous" and "dissolute" when applied to them by a man like Vincent de Paul do not bear quite the same meaning they would in the case of lay people. We have only to glance at the fierce denunciations which Rancé hurled at the Benedictines and the Carthusians to realise what small infractions of the rule were enough to arouse criticism. Really one would have to infer from this example that the only place where the religious life was being well lived was at La Trappe, which was by no means the case.

It was, however, Vincent's duty as a member of the Council of Conscience to remedy so far as he could these irregularities. This he did by sending priests as visitators to the monasteries and convents of which he had heard bad reports, and to find religious houses into which those who had been driven from their own abode by the troubles of the Fronde could be received. It is, however, no more than fair to add that, if a few religious took advantage of the confusion of the times to leave their cloisters and to wander at large among their relatives and friends, we have ample testimony as to the pathetic constancy with which many a community clung to its convent in face of famine and the devastation of war.

In all this work Vincent received little enough support from the all-powerful Mazarin. His attitude towards religion is perhaps sufficiently indicated by the reproaches he used to give his nieces for not being sufficiently devout. He told them that they ought to hear Mass daily—"If not for God, at least for the world." It may readily be imagined that he was not in intimate sympathy with one whose attitude towards devotion was of a different character. As Collet puts it, the principles of Mazarin and Vincent were so opposed that one might think they had studied two different gospels.

The consequence was that there very soon began to be friction between them. The fact that the sole accusation of bad temper brought against a man to whose gentleness everybody else testifies comes from the Cardinal speaks volumes. Vincent, though anything but self-assertive, was resolute in all that appertained to the glory of God. Even as early as 1644 a rumour reached him from one of the Missionaries at Rome that he was to lose his position on the Council of Conscience, to which his reply was, "It is true that there are some indications that I shall not be tolerated much longer in this employment." He was very willing to resign, just as he had been very reluctant to accept office; but Anne of Austria still insisted on retaining his services.

That Vincent did have a good deal of influence over the Queen was quite enough to arouse Mazarin's animosity, since the Cardinal wanted to have Anne completely under his domination. In the *carnets* written by Mazarin during 1643 we read such notes as, "M. Vincent . . . is the canal through which everything reaches her Majesty's ears"; "M. Vincent wishes to advance Father Gondi"; "Father Gondi has spoken against me"; "All the ladies are plotting together"; and the significant note, "Do not hold a Council of Conscience for some time."

The Cardinal nevertheless was not able to dismiss Vincent until 1652, when he sent him a curt intimation that he was no longer a member of the Council. By that time Mazarin had contrived to bring the infatuated Anne of Austria to the desired point at which she would do anything he told her. To Vincent his fall was an immense relief. He had carried out his duties without fear or favour and had been able to introduce many reforms. But for some time his membership of the Council had been made merely nominal because of the artfulness with which the First Minister contrived to nullify most of his proposals. From Court circles, in which he had never been at home, he was glad to retire.

There are many indications that his position had been difficult for some time. One of the hardest things for a man to defend himself against is a stealthy stab, yet such stabs were made. Though he had refused anything like the appearance of a bribe—even to the extent of refusing all those good offices on behalf of his Congregation which might have been, with a clear conscience, accepted—rumours began to be spread that he was amenable to benefits. These were carried to the Queen who, knowing Vincent as she did, refused to believe them and asked him why he did not answer his accusers. This on one occasion he was tempted to do when he heard that it was being said of him circumstantially that he had promised a benefice in consideration of some books and six hundred livres. But he laid down the pen he had taken up to write a denial saying, "Miserable man, what are you doing? Here is a slave in Tunis who was accused of a crime of which he was innocent and yet died without a word of complaint! No, I will not defend myself." If his abstention was that of a saint, it was also that of a wise man who knows that in the end calumny recoils on the heads of those who set it in circulation. Having accepted office, he stuck to his work. When his dismissal came it was clear to all the world that it was due to Mazarin's personal hostility. Though, as M. Madelin urges in his book *La Fronde*, it is likely enough that Vincent's fall was due, at least in part, to his disapproval of Mazarin's continuation of Richelieu's policy.

ℂ 21. In the Wake of War

IN COMING to what Père Coste calls "the most sombre epoch for all works of charity," we also come to the epoch in which Vincent's charity shone most resplendently and in which his genius for organization was most clearly manifest. Yet he could not have accomplished what he did had he not already had available in the Fathers of the Mission and the Daughters of Charity two disciplined regiments for the distribution of alms and the performance of other corporal and spiritual works of mercy, and in the Ladies of Charity a long-established society upon whose devotion he could count and upon whose wealth he might draw to the limit. That he was not the sole worker in this field is true enough, and happily true; it may also be true that, in the face of overwhelming misery, what he was able to do was relatively little. But there is no occasion, on that account, to disparage, as Michelet did, his relief work. For it was an effort on a scale quite without previous precedent. Sixty millions of francs, it has been estimated, passed through Vincent's hands for the war-devastated regions; there can be no estimate as to the number of people prevented from dying from starvation or of souls saved.

This period, from 1639 (when Vincent began his operations) until 1653, when the need for them ended, or at least was diminished, was one of confusion that inflicted bitter sufferings upon the innocent peasantry. With the political issues involved he refused to concern himself and made a strict rule that they should not be so much as discussed by his Fathers. We can hardly practise the same abstention if we are to evaluate Vincent's achievement: something must be done therefore by way of indicating the setting, though the military history may be set to one side. On that point it is sufficient to say that during these fourteen or fifteen years we have the French phase of the Thirty Years' War, upon which, in its later stages, the Civil War of the Fronde was superimposed, and in such a way that one hardly knew from day to day who was going to be on the opposing sides, so frequently did the protagonists veer in their allegiance. And though during the Fronde there was not a great deal of actual fighting, the incessant marching and countermarching of troops that plundered all the districts through which they passed was as ruinous to the peasantry—perhaps even more so—than would have been battles themselves.

In order to understand the Fronde one must go back to the ambitions of the *Importants*, who were now in their death-struggle against the centralised authority of the Crown. When Henry IV was assassinated by Ravaillac, Sully remarked, "The day of the kings has passed; that of the princes and great men has arrived." It seemed to be a shrewd judgment, and it came at times close to being realised, for there had been in the air during the wars of religion—and on both sides—a spirit that might easily have hardened into definite republican doctrine.

Nevertheless, the astute Sully was mistaken: the day of the political power of the nobles was over; that of an absolute monarchy was about to dawn, even though the *Importants* at once began to form themselves into a league to protect their own interests against the Queen Regent, Marie de' Medici. It is in this fact more than in any other that we shall discover the key to the events of the next forty years.

Richelieu's policy—one that was continued and brought to a completely successful issue by Mazarin—at any rate the *effect* of that policy, was to sacrifice the internal good of France for the sake of the power and glory of the throne. The positive political aim was twofold: on the one hand to suppress everything—whether religious dissension or secular ambition—which threatened that throne, and, on the other hand, to secure the weakening of Spain and the Empire. The Treaties of Westphalia and the Pyrenees may be said to have achieved the second aim, the outcome of the Fronde to have demonstrated that the first aim had been achieved.

The internal policy seemed not only wise but inevitable. The Huguenot "State within the State" obviously could not be tolerated, though the Huguenots were given an honorable and definite status. The old feudal system that split up the country into semi-independent areas was also equally obviously out of date; the nobles had to be reduced to a privileged class dependent upon the monarchy but without any political authority. And it may be said that Richelieu was far more drastic in dealing with political intrigues against his supremacy than he was in his treatment of the Protestant minority who, when at last finally defeated in the field, were handled with moderation. As for the foreign policy directed towards the weakening of the Hapsburg Emperor, that, too, was necessary if France was to relieve the pressure that Spain (under another Hapsburg) was bringing to bear both in the North and the South. If it had ultimate results very different from those calculated upon by Richelieu, these were veiled from the eyes of a man who, though strikingly able to deal with an immediate situation, could not be expected to be a prophet of what the future had in store. It appeared to be absolutely imperative to prevent Ferdinand—who, however laudable the religious objects he had in mind, had also the political purpose of turning the Empire into a consolidated and powerful state—from effecting his designs. Therefore the revolt of the Protestant princes of the Empire was backed against Ferdinand in order to prevent the further encroachments of the house of Hapsburg. Many Catholics naturally viewed this alliance with Protestants with misgivings, and even Richelieu was hardly comfortable about it; there was, however, nothing else that he could do. Or nothing that a prudent judgment, weighing only the political factors, was prepared to accept.

Yet it was not until 1635 that France formally entered the Thirty Years' War. Up to that year the Cardinal had contented himself with giving aid—mostly of a financial sort—to Ferdinand's enemies, and had launched against him Gustavus Adolphus, whose success was so thorough as to be embarrassing to his French paymasters. But, according to the conventions of the time, support of this sort given by a third party to one of two parties already at war, did not amount to a declaration of hostilities by the third party. Not until Richelieu had been First Minister for eleven years did he at last decide to take the field.

Meanwhile he had been obliged to meet a series of conspiracies and revolts at home. Each time he emerged triumphantly, and settled scores with drastic executions. But the very fact that there were these recurrent challenges to his power showed how widespread was the resentment against it. That was why, soon after his death at the end of 1642, when the conduct of affairs passed to his protégé Mazarin, internal troubles began again. Those who had been cowed by the terrible Cardinal thought that their chance had come under his milder and (as they supposed) weaker successor. Hence they were not inclined to submit without a struggle, and despite Mazarin's victories and the signing of the Peace of Westphalia, brought about a disastrous civil war even at the moment while Spain was still an enemy and threatening from Flanders.

Had Louis XIII and Richelieu lived it is certain that there would have been no Fronde. At the first sign of rebellion scaffolds would have been erected and heads would have fallen; nor would the Cardinal have hesitated—as is shown by his execution of Montmorency—to visit with condign punishment even the most exalted of rebels. But Mazarin was made of softer stuff. He preferred to seek his ends—which, after all, were those which he had inherited from Richelieu and which circumstances obliged him to accept—by means of elaborate finesse, the buying off of opponents with money or offices, and by making, when things got too hot for him, a strategic retreat that was always a prelude to re-establishment. All the same, one so universally hated could hardly have succeeded had he not possessed the unbounded confidence—and I think we must add, the passionate love—of the Queen Regent.

Yet if France hated Mazarin it was not solely on his own account. He was personally far from unattractive, except for his avarice; and the fact that he was an Italian adventurer—though here the memory of Concini was much to his disadvantage, as was Anne's Spanish birth to her—was the pretext rather than the cause of the detestation in which he was held. The truth is that he was saddled not only with Richelieu's policies but with Richelieu's many public and private enemies. Now they believed they had their chance for revenge. And though by a combination of skill and luck Mazarin was victorious in the struggle, the cost to France (except for the diplomatic outcome) was enormous, especially to the common people.

It would be impossible to deal in these pages, even in summary outline, with the tangled events of the Fronde. But certain facts should be pointed out: what was potentially a thoroughgoing revolution was due to many causes. The fatigue of the Thirty Years' War, so far from disposing men's thoughts to peace, made them restless. The struggle between King and Parliament in England seemed to many in France to sanction the struggle between the Parlement of Paris, jealous of its prerogatives, and a monarchy which was under the control of Cardinal Mazarin. There were indeed many legitimate grievances, in particular the crushing incidence of taxation, which fell most heavily upon those least able to support it. Had the

Fronde possessed a definite and consistent policy, and had it contrived to hold the royal family as hostages in Paris, it might well have happened that the later Revolution could have been anticipated in a bloodless fashion.

But no bond of union appeared except the general hatred of Mazarin. The Parlement hoped to reassert itself; Gaston hoped for the Lieutenant-Governorship of the Kingdom and Condé for command of the armies: that was about all. While Anne of Austria was personally gibed at for her supposed relations with her all-powerful First Minister, as Queen Regent she retained respect, even as her son, the young Louis XIV, was held in reverence. The French people—except in isolated instances—were not yet capable of formulating a republican doctrine. The Parlement in 1648 believed, or professed to believe, that it was fighting in the King's true interests—of course against Mazarin. But the princes and nobles who led the second phase of the Fronde, who hated Mazarin even more furiously than did the Parlement, were merely seeking more personal power. Accordingly all principles were soon lost sight of, and the issues degenerated into simple selfishness.

In Paris the populace was inflamed by de Retz, as yet only coadjutor Archbishop, a master of political oratory and intrigue. He humorously notes that on Maundy Thursday of 1649 the President of the Parlement remarked to him that at the blessing of the Holy Oils that day he must have used a generous mixture of saltpetre—which exactly hits off his relation to the events. He was the go-between of the Princes and the Parlement, but his main motive in the affair was the securing of a cardinal's hat for himself. His speciousness was typical of that of nearly all the Frondeurs. Had Louis XIV not been a minor, rebellion would have been unmistakably treasonable. As things stood, however, it could be represented as loyalty to the Crown and resistance to the encroachments of Mazarin.

It was for this reason that we find not only de Retz but Condé and Turenne turning sides with bewildering facility and even bringing in Spaniards to their support. And for a time we find the Parlement—disgusted at the arrogance of Condé who, though a soldier of genius (as we should guess from his hawk-like portrait, even if we lacked the witness of history), was hopelessly inept in politics—in favour of the momentarily less obnoxious Mazarin. Indeed the whole business is so confused that it is not easy to discover what it was really all about, or at any given moment just what was happening.

Perhaps it was the long tedium the Court had had to endure under Louis XIII that now partly explains the frantic desire to find any sort of excitement. Anne herself, whose boredom had been as extreme as the neglect her husband had shown her, found it delicious to have in Mazarin one who was solicitous in providing her with all the dramatic entertainments and frivolity she craved, and a master to whom she could abandon herself. As the Cardinal was to put it, "He who has the heart, has all." He certainly studied carefully the best means of holding Anne's somewhat silly little heart.

It was with infinite finesse that he gradually established his domination over her, so that for a long time the Court did not guess how complete that domination was. The courtiers at first regarded him as no more than a useful official whose services were required to clear up outstanding business, and who would then be dismissed; it perfectly suited Mazarin that they should think so. His consultations with the Queen Regent were held at night in Anne's oratory in order that they might not attract too much attention. The courtiers saw only that Her frivolous Majesty got plenty of amusements, and, as they shared in these, they were disposed at once to enjoy them and not to take their purveyor too seriously. Under such circumstances nobody could suspect the Cardinal of deeper designs. As de Retz expressed it, he let people think he was standing by their side until they found his foot upon their heads.

To quote de Retz again: "The first four years of the regency were in some sort carried along by the rapid motion that Cardinal Richelieu had given the royal authority." In other words, the administrative machinery functioned—or so those thought who did not know the truth—of its own accord. Meanwhile Mazarin, with his Italian cunning, went to the length—as we may see from some of the entries in his note-books—of instructing the Queen Regent to make public complaints about him, so as to throw people off the scent of what was really taking place. Docile to all he said, Anne did so; and, at the very moment that the vanity of the Princes was being flattered by this wily trick, the Cardinal was busily consolidating his power. When at last the world woke up to the actual state of affairs, it discovered that, though Mazarin was on the surface mild and flexible, as compared with the ruthless Richelieu, he was just as resolute in attaining his ends.

In spite of all this, the Fronde rebellion—whose essential triviality is indicated by its very name (stone-slinging)—must inevitably have succeeded had it possessed a purpose more definite than that of getting rid of Mazarin, or had its leaders been able to hold together. But the Frondeurs soon showed that in one way or another they could be bought. And its weakness appeared in what we are now accustomed to think of as its most picturesque element—the part women played in it.

It was in fact much too picturesque—and not serious enough. To be against Mazarin was the fashionable thing, one to be very much enjoyed. The wives and the mistresses of the nobles had, even more than the men concerned, only the vaguest notion of principle. It was such good fun for them to taste the delights of political intrigue or even occasionally—as in the case of "la Grande Mademoiselle," the valiant if absurd daughter of the craven Gaston—to take part, or make believe that they were taking part, in military action. Some of these ladies had their own devices for attaching men to the cause, and conferred their amorous favours freely. Dissolute, greedy, unscrupulous and fickle, they were bound to ruin the Fronde in the end. For as soon as these great ladies diverted the issue from the reasonable protests made by the Parlement that the royal power was being abused, constitutional rights infringed, and the burden of taxes too onerous to be borne, then only personalities were thought of and the matter became a *guerre pour rire*, a theatrical marching about with banners and trumpets. One killed one's enemies with epigrams in gilded salons to applauding laughter. But there were few military actions, and none that was decisive.

Even the arrest of Condé, Conti and Longueville in January 1650 was a comedy. Nobody protested, so great by then had grown Condé's arrogance. Yet a year later, when the situation called for one of Mazarin's self-imposed periods of exile, he went himself to release his prisoners, hoping to win them to his side—and was greeted with peals of merriment. Nevertheless Condé laughed too soon; the Cardinal's retreat was once again strategic. From long-range he continued to advise Anne of Austria, and by the end of 1652 he had re-established full control.

But however glamorous and exhilarating the affair was to the great nobles and their women, it brought only untold suffering to the mass of the people. Therefore Vincent's first action was to attempt to restore peace. He had already done something similar during the Thirty Years' War when he pleaded with Richelieu to bring hostilities to an end, only to be told, politely but coldly, that, before that could happen, a number of other people would have to agree. This time, however—since the continuation of the Fronde depended upon the will of the Queen Regent and her First Minister—he believed, or perhaps only hoped against hope, that a personal interview with them would bring about the desired results. Usually he moved with extreme slowness; on this occasion prompt action was called for. Accordingly on January 14, 1649, only a few days after Anne and her children had slipped away to Saint-Germain, he went there himself.

He was well aware of the risks that he ran. The inflamed Paris populace, which knew of his connexion with the Court, was only too likely to look upon him as a royal partizan—or rather "Cardinalist"—and did in fact during his absence plunder the granaries of Saint-Lazare. And from the other side there was equal danger, for Mazarin, because of Vincent's friendly relations with such dissimilar Frondeurs as Gondi, Olier and de Retz, held him in suspicion.[1] Nevertheless he was well received by the Queen, who sent him to see the Cardinal. And the Cardinal in his turn listened to what he had to say—showing no anger even at the pointed suggestion that, in view of the rage he inspired, he should resign—though he promised nothing except that he would consult Le Tellier, well aware that Le Tellier could be safely counted upon to echo his own decisions.

Very characteristically, Vincent used afterwards to set down his failure to the over-vigorous language he had employed. We may, however, be sure that, unpalatable as his proposal was, it was couched as gently as possible. The true explanation would seem to be that he was not temperamentally fitted for political negotiation, though it should be added that this was a situation in which even the most adroit politician might well have failed. Mazarin did not have the slightest intention of yielding; or Anne of letting him go. Further, any yielding on the part of the Court—at any rate after the Princes had begun to take

---

[1] If de Broglie is correct in saying that Vincent "belonged naturally to the Frondeurs," the Saint was careful not to give any indication of it. Instead, his constant aim was to remain on good terms with both sides.

their share in the Fronde—would have resulted only in hopeless civil disorder. The centralised monarchy, however unenlightened, at least was the only force in France capable of exercising authority. The Parlements could not have done it; the great nobles had no other concern than their selfish ambitions. Therefore the burlesque war had to drag to its close of exhaustion.

The two wars which, it must be remembered, could, during the time of the Fronde, be hardly distinguished from one another, may, for the sake of convenience, be considered here, as they must have appeared to all except the very wealthy, as a single long-drawn-out process of misery. The geographical areas were not quite the same—the Thirty Years' War being fought in the Eastern and Northern provinces (though the Spaniards got in 1636 to Corbie), and the Fronde manœuvres being closer to Paris (though there were operations at Orleans and Bordeaux). In each case, however, there were mercenary armies brought in—whether of Croats or Poles or Walloons or Hungarians or Bohemians or Swedes or Spaniards mattered little —and mostly these armies were under generals hardly to be distinguished from brigands.

Not that the French armies were much to be preferred, even by their own countrymen. All the soldiers lived in the only way they could live—by plundering the districts through which they passed. It was useless to make any protest against their behaviour, for the answer of the officers was that, as their men were not paid, they had to help themselves to whatever they were able to snatch. Such license was, not unnaturally, freely interpreted by brutal and undisciplined men to mean that they might torture the peasants for hidden hoards—which were more often than not non-existent—or force them to disgorge by ravishing their wives and daughters before their eyes. Anybody who objected to the proceedings got killed.

Sometimes, as in the case of a man named Oudard and nicknamed "Captain Grind-Iron," the peasants formed themselves into bands to resist these depredations. Then they were before long tempted to pillage on their own account. There really was nothing for the unhappy people to do except flee. If they attempted to raise any live-stock, these were commandeered; their grain-fields were trampled into mud, their barns robbed. And if they had nothing that the soldiers could steal, they were murdered.

The foulness of this kind of war is beyond description. The peasants were reduced to living upon the carcasses of dogs and horses and on grass, tree-bark, or a bread made from clay mixed with straw. We hear of a woman at Mirecourt being sentenced to death for having eaten a child she had strangled; of a mother making a bargain with another to eat her own baby on condition that the other woman did the same; of children devouring the bodies of their dead parents; and even of a group of children killing and eating a child younger than themselves. Some people, made desperate by hunger, tried to prolong their lives another day or two by feeding on their own hands. Even if these extreme horrors be discounted, there can be slight question that fiendish things were done or that the suffering of the poor over wide areas reached the very limit of human endurance.[2]

The letter Vincent de Paul wrote to the Pope towards the close of the Fronde sets out soberly and with exact knowledge (even if in general terms) what was happening. He describes towns, villages and cities burnt to the ground; the peasants unable to reap what they had sown and so making no further effort to look after their fields; and continues: "The soldiers indulge, with impunity, in the worst excesses, and expose the

---

[2] In Germany many cases of cannibalism were reported. It is actually said that in the Palatinate the bodies of hanged malefactors were regularly sold in the butcher shops.

people not only to rapine and plunder, but also to murder and all forms of torture. Such country-folk as have not been smitten by the sword are almost all dying of hunger. Priests, whom the soldiers do not spare any more than they do the rest of the people, are inhumanly and cruelly treated, tortured, and put to death. Virgins are dishonoured, and even nuns exposed to libertinism and rage. Temples are profaned, pillaged and destroyed; those that remain standing are, for the most part, abandoned by their pastors, so that the people are almost deprived of the Sacraments, Mass, and all spiritual succour. Lastly, a thing horrible to think of, and still more horrible to utter, the Most Holy Sacrament of the body of Our Lord is treated with the greatest indignity, even by Catholics, for, in order to plunder the sacred vessels, they cast down and trample on the Holy Eucharist. What, then, is the conduct of heretics, who do not share in these mysteries? I neither dare nor can express it. It is but a small thing to hear and speak of these things; they must be seen with one's own eyes." And while all this was going on, the great gentlemen and ladies on both sides, most of whom considered themselves very good Christians, thought war a pleasant diversion. It is the usual story: those who make wars are not the ones who have to suffer. They saw only the flags gallant in the breeze and heard the stirring trumpet; they did not see a scarecrow of a peasant gnawing a lizard or a snake in a ditch.

What Vincent de Paul told the Pope about the Fronde applies equally to the Thirty Years' War. In the face of such calamities he raised contributions and arranged for their distribution. During the earlier war Louis XIII put at his disposal forty-five thousand livres for the monasteries of Lorraine; the Ladies of Charity subscribed money and sold their plate; and while the Fathers of the Congregation went to the devastated areas to minister to the needs of the people, a lay-brother named

Matthew Régnard distinguished himself by carrying funds to the needy.

This was anything but an easy task, because of the roving bands of soldiery who were always looking for somebody to rob. But the good Brother was so skilful in outwitting marauders that he came to be called "Reynard." Dressed like a beggar, he often had upon himself huge sums, and when he saw soldiers approaching he used to drop his purse into a bush and return afterwards when the road was clear. Once, when he was carrying thirty-four thousand livres, a horseman appeared too suddenly to allow him to adopt his favourite stratagem. Yet even this time "Brother Reynard" was a bit too much for the bandit. Seizing a moment when the horseman's gaze was turned the other way, he quietly got rid of the wallet, and when he was searched there was nothing in his pocket but a knife. His dangers increased as the fame of his cunning spread, but his look of bland innocence and—as he put it—the prayers of Monsieur Vincent always brought him safely through. He distributed, mostly in small sums, about sixteen hundred thousand livres in all.

In order to excite interest in the conditions of the distressed people Vincent decided to make his appeal for funds through pamphlets which would give eye-witnesses' accounts of what was occurring. As the editor of the *Relations* (which was, in effect, a kind of newspaper), Maignart de Bernières, the Jansenist treasurer of the Company of the Blessed Sacrament, was appointed. This was no time for Vincent to enquire too closely into the orthodoxy of his helpers, and it should be added that Port-Royal contributed four hundred thousand livres to the work of relief.

In the cause of charity the opposed theological camps united their forces. And of course the Ladies of Charity had constant collaboration from the Company of the Blessed Sacrament, where the moving spirit, as usual, was the Baron de Renty. Though it would be false to say that everything was done directly at Vincent's instance—for there was a great deal of private charity, and many public collections came to him merely because he happened to be in the position to use them to the best advantage—it is no more than just to say that in everything he took the lead, that he stood in the popular mind as the very embodiment of public relief, and that he accomplished more than everybody else put together. It was to him that the Queen applied when she wanted nurses sent to the battlefields, and he supplied her with Sisters of Charity—probably the first attempt to have regular nursing in war. And when the Fronde disturbances broke out he had an accumulated experience which could be put to effectual use.

We have seen how he appealed in vain to Mazarin for peace. Having failed in his efforts, he then wrote to the Ladies of Charity begging them to raise money to help the poor. " 'Have you yet resisted unto blood?' " he asks. "Or, at least, have you sold some of the jewels in your possession? What am I saying, Ladies? I know for a fact that many of you—I believe nearly all of you—have given alms which would be regarded as great even if given by queens; the very stones would cry out against me if I were to be silent about this; and it is on account of your incomparably charitable hearts that I speak as I now do." The Ladies, as he was well aware, had in many instances been hard hit by the political troubles and could not lay their hands on ready cash; therefore he asks them to sell their jewels.

How they responded to his appeal is shown by the vast sums he was again able to raise. Yet the money at his disposal had to be dispensed very carefully in view of the widespread need. To make it go as far as possible he set up soup-kitchens under the charge of the Daughters of Charity and the Missionaries, and provided recipes for making a nourishing soup at an as-

tonishingly low cost—Mother Angélique Arnauld of Port-Royal
herself sending him one of these. If the actual recipe does not
strike us as very enticing, we must remember the French capacity for devising culinary wonders out of next to nothing, and
the fact that starving people were not likely to be over-fastidious
so long as they got something to satisfy their ravening hunger.

There were other things to be done—some of them very un-
pleasant. There was not only famine but plague at this time;
and after a battle the bodies of the slain were left to rot and
contaminate the air. Vincent charged his Missionaries with the
task of hiring grave-diggers and of officiating at burials. There
was no task so disagreeable that it could be neglected.

But the main task remained the care for the living. As the
soup-kitchens were only for immediate emergencies, Vincent organized the supplying of grain and farming utensils to the
peasants who had been despoiled, and he gathered together girls
who could be trained as domestic servants and boys who could
be taught a trade. Now the merely needy were not eligible for
help, only the destitute. So that the village priests might remain in their parishes, he found them small salaries; and to
women who had no other means of support he gave spinning-
wheels and flax. If all this no more than touched the edge of
the desolation wrought by the folly of the civil war, again it
saved thousands of people from death and other thousands
from final ruin. Day and night with all the means at his disposal Vincent toiled to save France from the disasters of the
Fronde. He cannot be blamed for not having performed impos-
sibilities; what he did perform looked like miracles.

Nevertheless this did not exempt him from public insult in
the streets of Paris by people who accused him of being responsible for the taxes levied by the government on the poor.
As one venturing upon the rôle of peace-maker, he inevitably
received blows from both sides. The wonder is how he escaped

personal violence; that he did so is a testimony to the fact that the majority both of the courtiers and the unfortunate sufferers from the war realised that he was doing all one man could do to alleviate the general misery.

Then once again, in a long letter written on September 11, 1652, he urged Mazarin to the only course that would bring about peace. Paris, he tells the Cardinal, is now crying out for the return of the young King and the Queen Regent. But he strongly advises Mazarin not to return to the city with the Court lest his presence should stir up strife anew. "It does not matter, My Lord, very much whether Your Eminence returns before or after the King does so, provided you do return, and that, once the King is re-established in Paris, His Majesty can recall you at pleasure. . . . But while men's minds are in their present condition, and because the foolishness of the public demands it"—it would be advisable for Mazarin to stay away. The letter was as friendly as it was sensible, and the Cardinal this time did follow Vincent's advice, and kept at a safe distance until the following February. All the same, he did not forget or forgive the letter: he took his revenge by immediately dismissing Vincent from the Council of Conscience. But the Fronde was over; peace had at last come to the stricken land.

It was just like Vincent to give others the credit for what he had done. But in this case his praise was deserved, for the Ladies of Charity had supplied the money for the relief he had inspired and organized. Characteristic, too, was his argument that they should be thankful to heaven for having given them the chance to perform these good works: "Are you not moved to gratitude for God's goodness towards you and towards these poor afflicted people? . . . History does not tell us that anything like it ever happened to the ladies of Spain, Italy, or any other country. That was reserved for you, Ladies, who are here present, and for those others who are with God, in Whom they have found an ample recompense for such perfect charity."

ℂ 22. The Widening Field

THE activities already mentioned would have been quite sufficient, it might be supposed, to have satisfied even the most energetic of men. Those that remain to be treated in this chapter, if dealt with in proportion to the details we possess—which, after all, are nothing compared to the mass of detail which has been lost—would easily fill a substantial book. Here I propose to condense in the most drastic fashion.

The Abbé Maynard has called Vincent de Paul "the most positive and efficient organizer the world has ever seen." And his achievements are all the more remarkable when we remember that he had to work without any of the appliances of modern efficiency, without typewriters or filing-cabinets or card-indices or any of the means of swift communication of our day. To a considerable extent he made up for this lack by a prodigious memory and a still more prodigious industry. Nothing seemed to be too insignificant for his consideration or for his personal attention. So that at one of the busiest periods of his life, when he was occupied both at Court and in the multifarious activities at Saint-Lazare, he took it as quite a natural thing that a tailor who had once worked there should write asking him to buy him some needles of a kind that could be got only in Paris. Imagine how the modern efficiency expert would have spluttered with wrath at being bothered with such a request, and how quickly the tailor's letter would have gone into the waste-paper basket!

But there had now come a certain physical slowing-down. As Vincent paid no attention to his increasing infirmities, the Archbishop of Paris had to take it upon himself to order him not to overtax a body that could no longer be expected to function as before. And Cardinal de la Rochefoucauld added his remonstrances. Unless somebody with the necessary authority had stepped in to restrain him, Vincent (the most prudent of men in all other respects) would have neglected ordinary prudence with regard to his health. His heart and mind were still young, and remained so until the end.

Thus we find him in 1649, when he was nearly seventy and ill, riding to the Court at Saint-Germain through a country full of undisciplined soldiers and charging on horseback across the Seine on a bridge flooded by the rising waters. The young Brother Ducournau, who accompanied him, confessed afterwards that his own heart was in his mouth all the time. When he went back to Paris the Duchesse d'Aiguillon saw to it that it was by a carriage she presented to him. Yet though he could not very well refuse to travel by it on that journey, he would not use it again until the Archbishop of Paris laid him under obedience. Then he consented at last to ride in it, humorously grumbling about his "disgrace."

The kind-hearted Ladies of Charity were obliged to use a high hand towards him, scolding him when he went out to preach a mission, or letting the Fathers know what they thought of them for letting the old man go. For he had long been ill with recurring fevers and with legs so badly swollen that in the end all excursions from Saint-Lazare became impossible. Nevertheless he never submitted to being bedridden or to a cessation from work. The fire of charity in his breast would not allow him to stop. When he could no longer personally take part in missionary work—a work he always felt so badly performed that it seemed to him upon returning to Paris that the city gates ought to fall upon his head—he continued to direct everything, accepting no more than the aid of a couple of secretaries for his enormous correspondence.

He not only went on with the old work of directing the Ladies of Charity and the Daughters of Charity and his Order and the seminary and the retreats and conferences, but he constantly added new work to the old. Never did he get into a rut. Yet no fresh scheme was ever started without his having first thought the whole matter out to its smallest details. In the same way he kept his finger upon everything that afterwards happened. The mere list of what has to be crowded into this chapter would be staggering.

The secret of it all is contained in a letter written about 1650: "The good which God wishes to be done is done as it were without our thinking about it; that is the way in which our Congregation came into existence, the way the missions and retreats for ordinands began, the way the Company of Daughters of Charity arose, the way the association of Ladies to assist the poor in the Hôtel-Dieu and the parochial sick was established . . . the way in which all the works of which we now find ourselves in charge first saw the light. Not one of these works was deliberately undertaken by us but God, Who wished to be served on these occasions, brought them about imperceptibly and, if He made use of us, nevertheless we never knew to what they were going to lead." Yet Vincent, as the instrument of Providence, never did anything haphazard but only after long consideration and a delay that often seemed to those associated with him to be unnecessary. This most indefatigable was also the least precipitate of men.

The new activities taken up by Vincent de Paul may be broadly classified as of four kinds: those extending the work of the Fathers and the Sisters to other Catholic countries; projects to re-establish the Faith in countries where it had been lost; missions to the heathen; and finally fresh charitable designs. It is interesting, and a little pathetic, however, to see how as time went on Vincent came at intervals to despair of Christendom, as he found it at home, and began to dream that the Kingdom of Christ would have to be founded in lands that had not yet heard His name.

There is a letter, for instance, written in 1646 to Dehorgny, then Superior at Rome, which (in part) reads: "I must confess I have, I think, a great affection and devotion for the propagation of the Church in infidel lands, which arises from the fear I entertain that God may gradually bring her to naught in Europe and that little or nothing may remain of her here in a hundred years' time, on account of the corruption of our morals, the new opinions which are spreading more and more, and the general state of public affairs. In the last hundred years the Church has lost, through two new heresies, the greater part of the Empire and the Kingdoms of Sweden, Denmark, Norway, Scotland, England, Ireland, Bohemia, and Hungary, so that only Italy, France, Spain, and Poland now remain to her, and there are many heresies both in France and Poland. Now, these losses of the Church during the last hundred years give us reason to fear that, in another hundred years, the Church in Europe may be totally lost and, bearing this fear in mind, blessed are those who can co-operate in the extension of the Church in other lands."

That is sufficiently explicit, though there is no need to take it for more than the expression of a very human mood of despondency. From such despondency, however, we may take heart; it was shared by many thoughtful Catholics in those days: to all appearances, the cause of the Church *had* been lost. And it had in large part been brought about by a man for whose high gifts and good intentions Vincent de Paul had sincere respect—Cardinal Richelieu. We know, however, from other letters and addresses, that Vincent considered that the reason for despair went deeper—and was due to what he saw of the corruptions of the Church, the corruptions that he was one of the chief means of correcting.

We have the advantage (though it is of course nothing to our credit) of living nearly three hundred years later. We have seen how in our time the two heresies so dreaded by Vincent—those of Calvinism and Lutheranism—have blown up, so that the Protestantism we are acquainted with is a vague and amorphous thing of no intellectual consequence and with no power of renewing itself.

On the other hand we have seen Catholicism come to regained life time after time in the very places where it seemed to be almost extinct. In Vincent's own France at the end of the eighteenth century there was virtually no man of learning and intelligence who did not consider the Church moribund; yet it was suddenly regalvanised. Ireland (as we notice from his letter) Vincent considers as good as lost, and Poland in danger. In both places the danger has passed, though it would be rash to say that it will not (in some form or other) show itself again even there. Meanwhile we are being threatened with a totalitarianism that would extirpate everything that interferes with the modern heresy, state-worship, system-worship and the myth of the sacred Aryan blood. And again some Catholics are in a panic.

But these things too will pass: the Rock on which the Church is built can be shaken but does not fall. So though one may exercise one's ingenious fancy in picturing a Pope in Alaska surrounded by a tiny consistory of Chinese and negro cardinals —"The Son of Man, when he comes, shall he find faith on the earth?"—all the lessons drawn from history ought to be heartening to a Catholic. Still there are foes without, and more insidious foes within the fold. Depression is likely to seize upon anyone who contemplates—not the kind of gross immorality prevalent in Vincent's time—but the general lack of fervour now shown even by those who are reckoned as good Catholics, and—though this is something that few like to face, still less admit—the ravages that the practice of birth-control is making. Nevertheless, Catholics may be of good courage: these things too will pass. The hunger for God is inextinguishable in man; fervour will return. Totalitarianism is not only anti-Christian but so anti-human that it already lies under sentence of death, though it may triumph for a while. And birth-control is the child of the present artificial civilization which in turn is the child of an economic order already dying. New foes will, of course, arise to the end of time and will make Christians as yet unborn again wonder whether the end of all is not upon them. They will have to meet their own terrors as these arise; let us not be dismayed by our own. Vincent, as we see, feared for the Church. But as Miguel de Unamuno has well said, "Many of the greatest heroes, perhaps the greatest of all, have been men of despair and . . . by despair they have accomplished their mightiest works." We may therefore draw courage from Vincent's fear—and from the advantage we have over him in experience. If we must indulge our imaginations, it had better be in trying to picture the development of Catholicism as it will be after the wisdom of India and China, the warmth of Africa, the energy of America and Australia, and the wistful mysticism of the Slav have made their contributions. I, for one, flatly decline to worry about Patagonian popes hiding their diminished heads in Alaska. The Church is still young.

But though I think Vincent de Paul wrong in his surmise, he was a thousand times right in his decisions. The patient persistence with which he went forward in the gathering gloom is perhaps the highest mark of his heroic sanctity. His period of greatest activity is the one that follows the period of his worst depression. Though to his human eye all seemed lost, or at least in danger of being lost, his supernatural insight was never keener. Because of the crumbling world, he trusted in God.

For the sake of order, though not of chronology, we may

now glance—it can be no more than a glance—at the four types of activity mentioned at the beginning of this chapter.

First, however, it would be as well to say a word about the extent of the Congregation of the Mission, since it was upon this that all of Vincent's other undertakings depended. Slowly but steadily—for Vincent always preferred solid upbuilding to showy adventures—good houses and seminaries were erected, of which there were twenty-three of the one and fifteen of the other at the close of his life. The chief establishments were the foundation at Richelieu (endowed by the Cardinal), and those at Marseilles and Rome, mainly supported by the Duchesse d'Aiguillon.

Generally all this new work went forward very placidly, but one celebrated "row" occurred which seems very amusing in retrospect, but was of course distressing to Vincent at the time. It was arranged by the Bishop that the Missionaries should establish a seminary in the decayed Abbey of Saint-Méen, an arrangement to which the Benedictines vigorously objected. They appealed to and were upheld by the Parlement of Rennes, while the Bishop, armed with the King's sanction, found support in the Duc de Meilleraye, the Governor of Brittany. The Duke sent a detachment of soldiers who rode into the abbey church and rudely ejected the Benedictines with shouts of "Outside, monks! Outside!" Vincent instructed the local superior to hold firm, though his argument that a bishop has a right to dispose of a religious house which has outlasted its usefulness may be open to argument. The correctness of his behaviour—apart from his theory—was upheld at the time of his beatification, when it was brought into question by the *Advocatus diaboli*, Prosper Lambertini,[1] afterwards Pope Benedict XIV. Rome

[1] Lambertini did not fail also to bring up Vincent's friendship with Saint-Cyran, and the alchemical experiments in Barbary. If he did not mention Vincent's getting ordained long before the canonical age, and his holding several benefices while he was still Curé of Clichy, this was only because

also upheld the Bishop and the Congregation of the Mission, it is worth noting, in 1646, but only after some years' consideration of the matter. Apart from this incident, the work went forward uneventfully, though once or twice (as in the case of the seminary founded at Alet) the Vincentians had to abandon their undertaking when they found that local conditions were such as to prevent their fulfilling their proper functions.

The first country outside of France to receive Missionaries was Italy, and this came about largely as an accident, though if the particular event which took them there had not occurred, no doubt another would have done so. In 1631 Vincent found it necessary to send a personal representative to the Holy See at the time when the authorization of the Congregation (at first refused) was under consideration. This was Du Coudray. His function was both to serve as a diplomatic agent and to demonstrate by the missions he gave the nature and value of the work of the new Society. Louis Lebreton, who succeeded him in 1639, was seldom called on to transact business at the Vatican and so was free to give all his time to preaching. The Roman Compagna at that time was a desert inhabited only by a few people whose spiritual wants (though they were so near the centre of Christendom) were completely neglected. The success of the Missionaries induced the ever-generous Duchesse d'Aiguillon to found a house at Rome—on condition that a daily Mass was said for the repose of the soul of her famous uncle, whom she had good reason to presume to be badly in need of prayers—and this brought invitations from the Cardinal Durazzo, the Archbishop of Genoa, and from the Archbishop of Turin, for the establishment of the Congregation in their dioceses. The work done was

he was unaware of these facts. In any case the weight of positive evidence in favour of Vincent's heroic virtue would have been overwhelming even against so adroit an ecclesiastical lawyer.

along the same lines as that directed from Saint-Lazare—not only missions to the peasantry but clerical retreats and conferences. It need not be recapitulated.

What is of special interest, however, is the series of missions given in Corsica. Here the Fathers encountered something very strange. Not only did all the men of the congregation come to church fully armed because of the constant vendettas, but the Corsican priests never laid aside their weapons even in church. Thus we hear of one cleric vesting for a procession of the Blessed Sacrament and sticking a pistol in the girdle under his cope. As he was about to take a second, Père Martin, who was conducting the mission, ventured to remonstrate, only to get the reply, "It's evident that you do not understand this country. When a vendetta is going on, the first person to be attacked is an ecclesiastic. However, to please you, I'll take only *one* pistol today." It was perhaps a rather curious fruit of grace.

The lay people of Corsica could hardly be brought to grasp the necessity for forgiving their enemies and for laying aside their national passion for revenge. Yet even that miracle was accomplished. During his last sermon, the preacher, who was determined not to leave the island with his work unaccomplished, dramatically held up the crucifix and called out, "Will all those who are ready to forgive come up and kiss the Saviour!" But though the congregation was visibly moved, no man could bring himself to do something so contrary to the Corsican code of honour, until a Franciscan came forward to lead the way, prostrated himself on the ground, kissed the proffered crucifix and announced that he was going to pardon the murderer of his nephew. Other priests followed his example, until everybody present came forward and publicly made reconciliation with his enemies.

Poland was the second Catholic country to be entered by Vincent's priests. This came about in 1651 because Louise-Marie de Gonzague, who had married in quick succession two Polish kings, asked for Missionaries. She had been one of the Ladies of Charity working among the sick poor at the Hôtel-Dieu, so Vincent could hardly refuse. But she also was a Jansenist, who had at one time lived among the solitaries of Port-Royal, and still kept up a regular correspondence with Mère Angélique Arnauld.

This fact did not deter Vincent. He knew that the Queen was pious and munificent and fully intended to support to the utmost of her powers both the Fathers and the Sisters he agreed to send. Indeed, a special arrangement was made under which the Queen had one of the Sisters as her constant companion, to whom permission was given to dress in a slightly different fashion from the other Daughters of Charity.[2]

Much valuable work was done among the poor, the spiritually neglected Catholics of the country districts, and among the heretics, of which Poland at that time contained a good many. The Queen realised that any attempt on her part to influence her guests in the direction of her own eccentric theological opinions would result in their withdrawal, and so left them free. It was from the Jesuits that a certain opposition arose when it was proposed to found a theological seminary. Nor was it unnatural that they should be suspicious of the members of an organization who had come to Poland at the invitation and under the protection of the Jansenist Queen.

Few as were the members of Vincent's Congregation, and many as were their varied projects in France, Vincent had nothing narrowly national about him. Indeed, to the day of his death he used to say that he would never lose the desire of going out to the Indies himself, old as he was. Therefore when the Holy See requested that he send priests to make an effort

---

[2] As this statement is likely to be questioned, I had better give my authority for it—Coste, Vol. I, p. 447. (English translation.)

to re-establish the Faith in the Scandinavian countries, he willingly consented. Circumstances prevented his actually supplying these Missionaries when the time came, but he did send a group of eight of his sons to Ireland, where it seemed that Catholicism was in danger of being extirpated by persecution. These men, five of whom were Irish, and one, English, worked with almost spectacular success in the dioceses of Cashel and Limerick, and we have from the Bishop of Limerick several letters to Vincent de Paul in which His Lordship, after telling of all the good that had been done among his people, adds that he owes his own hope of salvation to the Fathers' ministrations.

Eventually Ireland grew too hot under the Cromwellian persecution for men who were strangers in the country to continue their work. A lay-brother named Edward Lee was martyred—the first of the Congregation to achieve this honour—and the French priests returned to France, since they were too conspicuous in Ireland to be of any service. A couple of Irish Fathers remained until 1652, but even they had eventually to abandon the impossible task of attempting to preach missions in a country infested with Cromwell's spies.

Scotland, entered by the Missionaries in 1651, proved to be a more fertile field. The Highlands and the Hebrides were so remote from civilization that the Protestant ministers, after having—as they thought—stamped out Catholicism there, left the inhabitants utterly deserted. So that the Fathers found men of ninety who had never been so much as baptised. The lairds, indeed, had for the most part officially accepted Presbyterianism, but even their sympathies were vaguely with Catholicism, with the result that the chieftains and their clans were brought back to the Church *en masse*. If to this day the Hebrides and the Highlands remain the most Catholic parts of Scotland, a very considerable share in the credit of bringing that about rests with the Missionaries sent by Vincent de Paul.

The filth and savagery of the people, however, were a sore trial to those sent to evangelise them. Almost the only place where meat was obtainable was in the castles of the lairds, and there it was cut off in half-raw lumps and thrown to be eaten on the rushes of the floor. The delicate stomachs of those accustomed to French cooking revolted at such fare, though it is possible that, after a time, they came to accustom themselves to whiskey as a substitute for wine. Something of the sort was needed to warm those who travelled from island to island through wet mists in small boats, especially as about all they could eat was a little coarse oat-cake. They were fortunate when they could get as much as that; many days they had to go without food at all.

In the islands the Missionaries were at least relatively safe. On the mainland they were in constant danger. One of them, a Father White, was arrested in 1655, and though he was released after a six months' imprisonment, as no definite evidence could be found that he had said Mass, he was told that if he was caught again he would be promptly hanged. Undeterred by the threat, he serenely (if a little more cautiously) went on with his work, and died in his bed in Scotland twenty-four years later.

As we have seen, Vincent was constantly preoccupied with ideas about foreign missionary work. One of his heroes was Francis Xavier, and he dreamed of sending his own sons to the Indies. As this did not prove possible, he associated himself with the plans of the Society for Foreign Missions, then being formed in Paris, and signed the petition of 1653 to the Pope which eventuated in the consecration of three bishops to supervise what was being done in Tonkin and Cochin-China. But he still did not feel that he had done all that he should, so the next year he arranged to send out a couple of priests and a lay-brother to Madagascar. Several others followed in the years before his death, but the unhealthy climate and difficulties raised by the touchy officials of the trading Company hampered their work. The story of a dogged persistence in the face of almost insuperable obstacles is told in detail in the second volume of Père Coste's *Life and Labours of St. Vincent de Paul*.[3]

Crowned with more success, because nearer to home, was the mission to the slaves of Barbary. This was attended with the greatest possible dangers, and called for the exercise of consummate discretion. Having himself been a slave, Vincent well understood the risks that had to be run, as his personal experience filled him with compassion for the thirty or forty thousand Christian captives on the coast of north Africa.

To begin with, openly confessed Missionaries would not be admitted by the fanatical followers of the prophet. They had to be attached as chaplains to the French consulates, and, when this method did not prove very successful, the Duchesse d'Aiguillon purchased consular positions that the Missionaries could fill. But this scheme raised complications at Rome, which at first absolutely forbade priests to fill such offices, and then, under pressure, reluctantly consented to tolerate the arrangement.

Even so, the Missionaries were neither safe nor unhampered in their work. The Beys were given to bastinadoing consuls for the debts of defaulting Christian traders, and they would on no account permit conversions among their people—this meant death both to priest and convert—or even the reconciliation of renegade Christians, of whom a good many (including priests) had purchased their liberty by apostasy. Vincent's missionary consuls and chaplains had therefore to proceed with the utmost wariness. The following instructions were given as a guide to

[3] The religion appears from the Missionaries' letters to have been mere wizardry or Voodoo. In which connexion it is interesting to note the Madagascar name for witch-doctor as it is found in them—*Ombiase*. Can it be that the modern *Zomby* is a corruption of this word?

the methods to be followed: "It is easier and far more important to hinder many slaves from apostatising than to convert a single renegade. . . . You are not charged with the souls of Turks or renegades, and your mission does not extend to them but to poor Christian captives." Nevertheless, many were converted or reconciled, though this had to be done with extreme circumspection.

The main emphasis, however, was always laid upon preserving the faith of those who already had it but who were in constant temptation to renounce it. Priests among the slaves were, for a money consideration, allowed to exercise their ministry, so that now few of the hulks lacked Mass, and the Christian captives were encouraged to persevere in their religion. Instances of heroic fortitude even unto death occurred, and the cause of some of these martyrs has been introduced at Rome, though in most cases their names are unknown except to God.

One of the most touching features of this work was the redemption of captives, especially of the young women among them who were in danger of being put in harems. Abelly estimates that Vincent, during his lifetime, purchased freedom for no less than twelve hundred slaves at the enormous cost of a million, two hundred thousand livres, a sum contributed by the Ladies of Charity and by the Company of the Blessed Sacrament.[4] Moreover, those for whom liberty could not be

---

[4] A further word might be said here about the men's secret society, M. Raoul Allier having advanced the thesis in his *La Cabale des Dévots* that it should have the credit for much of Vincent de Paul's work, that Vincent was, in fact, hardly more than the agent for the carrying out of its decisions. That Vincent took suggestions from the members of a society to which he himself belonged is not only likely but virtually certain, as he was at all times open to suggestions. But the main lines of his work were already laid down before the formation of the society in 1627, and many of his later enterprises—notably the founding of the Daughters of Charity— were obviously outside the scope of the "Devout Cabal." The Company of the Blessed Sacrament did, however, contribute generously towards such schemes as foreign missions, the redemption of captives, and war-relief—

purchased at least were supplied with small sums of money from time to time; when sick they could be sent to a hospital erected for this purpose; and, above all, the consolations of religion could now be brought them.

Meanwhile in France the old activities of the Fathers and Sisters continued and new ones were begun. Vincent remained Chaplain-General of the galleys. And because he was unable in his later life, both on account of his physical infirmities and the duties that kept him in Paris, to visit the galley-slaves in person, he delegated his powers to the Superior of the house of his Congregation at Marseilles. In Paris, however, he and his priests kept a constant eye upon the prisoners at the Conciergerie who were waiting to travel by chain-gang to the ports. And the Ladies of Charity and the Sisters were always busy doing what they could to relieve these hapless wretches' sufferings. That Vincent's personal solicitude never wavered is shown by the frequency with which he writes to Marseilles sending on letters and small gifts from their families to the convicts. If their life remained miserable, at least they received sympathy and were now assured of release when they became disabled. The fact, too, that the new admiral of the fleet was the Duc de Richelieu, the nephew of the admirable Duchesse d'Aiguillon, also helped to alleviate their lot.

Reform was instituted in other jails in Paris. And again the

though this would seem to show rather that Vincent had managed to awaken the enthusiasm of his fellow-members for the good works he had himself initiated than that he was acting as their instrument. But there was, of course, constant cooperation and interchange of ideas, natural enough in view of the fact that the members of the Company of the Blessed Sacrament and the Ladies of Charity were often related and nearly always moved in the same social circles. As one instance of this, it may be pointed out that it was the wife of the founder of the men's association (the Duchesse de Ventadour) who bore the candle by the death-bed of Louise de Marillac. It is, however, safe to say that such charitable projects as did not originate with Vincent would have come to nothing had he not been at hand to carry them into execution.

Daughters of Charity were indefatigable in the charity they showed the prisoners. As for the Ladies of Charity, they formed a special branch to look after that large number of people who were guilty of no other offence than that of being unable to pay their debts. These were segregated from the criminals, with whom they had formerly been mingled, and in many cases it was found possible to pay off their debtors or to make a composition with them.

Then, too, schools were established in the country for peasant girls. This was something that in all probability would only have occurred to a man of Vincent's origin, one who realised how great a deprivation the lack of letters is, and how much it would mean to the poor to be able to read. The Sisters, after teaching from half past eight in the morning until half past five in the afternoon, were also ready to give night instruction to those children who had to work and so could not attend during the day. To this teaching Vincent attached as much importance as he did to the visitation of the sick, as part of the vocation of the Sister of Charity. Even in Paris such schools were founded, for at that time no provision was made by the State for education and therefore only the well-to-do received any instruction.

Because there was no poor law—except the generally evaded prohibition against begging—Vincent established an alms-house with accommodation for forty old men and women. If the help it gave was slight when compared with the need, it should be said that it pointed the way to what was required and had—like all of Vincent's works—a human warmth and a supernatural charity very far removed from that cold-blooded official (and officious) aid which the poor so very rightly loathe. The easy-going character of the place may be estimated from the fact that the old people were encouraged to do work fitted to their strength and that what they earned was used to supply them with the wine or beer they ordered. But as many of them drank more than they ever earned and as the profits of the work during the first year came to little over fifty livres, Louise de Marillac can hardly be considered a slave-driver.

This Hospice of the Holy Name of Jesus was looked upon by Vincent as no more than a beginning, in a small way, of a scheme to deal with a very great problem—that of mendicancy. Not that the old people admitted were, strictly speaking, beggars; rather they came from the class of the respectable indigent and included in several instances the fathers or mothers of the Missionaries and the Sisters. But Vincent hoped that his institution might serve as a model for dealing with those swarms of mendicants that had for so long constituted one of the greatest public problems.

The government had made several attempts to deal with the matter. As early as 1611 a royal edict had been published ordering all beggars to report to one or other of the five branches of the General Hospital. It had the effect of clearing Paris almost overnight. Less than a hundred beggars submitted to be interned.

After the civil war, however, the problem grew worse than ever. In the sixteen-fifties fifty or sixty thousand beggars were in the capital, perhaps more than half of whom were not professionally given to begging but had been driven in from the devastated areas where they could obtain no work. Yet of course among these there were many who took to this as an easy and, in some cases, a lucrative mode of life. In either event, some solution had to be found.

Vincent thought that other hospices along the lines of the one he had set up would be the best means of meeting the situation. He had already had some experience in this matter. For at Mâcon in 1621 he had induced the local authorities to handle the matter through the Confraternity of Charity. There the poor were aided from public funds, according to their necessities, but nobody got anything who solicited money from passers-by in the streets, and the able-bodied were found work. He would now have liked to have combined the methods which had proved so successful in Maçon with the provision of hospices for those who could be cared for in no other way.

The government took a different view of the question. Begging was to be forcibly suppressed; and though the threat made during Marie de' Medici's regency of the galleys for sturdy mendicants among the men and for whipping for the women was not now suggested, most of the official and wealthy classes considered that mendicity was something to be dealt with with a heavy hand. Those who did not belong to Paris were to be ejected; the others were to be interned and put to work, whether they liked it or not. Naturally they did not like it, and again there was a great exodus from the city. Only this time, as many of the beggars had nowhere else to go, they remained to accept their fate.

It was not a particularly hard one, even if Vincent's plan of compelling nobody and of going to the trouble of classifying the cases so as to adapt the assistance given to the individual needs was not adopted. He was over-ruled by the Ladies of Charity who, as even the most charitable ladies of high position are inclined, had little patience with what they regarded as a public nuisance. In this they were supported and abetted by the men's charitable organization, the Company of the Blessed Sacrament. Hospices might be all very well in their way, they decided, but the only method of getting the beggars off the streets was to intern them.

A number of barracks or strongly guarded houses were selected, among them the famous Salpêtrière, and in them were shut up all those found without visible means of support. It was drastic but, after a fashion, effective. Vincent's influence prevailed to the extent of getting them treated with some degree of humanity, and the Ladies were put in charge of the administration of the women's section—in which they were aided by the Sisters. His reward was what might be expected—ingratitude. The beggars accused him of being responsible for having them coralled into the Salpêtrière.

To Vincent's consternation, he was told that he was to supply chaplains from the Congregation of the Mission. He was obliged to refuse. Even if this had been a work that fell within the compass of the Congregation, he could have undertaken it only at the cost of giving up his project of sending Missionaries to Madagascar. So a compromise was effected with the Court, under which he was allowed to nominate chaplains from among the members of the Tuesday Conference. It is interesting to note that at their head was Louis Abelly, who was destined to become the first of Vincent's biographers.

Other charitable works that must be mentioned, if only in passing, are the orphanages conducted by the Daughters of Charity, and the lunatic asylum in Paris known as *Les Petites Maisons*. For the deranged in mind Vincent had a special devotion which will probably strike most people as extremely odd. It was, however, very characteristic of him, and to this day the Sisters gladly accept among their many activities the one which their Founder always insisted was a "noble vocation." Just because it was a thankless task it appealed to him.

Almost as thankless were his efforts on behalf of the Irish exiles in France who had been driven out by the Cromwellian persecution. Many of these found employment in the army, which of course perfectly fitted their temperament. It was not so easy, however, to deal with the refugee Irish priests, since these had no definite employment and appeared to wish for none. When Vincent tried to form an association for them under the direction of one of the Irish Fathers in his own Congregation, the Celts, morbidly sensitive to what they construed as criticism, told him to mind his own business. Nevertheless, for these, as for the handful of English Catholics who had gathered around King Charles I's Queen, Vincent collected funds and tried to provide in other ways. It would be interesting to know whether he encountered Richard Crashaw in Henrietta Maria's circle at this time.

What is in many respects the most appealing of all of Vincent's charitable schemes is left to the last: his work for the foundlings. Because it lends itself to pathetic descriptions, there has been a great deal of romancing on the subject, in which perhaps the worst offender is Vincent's brilliant but quite unreliable biographer, the French Academician, Henri Lavedan. He grows positively lyrical in picturing his hero going out late at night, night after night, into the most ruffianly haunts of Paris and tottering back with two, three or even four babies in the cloak he wore only for such occasions. But the truth must be told, and Vincent's glory is not in the least diminished by the fact that there are no authentic records of his *ever* going out to pick up deserted babies. What he did was to found and to sustain under very great difficulties a foundling hospital.

Lavedan's raptures have this much of excuse: he did not invent the story. It appears to take its origin from Jean-Baptiste Capefigue who quoted in his Life of Vincent de Paul, published in 1827, what purports to be a diary kept by a Sister of Charity. This seems to be very circumstantial in its account of the Saint arriving with his nightly cargo of babies. The trouble is that Capefigue, though he says he actually saw this diary, does not say where it is to be found; and nobody else has ever seen it. On the strength of this the Abbé Maynard embroiders a bit, according to his wont, and quotes from Capefigue's diary, though not verbatim.[5] But when Maynard was chal-

[5] Cf. Vol. III, pp. 331-333 (the 1860 edition).

lenged to say whence he had derived his material, he gave the extremely unsatisfactory answer that he could not remember.

There is no need to impugn the good faith of either of these men; probably enough they were merely imposed upon and did not show much critical sense. Nevertheless what might have escaped Capefigue, or even Maynard, should not have escaped a distinguished literary man like M. Lavedan—namely, that the style of the diary suggests nineteenth rather than seventeenth century French. Quietly but decisively Père Coste points this out and relegates the cloak-fulls of rescued babies to the legends.

The facts are as follows: seventeenth century Paris had a foundling hospital known as the *Couche*. It was nothing but a baby-farm run by a few disreputable women who made their profit by selling what infants did not die under their tender care—which included laudanum to keep the poor children from crying—to anyone who wished to buy them. Sometimes a person wanted to get hold of a child to palm off as his own; almost as often the purchasers were the strolling mountebanks who deliberately deformed a child so as to make it a monstrosity for a circus. Abelly goes so far as to say that they were even sold to wizards who needed human sacrifices, though that perhaps may be taken with a grain of salt.

It is true, however, that, whatever allowances are made for exaggerations, the *Couche* was abominably mismanaged. So in 1638 Vincent and Louise contrived to get a small house and the financial support of the Ladies of Charity and put the children under the care of the Sisters, or boarded them out with carefully selected women. By the end of December 1643 we find that they had rescued twelve hundred children, or an average of two hundred and forty a year—though we must remember that the number was much smaller than that in the beginning— and that by 1644 the annual cost of this work was forty thousand livres. In 1645 Vincent invested sixty-four thousand livres left him by Louis XIII for missionary work in building a row of thirteen small houses at the north end of the Saint-Lazare property, and rented them to the Ladies of Charity as homes for the orphans.

The children were brought up in what we should consider today a rather spartan style. But of course if this work was to be maintained at all in the hard times of the Thirty Years' War and the Fronde—when all kinds of other pressing demands were made on the Ladies of Charity—the cost had to be kept down. Moreover, it was inadvisable to accustom children to luxury who would, as soon as they grew old enough to work, have to be put to domestic service in the case of the girls and, in the case of the boys, taught some not-too-difficultly-learned trade. But Vincent's tender affection for his foundlings shines with an exquisite radiance in an address he gave to his Daughters on December 7, 1643: "If persons of the world consider themselves honoured by serving the children of the great, how much more should you who are called to serve the children of God. . . . He takes pleasure in their little prattlings, nay, even in their little whimperings and complaints." That last stroke may be something that mothers would understand; it is what very few men, even those who are fathers, could be expected to see at all. And yet it only has to be pointed out to touch every human heart.

Then, when this work was on the point of being given up in 1647 for lack of funds, we had that most moving appeal to the Ladies of Charity who had assembled to decide the matter. It has already been quoted in this book as an example of Vincent's power of natural oratory, but it will suffer being quoted again. "Ladies, sympathy and charity led you to adopt these little creatures as your children. You have been their mothers according to grace, ever since their mothers according to nature

abandoned them. Cease to be their mothers, and now become
their judges. Their life and death are in your hands. I am now
about to collect your opinions and votes; the time has come
to pronounce their sentence and see if you still desire to have
mercy upon them. They will live if you continue to take charitable care of them; and, on the contrary, they will infallibly die
if you abandon them."

The work, after such an appeal, had to be kept on. It survived not only the dark days of the Fronde, but continued—
with about four hundred children being added every year—up to
the outbreak of the Revolution.

ℂ 23. The Seal on the Work

As WE have seen, Vincent de Paul had no intention of founding the Congregation of the Mission. On the contrary, when Philippe-Emmanuel Gondi and his wife set aside a sum to endow the preaching of missions to the peasantry, Vincent did all he could to get one of the existing orders to accept the charge and only undertook it himself because nobody else would come forward.

But having gathered his little group of Missionaries, he still refused to consider them as more than a band of secular priests bound to a particular task, and this conception remained to the end. Though afterwards rules had to be drawn up and some definite bond devised to hold them together, he never for an instant regarded his Congregation as a religious order. Indeed, to have sought to have formed a new religious order would have presented difficulties which, in view of the feeling at Rome against new establishments of the kind, would have almost certainly proved insuperable. For what Vincent wanted was something that had virtually all the distingiushing marks of a religious order except the habit, and yet was not to be a religious order. He was clear in his own mind, but there is little wonder that the Holy See was somewhat puzzled by his proposals.

Most founders of religious institutes are careful to draw up their rules as early as possible. The advantages in doing so are obvious: those who join, join for a definite purpose and know from the beginning just what they have to expect. Further, as no man can tell how long he is going to live, it is no more than prudent to lose no time in defining the nature of his work and getting it approved. For Rome is always given to moving slowly and to weighing all questions before issuing a pronouncement;

and the amount of business before the Papal officials often results in a congestion that is exasperating to anyone not highly endowed with patience.

Vincent de Paul, however, was not like most founders. No man was less precipitate or more patient. The matter was momentous and urgent—and especially urgent owing to the fact that he was already well into middle age before he began his life's work. It is true that the general purpose of the Congregation was clearly indicated in the Gondi contract. But that contract was insufficient to give permanent assurance that the original purpose would be carried out. Besides, it had made the main obligations those of preaching missions and of caring for the galley-slaves. Before long new activities, no less important than these, came to be added. The seminaries and the retreats for ordinands had been established, and a quasi-religious order of women, dependent upon the Fathers, had come into being. Therefore it was extremely important that the life of the members of the Congregation be regulated by explicit law, and their juridical status indicated.

In spite of all this Vincent apparently was content to let the matter drift. As a matter of fact he was thinking about it all the time, but he did not wish to act rashly. It was his principle to be guided by experience, which he did not regard as being merely an opportunity to garner prudential knowledge but as a willingness to wait for the manifestation of the will of God. He was aware that rules of religious orders often have to be modified in the process of time. He knew that the Dominicans had maintained their unity because their formal rule—that of St. Augustine—was no more than a set of general principles, and that these were made operative by the elasticity of a system which permitted, in the constantly remodelled Constitutions, such regulations as the age required. The Franciscans had split into several divisions because of varying interpretations of their rule. The Benedictines had suffered a series of reforms, and among them each monastery was to all intents and purposes free to give its own interpretation to the rule of the founder. Vincent therefore believed it inadvisable to draw up any rules until the whole community was quite certain as to what those rules should be.

In 1642, however, a serious illness that came upon him made him anxious to defer the decision no longer. He was already sixty-one; we know that from this time he was daily prepared for death; and he knew that, however speedily he acted, a great many complicated questions would have to be thrashed out among the Fathers before they could approach the Holy See for approbation. As a matter of fact it was only shortly before his death at the age of eighty that the rules were, to his great joy, finally approved and he could say his *Nunc dimittis*. Yet in the interval he and his Congregation were always (though with many interruptions) preoccupied with this important concern.

A beginning was made when he and Père Portail, his first disciple, drew up a tentative draft which was discussed at length by the community at Saint-Lazare. As no conclusion was reached, a committee was appointed to act. But after they had done their work, there still remained the question of approbation. The Archbishop of Paris had been delegated at the time of the acceptance of the first regulations to handle the question on behalf of the Pope; but the Archbishop had ideas which were not always in conformity with Vincent's own. It seemed, therefore, better to go direct to Rome.

Then, while negotiations were still in progress, the Archbishop left Paris and his authority was, for the time being, in the hands of his coadjutor, the future Cardinal de Retz. And though Vincent's former pupil showed himself willing to do what was asked of him, unluckily just then Portail was away on an extended tour. Meanwhile Rome refused to do anything at all.

In 1651 the rules were again revised and the Archbishop again approached. This time he proved more amenable, so that the document was sent to the printer, but came back too full of typographical errors to be of any use. But in the interval something very important had happened: the Archbishop of Paris had died, and from his successor, de Retz, Vincent felt sure that he could obtain a good deal more than he had first dared to ask for.

But again mishap occurred. De Retz had been arrested, imprisoned and induced by Mazarin to resign the archbishopric in consideration of receiving as compensation seven enormously wealthy benefices. The Cardinal felt uneasy at the prospect of so redoubtable an enemy being not merely coadjutor but titular Archbishop of Paris. Philosophically de Retz, as he records in his *Memoirs*, bowed to what seemed to be inevitable and made himself as comfortable as he could in the prison at Vincennes, where he brushed up his Latin, and, as he adds, "Composed the *Consolation of Theology*, wherein I shewed that every prisoner ought to endeavour to make himself the *Vinctus in Christo*, of which St. Paul speaks." However, this outburst of piety did not last long; a little later he managed to make a spectacular escape and finally got to Rome, where he was *persona grata*—largely for the reason that Mazarin was not. There he repudiated his resignation and was not only sustained in this action by the Holy See but created a cardinal.

The friendly relations existing between Vincent and de Retz are indicated by the fact that the fugitive, upon reaching Rome, was lodged in the house of the Congregation of the Mission, much to Mazarin's annoyance.[1] In return he did what

---

[1] There was a little comedy played here. Père Berthe, the Superior at Rome, felt (or pretended to feel) some consternation at being asked by de Retz to be given an apartment at the Missionaries' house. And in fact Mazarin was so furious when he heard of it that he insisted on the recall of all the French Fathers at Rome. Not content with that, Mazarin drew

he could to further the approbation of the Vincentian rules. The series of mishaps had turned out to be providential. Innocent X, who had shown a rooted objection to anything in the nature of a new religious order, had recently died and had been succeeded by Alexander VII, whose prejudices on this point were not so strong. The new Pope signed the Brief, *Ex Commissa Nobis,* on September 22, 1655—and the long struggle was won.

It must be admitted, nevertheless, that Innocent X was not without reason for his opposition. What Vincent asked was, or seemed to be, a constitution for his Congregation so strange as to be almost without precedent. The main issue turned on the question of vows. Vincent was resolutely set against turning his foundation into a religious order; upon that he and all the Fathers were agreed. On the other hand, he wanted the members of the Congregation to take vows, though the taking of vows (of the sort he had in mind) appeared to constitute them religious. If he had asked merely for simple and private vows no objection would have arisen; but he demanded vows which, though they were not to be formally received by the Superior General (and as such seemed to be only simple and private), yet had the binding force of solemn vows, in that they could be dispensed by no one save the Pope and the Superior General. And this looked very much as though he wanted to have it both ways.

That he did want to have it both ways may as well be admitted. He was insistent that his priests should be seculars and not religious; at the same time they were to be bound exactly

---

up an indictment of his new colleague in the Sacred College, setting out the full details of his scandalous life, and demanded that he be brought to trial by an ecclesiastical court. By way of completing his persecution, he forbade any subject of the French Crown to have any dealings with de Retz. Nevertheless Mazarin's spite did his enemy little harm: de Retz in due time returned to the Archbishopric of Paris, successful in his main objects, if also politically discredited.

as though they were religious and were to enjoy—in their freedom from the jurisdiction of bishops in temporalities—the privileges of a monastic order. It can therefore be hardly wondered that a Pope who was opposed to establishing new orders in the Church should oppose so novel a project. Innovations rarely find much favour at Rome.

Vincent, however, was well aware that the Pope, if he chooses to do so, can always make special arrangements. The Jesuits were accorded the status of religious even though they took only simple vows. If so, why could the thing not be made to work the other way? Vincent must have had the case of the Society in mind, for the rules of the Mission were to a great extent based on those of the Jesuits, often using even the same terminology; and the Vincentian practice of having priests return to the novitiate after some years of active service is nothing else than the Jesuit "tertianship."

His fundamental conception of the relation between vows and status is, however, almost exactly opposite to that of the Jesuits, and is closer to that of the Redemptorists, who make their vows solemnly and to their Superior, but, for all that, are classed as seculars. So another rare exception was made, under which, as Father Leonard points out, "The actual status of the Congregation from that day to this is rather paradoxical. Its members still form part of the pastoral clergy, yet they take the simple vows of religion, and it has been decided that if a man made a vow to become a member of a religious Order, he would fulfil it by entering the Congregation of the Mission." Vincent had known just what he wanted—a canonical position that was to him quite clear, though to others anomalous. He had to fight hard to get it; in the end he succeeded.

On this question there had been a good deal of discussion in the Congregation. Some Fathers took the not unreasonable ground that they ought to remain, like the Oratorians and Sulpicians, a group of secular priests living without vows in community. It was argued, indeed, that a free attachment to the community would be more perfect than one that was enforced. And among them were a few who had not so far taken vows, as there were one or two cases of men who did not take them until several years after the rules had been ratified.[2] As they were able to plead that these did not form part of the conditions under which they had joined the Congregation, their attitude was tolerated.

Now at last the seal was set upon Vincent's work; his Missionaries had their rules and the approval of the Holy See. He could die content. On May 17, 1658 the ailing old man was able to distribute printed copies of the rules at Saint-Lazare. As there were not enough of these available for everybody—even after that unconscionable delay—the students and lay-brothers had to wait a few days for another printing. But, to the priests assembled it was Vincent's wish to give each a copy with his own hands, only he found when he attempted to walk around with the pile of little books that he was obliged to give up the task as being too much for him. Therefore the Fathers went up in turn to their Founder and took the rule from him, kissing the hand that gave it. To each Vincent murmured, "May God bless you!"

The settlement of the rules for the Daughters of Charity had also occurred in 1655, though they had been signed by their banished Archbishop, the Cardinal de Retz, in January, whereas the Fathers' Constitutions received the Pope's endorsement in September. But, as we have already seen, there is a curious story attached to this.

The difficulty here was similar to that of the Missionaries' rule

---

[2] One of them, Père Tholard, even became head of one of the four provinces into which the work of the Congregation was divided, so it is clear that there was no insistence on uniformity in the matter of vows.

in that it was largely concerned with the question of vows, a question which did not receive its final answer until after the death of Vincent de Paul. When Louise de Marillac gathered in her house in Paris the first of the Daughters of Charity, neither she nor Vincent had any very clear idea as to what the status of these village girls was to be. About their function they were definite enough: the girls were to assist in every possible way—especially in that of hard manual work—in the service of the poor. But they were looked upon as mere auxiliaries to the members of the Confraternities, to do what the Ladies of Charity or Mademoiselle or Vincent or the parish priest or the doctors at the Hôtel-Dieu told them to do.

As time went on, however, they began to be regarded as a species of nun, and perhaps some of them even regarded themselves in that light. Vincent would not hear of it: they were not religious, he told them, but seculars, and their uniform was not a habit. It was a little bewildering for some people to know just what they were.

Moreover, as they had dedicated themselves to the service of God through the service of the poor they came to ask whether they might not take vows. And there lay the crux of the whole matter. Vincent told them that by taking vows they would become religious, and that even if they took private vows—such as were capable of being dispensed by a bishop—it would be better not to take them at all than to do so with the idea at the back of their mind of getting released whenever they chose. There seemed for a while to be no way out of the difficulty. For, once they were religious, they would have to be cloistered and therefore unable to do their distinctive work.

All the same, they were persistent, and Vincent was ingenious. On March 25, 1642, Louise de Marillac (Mademoiselle Le Gras) and three other Sisters about whose vocation there was now reasonable certainty, were permitted to take perpetual vows, though only as a private act. If made a general custom it would have defeated Vincent's purposes for his Daughters. Vows for everybody renewable yearly, such as afterwards came into effect, proved to be the solution.

In 1645 the Archbishop of Paris (or rather his coadjutor signing in his name) formally recognized them as an organization in these terms: "We have erected and hereby do erect, by these presents, the group of aforesaid girls and widows in this diocese into a special Confraternity under the title of Servants of the Poor of Charity. We desire and ordain that all those already admitted, and who may hereafter be admitted, shall be free to do all in their power to comfort and console the aforesaid sick poor, on condition that the aforesaid Confraternity shall be and shall remain in perpetuity under the authority and control of His Grace the Archbishop and his successors, and that it shall exactly observe the statutes annexed, which we have approved and do hereby approve by these presents. And inasmuch as God has blessed the care and toil which our dear and well-beloved Vincent de Paul has taken to bring this pious design to success, we have confided and committed to him the government and direction of the above-mentioned Society and Confraternity, as long as it may please God to preserve his life."

The rigmarole of this legal phraseology makes clear, however, that it was the intention to confer the authority upon Vincent de Paul for life—but left it an open question as to who should succeed him. Louise de Marillac did not like the terms of approbation, and perhaps it was for this reason that, though the document was signed on November 20, 1646, the Sisters were told nothing about it until six months later. Then Vincent said, "Up to the present, you have not formed a separate body to that of the Ladies of the Confraternity of Charity; but now, my Daughters, God wishes you to be a separate body." That much of their status had been fixed.

There had been some discussion as to who should be their Superior (or "Sister Servant") after the death of Louise. As she was herself a Lady of Charity, wearing her widow's weeds instead of the grey dress and white toque of the Sisters, the logical inference was that, after her death, another of the Ladies of Charity should take her place. But this, however logical, would not have been practicable; for no extern, unacquainted with the spirit of the community, could have carried on her work satisfactorily. By separating the two organizations and providing for the election of a Sister as Superior, another problem was solved.

But another problem remained. When Mademoiselle took the document in April, 1650, to be registered by the Parlement of Paris, the question was at once put, "Are you regulars or seculars?" And when Louise answered "Seculars," the Procurator, Blaise Méliand, was puzzled, and asked for time to study the matter. He assured Louise of his highest respect for the work the Sisters were doing, but could find no precedent for a community of uncloistered women, and received the perhaps not altogether tactful answer, "If our little Company does not deserve to live, destroy it entirely; if the design is praiseworthy, establish it on a firm footing."

Then, as happened so often in the case of those concerned with Vincent's projects, Méliand died suddenly before he had made up his mind, and his successor as Procurator General, Fouquet, could not find the document. It might be noted that its not quite satisfactory nature had led Anne of Austria in 1647 to petition the Pope to appoint as Superior of the Sisters, not Vincent in his personal capacity, but the General of the Congregation of the Mission. If the document disappeared (as has been suggested) by design and not accident, the finger of suspicion would seem to point to the Queen-Regent. It is not unlikely that Méliand took the Archbishop's approbation to her to ask her advice, and that after his death she quietly got rid of the charter.

Ironically enough, it was her great enemy (or rather the great enemy of Mazarin) who brought the issue to the desired termination. Whatever faults he had, de Retz was sincerely attached to Vincent de Paul and time and again showed himself a true friend. John Francis Paul de Gondi in the days when he was Vincent's pupil proved himself to be what his aunt called him, a "little devil"; as Abbé and coadjutor Archbishop of Paris, he was anything but an edifying ecclesiastic; but as Archbishop in his own right and Cardinal he had a great deal to do with getting the rules of the Congregation and the Daughters of Charity approved. Again one sees the finger of Providence operating. The new document read, "Inasmuch as God has blessed the work undertaken by our dear and well-beloved Vincent de Paul to bring this pious design to success, we have accordingly confided and committed and, by these presents, do confide and commit the government and direction of the above-mentioned Society and Confraternity for the course of his life and, after him, to his successors, the General of the said Congregation of the Mission."

That was all that was needed; Louise de Marillac could now be sure that the direction of her Daughters would not pass to any priest the Archbishop of Paris took a fancy to appoint.[3] The royal signature was given in November, 1657, and the registration made by the Parlement a year later. Both civil and ecclesiastical authority had ratified her design.

The Sisters in Paris, overjoyed with what had been at last accomplished, assembled to sign the Deed of Foundation. The

---

[3] The final draft of the rules of the Daughters of Charity was not, however, made until after Vincent's death.

names of those who could not be present in the body, but whom everybody knew to be present in spirit, were not left out. Even with these, there are only about thirty names, beginning with that of Louise de Marillac and ending with that of Vincent de Paul. Nine sisters were able to sign only with a mark.

ℂ 24. Sunset at Sunrise

A NUMBER of books have been written which are not so much lives of Vincent de Paul as anthologies of his sayings or exemplifications of the special quality of his sanctity. No saint has left more abundant material suitable for such works. The Abbé Maynard's *Virtues and Doctrines* was the first of these, and is still the best known; but others that have the advantage of being rather more concise are Boudignon's study of Vincent as a model for men of action (with its correct but what will appear at first glance to be somewhat misleading title) and Arnaud d'Angel's *Saint Vincent de Paul: a Guide for Priests*. All offer a good summary of Vincent's very practical teaching, but have a hortatory and edifying purpose.

My purpose has been rather different: it has been that of trying to show Vincent in action and at the same time to keep close to the ascertained historical facts. But since the saint may have to some extent escaped in the process—action being an external thing—it would be as well to say something now about the inner life of this great man.

Yet we know very little except what we can infer from the addresses Vincent gave to his Fathers and Daughters; and, on his own confession, in these he often refrained from giving them the more lofty thoughts that had occurred to him, partly, one may suppose, because he considered this more practical than indulgence in speculative theology, but partly, one may be sure, in order to exercise that virtue of humility which made him seem—on account of its extravagance—as the admiring Abelly remarks, a little queer to some of his contemporaries.

The extant letters are mainly those of a very busy man of affairs. Not that he often failed to reveal in them his spirituality, but they are for the most part primarily confined to matters of business. We do not find in them—though there are important exceptions—the kind of spiritual direction Francis de Sales gave.

In private, however, he gave a great deal of the most patient spiritual advice to the Fathers and the Sisters, so that, as the Abbé d'Angel truly points out: "Centuries before Freud, he practised psycho-analysis, and he led his patient on, from hypothesis to hypothesis, until they put their fingers, so to say, on the cause of their troubles." He used to declare that spiritual direction was the art of arts, and especially did he employ it in dealing with the difficult spiritual malady of scrupulosity. Even when engaged in the transaction of business of the highest importance, he was always ready to take a troubled Father off into a corner to listen to what he had to say and to offer a solution of his difficulties. He was ready to do this even if, as sometimes happened, the unhappy man came back several times during the course of the day to present some new aspect of the scruples torturing him. Vincent knew very well that there is no disease more dangerous or more painful than such affliction of soul, and therefore always made himself available to do all in his power to prevent it from developing into despair.

In the nature of things we can get no more than glimpses of his method, and these usually from his letters, which are so often signed "Vincent, Unworthy Priest of the Mission," or with initials that stood for the same. As for what he said or wrote about himself, this—though he gives us some biographical details we should not otherwise have—he brought in only to illustrate a point and then as it were inadvertently. Afterwards he would exclaim, "Miserable man that I am! Always talking about myself!"

About his spiritual life he was extremely reticent. And when he did somehow get on to that subject, his listeners—had they not known him so well—would have thought, to hear him, that he ought to be at once handed over to the civil authorities and executed as the greatest rascal on earth. In fact, he used to protest in so many words that he always felt after his evening examination of conscience that he deserved to be hanged at Montfaucon. If he caught himself talking in a different strain, he would immediately check himself and explain, "I am a wonder of wickedness worse than the devil, and I deserve to be lower in hell than he is." This, though it was evident that he really meant it, struck a good many of his listeners as a somewhat amusing eccentricity, however charming and touching they also found it to be. Nothing is more beautiful than genuine humility—even to those who lack it.

Indeed, as we have seen, he would not permit the Congregation of the Mission to be praised. While unwearied in exhorting his priests to the practice of perfect virtue, he spoke to those who were thinking of joining the Congregation in such terms as to leave the impression that Saint-Lazare was the den of a gang of scoundrels. This of course was a kind of extension of his own humility. The Ladies of Charity escaped, but that was because they were a purely voluntary association—and perhaps because of their sex. Yet even to these aristocratic and wealthy women he constantly inculcated humility. His Daughters of Charity, however, received frequent reminders that they were—like himself, as he never failed to add—only poor peasants. His habit of self-deprecation sounds at times like the formulas of Chinese politeness—as they are popularly imagined to be in the Western world.

All this was not merely talk; it was noticed by those who lived with him and who had ample opportunities for catching him in his unguarded moments, that there were no unguarded moments, so far as humility was concerned. In all kinds of small ways, which he thought nobody would be likely to observe, he abased himself. Even on those occasions when, as Superior, he had to correct some fault, or reprimand one of the Congregation, he would usually summon the man to him afterwards—even if he happened to be the most mulishly stupid of the lay-brothers—and astonish him by kneeling down to kiss his feet. Incidentally of course such penitence was more stinging than reproof.

Or if, as now and then happened, he was met by some beggar at the gate of Saint-Lazare and, having been asked for an alms, was obliged to request that person to wait while he went to get some money, and if—as frequently was the case in such a hive of activity as Saint-Lazare—he was pounced upon by one of the priests who had some urgent business to discuss, and so forgot his promise to the tattered old man or woman waiting in the porch, he would go down himself (as soon as the matter came back to his mind) with both alms and abject apologies. Anybody else would have thought it quite sufficient to send a lay-brother; but not Vincent. Christ, in the person of the poor, had been neglected. Kneeling and in tears he would kiss the weary feet. Though isolated acts more heroic than any he performed, or even more extreme instances of humiliation, may be found in the lives of other saints; surely with none was humility such a settled habit.

Moreover, he often gave when he had nothing to give. The Procurator would expostulate that there was no money in the house and that Monsieur Vincent was ruining them all. Nothing seemed to please him better than such news, for it gave him a chance to turn to God. For immediate purposes, however, he would send across the road to Louise de Marillac to ask her to lend him a little to go on with. The needy were not to be turned away on that account.

Yet Vincent must not be thought of as being merely sweet and kind and good-natured; that would be to misunderstand him. Abelly notes his resolute look, and this appears, mingled with the kindness, in such portraits as we possess. Besides, it is shown in the whole history of his life. Only a man of iron determination could have succeeded in carrying through, in the face of such difficulties as he had to encounter, the many projects he took up, not one of which was ever abandoned. Ready as he was to receive suggestions and to defer to other people's opinions, he showed an unrelenting pertinacity in following his object, once he was perfectly sure that it was what God wanted. But he obtained his objects not by bluster, nor even by the giving of quietly decisive commands. His normal method was one of indirection. Thus he would say to the disobedient, "Don't you think, Sir, that perhaps if you had been just a little more careful not to do things in your own way, you might have been a trifle more successful?" Or he would drop a hint to the Superior of a house of whom he had heard—let us say—that he was inclined to be niggardly, that a report had come to him to the same effect about some other unnamed house. As for the lay-brothers—among whom were a few men rather rough-mannered and dense—he would patiently explain over and over again what needed to be done, and just how—never losing his patience, but seeming to take delight in what would have caused anybody else exasperation. Nor did he hesitate to help them when he could in their work in the kitchen or refectory, not with the purpose of officiously showing them the best methods of performing their allotted tasks, but rather out of pleasure of being among them; there he always wore a radiant look on his face.

He expressed so much gratitude for even the smallest of courtesies that people went out of their way to do him some slight service merely in order to get this flash of thanks. If he never seemed, on the other hand, upset at anything, but always kept his serene look and a voice which, though it had at times a firm tone, never took a rasping one; if, as Abelly puts it, his heart by always dwelling in the same disposition, preserved his interior equanimity—it was the result of grace not of nature. Francis de Sales was affable by constitution, a handsome and well-bred man; whereas Vincent de Paul was temperamentally inclined towards irritability and impatience. The grace of God of course adorned in the case of Francis what already existed; but with Vincent grace had to achieve, as the result of a slow and laborious process, the gentleness that was among the most marked of the characteristics of his sanctity.

He wanted to have meekness for its own sake; he was also clever enough to understand its practical efficacy, and, in fact, sometimes spoke of it in these terms, saying that the only occasions when he had failed to get obedience were those on which he had insisted upon getting it. We must remember that, however much he praised simplicity, he was not a simpleton or even what can be called a simple character. Instead we see in him the union of qualities that are very seldom united—humility and determination, self-abnegation with a prudence that would be canny were not his peasant shrewdness elevated to and merged with his dependence on the guidance of God.

The most remarkable fact about him was that, as his external activity increased, so did his activity in God. Perhaps the statement might be put conversely: the more completely he was absorbed in God, the more intense became his activity. This never stopped. Rather he made of his bodily disability an opportunity for further work, and during his last years, when he could no longer walk to the room where he had been accustomed to spend an hour of recreation with the Fathers, he sat in his cell and wrote or dictated letters.

It was noticed that he never seemed to lose the sense of the presence of God. Even walking down the street, he was completely recollected, and when a church clock struck the hour he would take this as a signal for renewing the resolutions he had made at prayer that morning. Not that he was ever in a dream; no man less so. If anyone spoke to him, his attention was fully fastened upon the business brought forward or the question asked. Yet he would not give an answer until he had raised his thoughts with a greater intensity to heaven to receive from the divine source the enlightenment of mind he needed.

Had he been a fussy and bustling man, driving himself and driving others, he would not have accomplished what he did. It was his quiet unhurriedness that was the secret both of the volume and the stability of his work. Multifarious and complicated as were his constantly growing enterprises, he never became in the least flustered. In slowness was his strength; he took sufficient time to look into every corner of a problem, and all around it, before he came to a decision. He was not greatly handicapped by lacking the modern paraphernalia of efficiency—except the means of swift communication; not with that wonderful memory and that orderly way of going about things. Though he would have said—and said rightly—that he owed more to divine inspiration than to his natural gifts, we must recognise that in him grace was, as usual, making use of natural endowments. Père Coste describes the natural (and perhaps the supernatural) man as one who never lost a moment. "His success was due to the fact that none of his labours was wasted; once he took up an enterprise, he pursued it without further delays, never looking backwards or retracing his steps; he was not the type of man who destroys a scheme drawn up the evening before and then launches upon a perfectly new one the following morning. His practical, penetrating and critically acute mind weighed the arguments for and against any undertaking before beginning it; he examined every question to the roots, both as a whole and in its parts, with all its advantages and disadvantages, and all that could hinder or further its progress."

Qualities of this sort are not those usually thought of in con-

nexion with genius, yet genius, and of a high order, Vincent
must be admitted to have possessed. But it was of an order that
many will not think to be genius, even after it has been pointed
out as such. The dash, the brilliance, the poetry we look for—
these we shall not find in him. Rather it is a case of Gerard
Manley Hopkins's "Sheer plod makes plough down sillion
shine." Indeed, I confess that (setting aside sanctity, which
has a close kinship to genius) I do not ordinarily consider administrative talents, however useful they may be, as among the
clearer marks of the divine fire. But, because Vincent's capacity
for organization was so thoroughly subordinated to his sanctity
that one can hardly distinguish between them, I recognise genius
in him, though it is of a kind that stands almost alone, and
for that very reason is only too likely to be thought of as merely
goodness of heart and steady industry.

He was above everything else a man of prayer, a mystic.
Nevertheless Abelly, who was for a long time a member of the
Tuesday Conference, has to say, "One was never able to discover what kind of prayer was Vincent's, whether it was ordinary or extraordinary, as his humility always led him to
conceal the graces he received from God, so far as this was possible . . . All that one can say is that it must have been perfect
because of the disposition he showed and the fruits which sprang
from it." We may couple with this Vincent's own saying, "Give
me a man of prayer, and he will be capable of everything."

Even in the spiritual life, however, he showed little or nothing
of what is called originality. Instead he largely followed Bérulle
and Francis de Sales—whose *Introduction to the Devout Life*
and *Treatise on the Love of God* he never tired of recommend-
ing, and which he made the staple of his Daughters' spiritual
reading. Luis of Granada and the stodgy (if classical) Rodriguez
are now and then mentioned with some approval, but de Sales
and Bérulle must be considered his masters. At the same time he

used them all rather freely, and was by no means a rigid adherent of any system. The originality of the Vincentian spirituality consists rather in an unprecedented practicality. There are reasons for believing that not even in his private prayers did he permit himself the eagle flights of a Teresa or John of the Cross but gave himself to a consideration of the practice of virtue and conformity to the will of God. It is quite certain that these were almost the only considerations he wished to impress upon his disciples.

That he practised external mortifications on his poor old ailing body we know from the hair-shirt and scourge and iron girdle found in his room after his death. These were traditional at the time, and so Vincent used them, though not to any excess. He was sufficiently of the new, the Salesian school, not to attach nearly so much importance to the implements as to the mental habit of mortification. Therefore even in prayer he mortified his inclinations. "Some," he remarked, "have beautiful thoughts and sentiments, but they do not apply them to themselves. They do not reflect enough upon their interior condition."

What little could be seen of his interior life was this: that though he was nearly always the last person at Saint-Lazare to go to bed—for he usually worked at his correspondence and accounts late into the night—he was invariably the first to be up. When the bell struck four, he did not wait for the second stroke. Then with the community in the church he made an hour's meditation before vesting for Mass. But in all this, he was distinguished by no more than a punctilious regularity in doing what all the Fathers were expected to do. What set him entirely apart was his unwillingness to ascend the altar if he could recall even the slightest shade of unremoved misunderstanding with one of his fellow-creatures. Once, when already vested, he had to unvest and seek out a member of a religious order with whom he had had a disagreement—going some distance on foot—before he felt free to proceed with the saying of Mass.

Nobody could fail to perceive his rapt expression while offering the Holy Sacrifice, or how deeply he was moved when he recited the *Confiteor* or the *Domine, non sum dignus*. In reading the Gospel he would make a slight pause, as though of astonishment, whenever he came to the actual words of Christ. Especially did he seem to pay a personal attention to the double affirmation, *Amen, amen, dico vobis;* here he found something that called for an immediate and loving submission. The familiar words came forth as though they were being pronounced for the first time; as such they were to be laid to the heart and applied. Prayer, to him, was the preparation for all the business of the day. It strengthened mind and heart, purified the affections, and gave resolution to the will.

Nor did he cease to pray after the morning's devotions were over. More completely perhaps than anyone else he exemplified the old monastic proverb, *Orare est laborare*. Thus he told his Daughters how they might turn all the duties of the day into prayer, and advised them to say to themselves, "I will set out to serve the poor. I will try to do so in a gay and modest manner, so as to console and edify them; I will speak to them as though they were my lords and masters. There are some people who seldom speak to me: I will bear it. I have a way of grieving a Sister: I will avoid doing so. She annoys me at times; I will bear with her. One lady scolds me; another finds fault with me: I will try not to omit the fulfillment of my duty but pay her the respect and honour due to her. When I am with so and so I nearly always receive some hurt to my perfection; I will, so far as is possible, avoid that person." That was in his eyes both prayer and its fruit.

Such practical results were what he was after both for himself and for those under his direction. Because of his union with God we cannot refuse him the title of mystic, although he bore slight resemblance to the generally received picture of one. If he never undertook anything without praying about it for a long time—once he took five months before deciding to recommend a man for a merely secular position—sudden illuminations were not at all in his line. In his view, as Père Coste well says, "Prayer should be accompanied by the precautions demanded by prudence." Not by shafts of light but by a preparation of the way did God indicate what he called on Vincent to do. This explains the delay many impetuous people found hard to put up with in him. Hence when what is called a bright idea occurred to him, he was invariably distrustful of it. An axiom he repeated over and over in a hundred forms was that "God always gives a greater blessing to humble beginnings than to those that start with a peal of bells."

So it went on until this man who began so late—late enough in positive sanctity, and still later in what was to be his life's work—rounded out in old age all his designs. During his most fruitful years he was more or less ill. Once, to encourage a patient in a hospital, he told him that he himself had suffered (and had recovered from) hernia, asthma and consumption.[1] The diseases of his later life were of a different character. For a long time he had had festering sores in the legs, which obliged him first to ride on horseback instead of walk, and then to use the carriage he so hated, and finally made it impossible for him to leave the room. In 1658 he was thrown headlong from his carriage in a collision, and his life was despaired of. But he rallied, though his disabilities increased. He had now a kidney disease, and the pain of his swollen legs was added to a recurring fever which he had been accustomed to disregard but which

---

[1] This, however, is the only record we have of his having been afflicted with these particular ailments.

could no longer be ignored. His "tiny little fever," as he styled it, had to be treated.

The treatment was worse than the disease. The Fathers moved him from the little bare cell—unfurnished except for a truckle-bed, a plain table and a couple of wooden chairs—into a larger room, and gave him, though he grumbled at the luxury, a canopied bed and a Brother to look after him. But the fact that there was a fire-place in the new room could hardly have increased his comfort. For the treatment he had to suffer was the strange one of having the room baking hot and of being covered, even in summer, with several blankets. As though this were not enough, they added hot-water bottles, so that the unfortunate old man sweltered in distress all night waiting for the coming of the morning.

Moreover, at night pus used to gather in the joints of his knees and give him exquisite torment. Some little relief could be obtained by his turning from one side to the other. But as it was almost impossible for him to move, a cord was hung from the ceiling, and to this he was obliged to cling whenever he wanted to shift his position. Nevertheless, he still refused to consider himself as bedridden, and at break of day he was up as usual.

Since it was no longer possible for him to walk to the church, an adjoining room was turned into an oratory. There, no longer able to say Mass, he heard it and made his meditation. When the time came that he could not hobble even so far as that, he was carried along the corridor in a chair.

He knew he was dying; only the toughness of his constitution had kept life within him years after he should have been dead— that and his indomitable courage. If any further sign of his imminent departure was needed, it was supplied by the death within a month of one another, early in 1660, of his first and closest disciple, Anthony Portail, and of Louise de Marillac.

Vincent found himself unable to visit either, but to Louise he sent a message to say that he would soon be joining her in heaven. With her son and his wife and child, and her Daughters, and the Duchesse de Ventadour (for the Ladies of Charity) at her bedside, Louise, nervous and scrupulous to the last, died. To the officiating priest who was about to pronounce the Apostolic Benediction for the hour of death, she whispered that he should wait: it was not yet quite time. A few minutes later she let the words be spoken: they had to synchronise exactly with the passing of her soul.

Knowing that he had not long to live, Vincent wrote farewell letters on January 9, 1659, to both the Comte de Joigny (now Father Gondi of the Oratory) and to the Count's son, the Cardinal de Retz. He thanks Gondi for all his kindness and begs forgiveness for the "displeasure I have given you by my uncouthness," promising to pray for him in this world and the next. To the Cardinal-Archbishop he recommends "Your little Congregation of the Mission which you have founded, favoured, and maintained"; and of him also he asks forgiveness "If I have in any way displeased you." Again there is a promise of prayers in heaven—prayers the Cardinal badly needed and to which he was probably indebted for the grace to end his life more becomingly than he had spent it.

Every day now Vincent's physical condition became weaker and his pain greater. Yet he did not show any sign of what he was suffering, and when asked how he felt, would answer serenely, "Our Lord suffered more than I do." He continued to attend to his correspondence and to the business of his foundations, and it was remarked that, whenever he addressed the Fathers in conference, his matter was arranged as orderly as ever and that energy seemed to come back to him. At the beginning of July he met, as he thought for the last occasion, the Daughters of Charity to give them an address on the virtues of Louise de Marillac. This had been put off from the Spring only because he hoped that during the Summer he would recover enough strength to go downstairs to the parlour. When he found that that was out of the question, he broke for the first time his rule of never allowing women into his room. Yet because he detested anything in the nature of a "scene," he refrained from saying goodbye in so many terms.

The self-imposed rule having been broken once, Vincent allowed it to be broken again, and received the Sisters a second time at the end of the month (on the 24th) and on August 27, when an election of office-holders had to be held, which permitted them to come up once more. That was the last time he saw them. Already he had written to one of the nuns at the Visitation convent to say that his illness had deprived him of any hope of ever going there again.

Even the Ladies of Charity were allowed up. They were putting their rules into more permanent form, and it was necessary for him to be present. They, too, knew that they would never see him again in this world. But the Duchesse d'Aiguillon tried to persuade him to consent to be moved to her house so that he could be nursed better than was possible at Saint-Lazare. The kind offer was similingly refused, as no doubt the Duchesse knew it would be. Over a long period she had shown herself the most generous of all of Vincent's many generous supporters, though now and then her wealth and her position had led her to be a trifle domineering. To please her, the slowly dying man accepted the medicines and delicacies she insisted upon supplying.

By the beginning of September his condition improved somewhat, and hope was renewed that his life might still be spared for a while. But it was only the flaring up of the candle; by the middle of the month he sank again, and now the watchers knew that the end was near.

The ominous sign of continual drowsiness appeared, so that by the eighteenth he could not keep awake even at Mass or long enough to receive Holy Communion. In his brief waking moments he would explain, "The brother has come and is waiting for his sister." But on the twenty-sixth he was taken to the chapel and heard—or rather slept through—Mass, but could be sufficiently roused to communicate. The effort drained what little strength he had; death was now at hand.

The doctor was summoned but had to shake him to get him out of sleep, whereupon Vincent smiled, murmured a few words, and dropped off again. They left him in his chair, for they saw it was useless to move him.

By way of stimulating his failing faculties he was given— no doubt at the doctor's suggestion—a powder in his nostrils. Then the Fathers and Brothers crowded in to ask his blessing.

The scene has been recorded for us in minute detail, but is likely to read rather painfully to most people of our time. All those who had lived with him so many years knew perfectly well that he was a saint and that in his heart he blessed them one and all, as for that matter he had a blessing in his heart for the whole world. Nevertheless they pestered him with specific questions: "Do you bless the Tuesday Conference?" "Do you bless the Ladies of Charity?" "Do you bless the Foundlings?" It all seems very unnecessary. Drowsily he blessed everybody in turn whom he was asked to bless.

They also dragged from him, point by point, the profession of his belief in the various articles of the Christian creed. It was hard work for them, as they had to shout in his ear and keep putting powder up his nose. But he answered as well as he was able. When they wanted to know whether this man whose whole life had been one of charity forgave everybody, he could only mumble, "Nobody has ever . . ." and dropped off to sleep once more. Again the blessing was demanded, and Vincent managed to get out, "It is not for me . . ." before the "brother" Sleep took him again. No doubt they knew that this was what he would have wished had he been capable of expressing any wish, though one also suspects that the Fathers, however unconsciously, were "staging" his death and taking a full report of it with a view to the eventual process for beatification.

At four in the morning the "sister" came. Seeing the change in his face they shouted at him, *Deus in adjutorium meum intende;* and he answered in the same words. Then, so that he should die with the Holy Name upon his lips, Père Berthe, who had taken the place of a priest exhausted from this ordeal, cried "Jesus!"; and "Jesus" came the response. It was Vincent's last word. Almost immediately the death-rattle began, and within a quarter of an hour his spirit had ascended to God. The agony of his long-drawn-out illness had departed and had been succeeded by a vast and merciful weariness. There was no struggle. Sitting in his chair and wearing his priestly cassock—and this surely was what he would have wished—he died.

He had always been punctilious about rising at the first stroke of four; and half-past four always found him in his place in chapel for prayer. Almost to the minute, he passed from the world. Those gathered around him saw another change in his countenance; it was now that of a man fixed in unchanging contemplation of the divine.

ℂ Index

Abelly, Louis, 3-6, 24, 26, 29, 30, 32, 39, 43, 49, 56, 66, 93, 94, 188, 190, 227, 232, 238, 279, 281, 296, 298, 299, 303
Acarie, Madame, 53
Adolphus, Gustavus, 18, 19
Adour, The, 23
Adrian le Bon, 120, 121
Aiguesmortes, 46
Alet, 268
Alexander, VII, 288
Alméras, Pêre, 29
Anne of Austria, 10, 110, 111, 113, 114, 137, 141, 147, 176, 220, 223-30, 242, 249, 251, 253, 293
Anneçy, 107, 109
Antraguet, 71
Arnauld, Mother Angélique, 205, 213, 259
Arnold, Antoine, 213-17
Arnold, Matthew, 221
Augustinian Canons, 119
Augustinian nuns, 134
Augustinians, 120
Augustinus, 204, 212, 216-18
Aurelius, Marcus, 221
Avignon, 48

Barbary, 41, 42, 48
Barberini, Cardinal, 240
Bastille, 89
Béarn, 28
Beauvais, 87, 128, 174, 175
Beauvais, Bishop of (*see Potier, Augustin*)
Belin, 90, 115
Belley, Bishop of (*see Camus*)
Bence, Père, 78
Benedict XIV, 267
Benedictines, 241, 267, 286
Berthe, Père, 311

Bèrulle, Père Pièrre de, 52, 53, 56-58, 60, 61, 64, 65, 69, 70, 75, 76, 78, 79, 95, 101, 117, 175-77, 207, 303
Beynier, John, 70
Beys, the, 273
Boccaccio, 88
Bordeaux, 39, 95
Borromeo, St. Charles, 191
Bossuet, 104, 180, 186, 202, 218
Boudignon, 130, 296
Bougaud, Louis-Emile (*see Bishop of Laval*), 5, 7, 55, 68
Boulenger, M., 217
Bourdaise, Toussaint, 201
Bourdoise, Adrian, 53, 102, 176, 177, 184
Bourgoing, François, 57
Bremond, Abbé, 9, 60, 104, 195, 213
Bresse, 70, 77
Buddha, 97
Buglose, 96
Bull of Canonization, 94, 95
Bull of Condemnation, 217
Buzet, 37

Calvin, 208
Calvinism, 14, 206, 265
Calvinist, 217
Camus, 143, 145, 146, 197
Canon law, 157
Capefigue, Jean-Baptiste, 280, 281
Carmel, 106, 107, 110
Carmelites, 53
Carthusians, 241
Catholic Church, 88
Catholicism, 14, 18, 206, 265, 266, 271
Catholic League, 14, 61
"Catholic Puritanism," 206, 207

INDEX

316